SOMEONE ELSE'S TWIN

OTHER BOOKS BY THE AUTHOR

Indivisible by Two: Lives of Extraordinary Twins

Entwined Lives: Twins and What They Tell Us about Human Behavior

Uniting Psychology and Biology:
   Integrative Perspectives on Human Development
   (edited with Glenn E. Weisfeld and Carol C. Weisfeld)

Born Together—Reared Apart: The Landmark Minnesota Twin Study
(forthcoming)

Nancy L. Segal

SOMEONE ELSE'S TWIN

The True Story of Babies Switched at Birth

Prometheus Books

59 John Glenn Drive
Amherst, New York 14228–2119

Published 2011 by Prometheus Books

Cover image © Media Bakery
Cover design by Nicole Sommer-Lecht

Inquiries should be addressed to
Prometheus Books
59 John Glenn Drive
Amherst, New York 14228–2119
VOICE: 716–691–0133
FAX: 716–691–0137
WWW.PROMETHEUSBOOKS.COM

15 14 13 12 11   5 4 3 2 1

Library of Congress Cataloging-in-Publication Data

Segal, Nancy L., 1951–
    Someone else's twin : the true story of babies switched at birth / by Nancy L. Segal.
        p. cm.
    Includes bibliographical references and index.
    ISBN 978–1–61614–437–1 (cloth)
    ISBN 978–1–61614–438–8 (e-book)   •
    1. Twins—Psychology—Case studies. 2. Twins—Canary Islands—Case studies.
3. Infants switched at birth—Canary Islands—Case studies. 4. Mistaken identity—
Canary Islands—Case studies. I. Title.

BF723.T9S45 2011
155.44'4—dc22

2011014988

Printed in the United States of America on acid-free paper

To my fraternal twin sister, Anne,

and

In loving memory of our parents, Al and Esther Segal

CONTENTS

FOREWORD

No one else on planet Earth knows more about twins than Dr. Nancy Segal. She has personally participated in studies dealing with (a) the biology of twinning, (b) the psychological consequences of twins having been separated early in life, (c) the psychological consequences of twin loss, (d) the experience of being a member of a pair of twins (or triplets), (e) the evolutionary aspects of twinning, (f) the psychological development of twins over time, and (g) the behavioral genetic findings from twin and adoption research. She even invented and implemented a new twinlike research design—the study of virtual twins (unrelated individuals very close in age who are reared in the same family). Dr. Segal has also worked as a consultant on numerous legal cases involving controversies that have arisen because the participants were twins (e.g., wrongful death, injury, custody, accusations of cheating, and controversies regarding twins' placement in the same or different classrooms). Finally, Dr. Segal brings to bear a depth of understanding and empathy that can only come from being a twin herself.

The psychological consequences of switching and consequently separating a pair of twins at birth are profound for all participants. In addition, such an event has legal and ethical implications. No one else comes close to being as qualified as Dr. Segal to elucidate the underlying issues and explain their relevance to a variety of contemporary societal practices. Consider just two of the many issues discussed in this book:

parental certainty about a child's paternity and maternity and genetic and environmental influences on psychological development.

In the past, a new mother never worried over whether or not her child was really hers. Only fathers worried, generating an entire literature on cuckoldry, a topic well developed in the works of Shakespeare. Evolutionary psychologists have asserted that this "problem" led to the development of mechanisms for mate retention, such as denigrating competitors. As Dr. Segal points out, possible baby switching now presents us with a novel problem for mothers, raising a host of interesting psychological issues even Shakespeare did not imagine. Indeed, in spite of the clear elucidation of the problem by Shakespeare, not long ago psychology was so dominated by behaviorist arguments that the rearing environment was everything (the Professional Blank Slate Theory) that psychologists would have asserted that it did not matter who the child's biological parents were. Indeed, some psychologists even argued that a child's gender was simply a social construction.

Children change as they grow and develop, and there are correlations between the parents' behavior and children's behavior (e.g., parents who talk to their children more tend to have children with larger vocabularies than parents who talk to their children less). Therefore, many parents believe that their child-rearing practices are the principal cause of the way in which their children turn out (the Lay Blank Slate Theory). This theory, while clearly in part correct (children require a supportive environment in order for normal development to follow an orderly course), mistakes correlation for causation and ignores the fact that parents also transmit genes that influence behavior.

Today, in part because of Dr. Segal's work in evolutionary psychology, social genetics, and developmental behavior genetics, we know that both Blank Slate theories are seriously flawed and a much broader frame of reference must be brought to bear on virtually every important psychological issue. Evolutionary mechanisms, quantitative genetic mechanisms, and environmental influences all underlie human development and the adult manifestation of psychological traits, as well as emotional response systems and the development of one's identity. Dr. Segal brings this broad frame of reference to the issues discussed in this book.

Because she is both a gifted psychologist and a gifted writer, the story of this unusual experiment is told with verve, insight, and empathy. It is a story that has relevance to each and every one of us, as each and every one of us could have been *Someone Else's Twin*.

Dr. Thomas J. Bouchard Jr.
Professor Emeritus
University of Minnesota
Department of Psychology
Director, Minnesota Study of Twins Reared Apart (1979–1999)

1

INTRODUCTION
Discovery in Las Palmas

Every once in a while a researcher discovers a problem, event, or situation that is irresistible, something so compelling that she drops everything to study it. This happened to me in June 2008 when I learned about Delia and Begoña, a pair of switched-at-birth identical twins from Spain's Canary Islands (Islas Canarias), located off the Moroccan coast. In 1973, newborn twin Delia, born on January 18, was accidentally switched with unrelated infant Beatriz, born on January 15, in the crowded nursery of the Nuestra Señora del Pino Hospital. It is likely that the three infants were placed in the same incubator, making an exchange of babies likely by either of the two nurses in charge of sixty newborns. In that instant, Begoña and Beatriz became a fraternal "twin" pair, and Delia became a first-born "singleton" child raised by a family with whom she had no biological connection. No one discovered the mistake until 2001 when the twins and Beatriz turned twenty-eight, at which time two chance encounters, two incidents of mistaken identity, and more than a little curiosity finally revealed the truth.

Lawsuits filed against the Canary Islands Health Service by the twins and their families continued for years. The case drew little attention until 2008, when it was allegedly leaked to reporters in the capital city of Las Palmas on the island of Gran Canaria. News spread quickly through the seven islands comprising the Islas Canarias, across Spain, and throughout the world. Psychologist Payam Heidary from California

Fig. 1.1. (a) Delia as a three-month old infant, (b) a three-year-old child, and (c) an eight-year-old girl, shown at communion; (d) Beatriz (left) and Begoña (right) at about age seven. The twins' hair was fair when they were born but turned darker as they grew up. Courtesy of the twins. Adult photos of the twins and Beatriz have not been included because they and their attorneys wished to protect their privacy.

sent me a link to the online story.[1] Minutes after reading it I was riveted and knew I would go to Las Palmas to meet the twins, their families, and their attorneys. I wanted a closer look at the circumstances and consequences of this incredible case—my only fear was that another investigator would get there first. I learned that Delia and Begoña were only the sixth pair of switched-at-birth twins ever identified; I learned of a seventh pair shortly after I discovered them.

Fig. I.2. The twins' and Beatriz's attorneys: (a) Sebastian Socorro Perdomo (for Delia) and (b) José Antonio Rodríguez Peregrina (for Begoña and Beatriz). Courtesy of the attorneys.

I was fortunate that the families' attorneys, Sebastian Socorro Perdomo (for Delia) and José Antonio Rodríguez Peregrina (for Begoña
and Beatriz) gave me full access to their clients while they turned away
most reporters, journalists, and other individuals seeking information
about the twins. The lawyers reasoned that my professional background
in twin research might help their case. I sent Socorro several articles
about twins reared apart and a 2005 book chapter I had written about
switched-at-birth twins before I arrived.

The Spanish press and other newspapers in mostly Latin countries
began covering the twins' story in 2008. In June of that year Socorro's
office arranged for me to be interviewed by Mónica López Ferrado, a science reporter from Spain's leading national newspaper *El Pais*.[2] I received
Ferrado's e-mail message while changing planes in Dallas en route to
Louisville, Kentucky, for the annual Behavior Genetics Association
meeting. Ferrado produced what must be the best, most comprehensive
newspaper coverage of this case outside Gran Canaria. When I arrived in
Las Palmas in September 2009, I was interviewed by Antonio F. de la
Gándara, a writer from the local Canarian newspaper *Canarias 7*, who
also covered the case extensively.

I traveled to Las Palmas in September 2009 to spend twelve days
gathering material. I stayed at the Tryp Iberia Hotel, just three kilometers (two miles) from the city's popular beach, Playa de las Canteras, and
marveled at the hotel's gorgeous views of the ocean. Scenery aside, the
hotel is also situated approximately midway between the two attorneys'
offices, located, respectively, in the old town of Triana Vegueta (Socorro)
and the newer development along Calle Luis Doreste Silva (Peregrina).
With much to be done, I had only one free weekday. I used it to visit the
old Cathedral Santa Ana and Casa Colon (Columbus Museum) in the
historic scenic section of Vegueta and to explore the bustling shopping
promenade Calle Mayor de Triana (see figures 1.3 and 1.4).

Before I got to work, I wanted to understand a bit more about where
the twins grew up. On Calle Alcalde José Ramirez Bethencourt, not far

Fig. 1.3. A street in the old town of Triana Vegueta. Courtesy of Nancy L. Segal

Fig. 1.4. A street performer on the promenade Calle Mayor de Triana.
Courtesy of Nancy L. Segal

from the hotel entrance,[3] is a statue of a large canine, shown in figure 1.5. Most people assume that the seven Canary Islands were named after the bird, the canary, but the islands were instead named after the dogs that figured significantly in their history. Canary birds were, in fact, later named after the islands to which they are native.[4] There are many historical references to dogs on these islands and many different stories about how the Canary Islands were named. Archeological excavations on one of the islands, Tenerife, showed that dogs were buried with their masters to lead their souls to the place of the dead.[5] As for the name, it may derive from the North African tribe the *Canarii* who once inhabited the island of Gran Canaria, the twins' birthplace. The name might

Fig. 1.5. Bronze statue of the *Perro de Presa Canario* (Canary dog) outside my hotel on Calle Alcalde José Ramirez Bethencourt. This breed originated in the Canary Islands and is relatively new to the United States; several animals were imported in the late 1980s.[6] Several such statues appear throughout Las Palmas, each sponsored by a particular business or organization. The yellow garment depicts one of the colors of the flag of Gran Canaria, signifying the sun and the sand. Yellow is also the color of the local soccer team. The blue on the garment and platform also comes from the Gran Canarian flag. Courtesy of Nancy L. Segal

also come from the Latin term *Insular Canaria,* which means Canary Island. Whatever the reason, eventually people began calling the islands the Islands of Canaria, then the Canary Islands.

I do not speak Spanish, so I worked closely with interpreter Jessica Crespo. She accompanied me to the attorneys' offices, the twins' homes, the judge's office, the shopping mall where the twins first met, and many other locations. I found Jessica through the American School in Las Palmas, where she teaches English. I hired Jessica based largely on her credentials—she holds a bachelor's degree in translation and inter-preting with a major in law and economics and a master's degree in audiovisual translation from the University of Las Palmas. Jessica is also a sworn translator, as named by the Ministry of Foreign Affairs, and has studied children's literature translation at the University of Surrey in England. She showed an impressive command of English, evident to me during telephone interviews prior to my leaving for Spain. I met Jessica in person on September 13, the day before our interviews with the twins began. Jessica was a stunning, twenty-seven-year-old woman who spoke French as well as English and Spanish. She had shoulder-length brown hair and brown eyes and stood taller than her five-foot, eight-inch height because of the shoes she wore. I was lucky to have found Jessica because her wonderful social skills put the twins and their families at ease during the interviews, and we became friends as well as colleagues. Jessica is pictured in figure 1.6.

The result of my research in the Canary Islands is this book, *Someone Else's Twin*, in which I examine and describe the traumatic life changes with which Delia, Begoña, and Beatriz still grapple. I also intro-duce other switched-at-birth twins and singletons whose life stories were similarly altered beyond recognition. This book is also about the signif-icance of the families' experiences for women having babies, parents raising children, lawyers protecting justice, and researchers studying behavior. I chose the title *Someone Else's Twin* because it captures the switching of the twins from the perspectives of everyone involved.

Fig. 1.6. Jessica Crespo, my interpreter par excellence, on our first walk to Peregrina's office from my hotel. Courtesy of Nancy L. Segal

For readers to understand my immediate response to news of the Canary Islands twins, I must go back in time. I am a fraternal twin. My sister Anne and I were the only children born to our parents Al and Esther Segal, both in their early thirties. The double conception was natural—my mom was just approaching the age at which the chance of having fraternal twins starts to rise.[7] She had an easy pregnancy, although we were born prematurely at seven-and-a-half months, as are many multiple-birth infants. One could also say that we were an early reared-apart pair—Anne, the larger and more robust baby, went home after a few days' stay in the incubator, while I was a month-long incubator occupant.

Over the years, friends and relatives sent us the usual matching out-

Fig. 1.7. Nancy (right) with her mother and twin sister, Anne, as
(a) young children and (b) adults.
Photos taken by (a) my father, Alfred M. Segal, and (b) Michael Keel

fits, but they did not look adorable on us. I discovered several photographs taken when we were two, three, and four showing us in identical T-shirts, shorts, and dresses. Seeing them today gives me the
impression of two kids trying to look like twins, making it easy to understand why my mother rarely dressed us alike. Our physical differences
have persisted—since childhood, Anne stood four inches taller than me,
so I often received her hand-me-downs. Anne's hair is short and wavy,
while mine is long, straight, and slightly darker than hers. No one ever
confused us or suspected that we were twins, although some people
forget which name goes with which twin.

The differences between Anne and me extend beyond our looks.
Anne is a corporate attorney; I am a psychology professor. Anne is
slightly introverted; I am fairly extroverted. Anne is married; I am
unmarried. Anne lives in New York; I live in California. But we are close
sisters who trust each other more than any other person in the world and
laugh together at jokes no one else would follow. However, it was our
differences, not our similarities, that captivated me and caused me to
think hard about how children growing up together can be so dissimilar.

My dual interest in twins and psychology has defined my career, and I've had more fun than many of my colleagues trying to answer all sorts of human developmental questions. For me, twins bring human interest and personal relevance to a scientifically significant research subject. Their personal stories illuminate the test data in many ways. It is amusing to hear that identical twins independently choose similar outfits, buy the same birthday cards, or make the same unusual mistake on an exam. But these events are consistent with research showing that identical twins have similar tastes, preferences, and abilities.

There is another small piece to this story. Just for fun, Anne and I had our DNA tested at Affiliated Genetics, a Salt Lake City, Utah, laboratory that performs paternity and twin-typing (identical and fraternal) tests. The staff distributes special kits that allow clients to prepare saliva samples at home and mail them to the laboratory for processing. I often use their services for determining whether twins in my studies are identical or fraternal.

Our results were perfectly reasonable, but gave me a slight jolt. Anne and I had fewer than the average eight out of fifteen matches expected for fraternal twins and full siblings. The results are certainly consistent with genetic relatedness. In fact, it is possible for fraternal twins and full siblings (both of whom share half their genes, on average, by descent) to differ on all tested DNA markers because they have only a 50 percent chance of inheriting each gene in common. Because I knew this in advance, my momentary concern quickly subsided. Delia, Begoña, and Beatriz's case has heightened my awareness of how previously unknown birth events can so profoundly alter lives years later.

Knowing who your relatives are is a fundamental part of personal identity and developmental continuity, as the switched-at-birth twins have clearly shown. What happened to the Canary Islands families could happen to anyone.

TWINS IN SCIENCE

Scientists see twins as natural experiments that reveal how and to what degree genes and environments shape human behavioral and physical traits. This natural experiment derives from the availability of two types of twins, monozygotic (identical or MZ) and dizygotic (fraternal or DZ). MZ twins originate from the splitting of a single fertilized egg or zygote within the first two weeks after conception. Most textbooks state that MZ twins share 100 percent of their genes, and that is theoretically correct. However, errors in cell division, mutations, copy number variations (presence of more than two copies of some genes), differential X chromosome inactivation in MZ female twins, and other events make MZ twins not strictly identical.[8] Still, MZ twins are as close as possible to natural human clones. It is generally believed that MZ twinning is a random event, meaning that anyone is equally likely to conceive such a set. However, some studies have questioned this wisdom, suggesting that the predisposition for having MZ twins is genetically transmitted within certain families.[9]

DZ twinning is genetically passed down within families.[10] The specific genes involved are as of yet unknown, but some good candidates for these genes have been identified.[11] The conventional wisdom is that DZ twinning "skips" generations, and while this can happen in some families, this type of transmission has never been scientifically confirmed. DZ twins result when a woman simultaneously releases two eggs that are fertilized by two separate sperm. As I explained above, DZ twins share 50 percent of their genes, on average, making them genetically equivalent to full siblings. DZ twins may be same-sex or opposite-sex, events that occur with approximately equal frequency. DZ twins occur more frequently among Black populations, followed by Caucasian populations and Asian populations in succession, further supporting the presence of genetic effects on nonidentical twinning. DZ twins are also born more frequently, on average, to women conceiving in their midthirties and later and more frequently to women who are taller and heavier.[12]

Spontaneous DZ twinning has, in fact, been associated with increased maternal levels of follicle-stimulating hormone (FSH) found in relatively taller, heavier, and older women.[13] The link between DZ twinning and maternal age partly explains recent changes in the frequency with which twins are born.

The twinning rate in the United States in 2008 (the latest year for which statistics are available) and in other Western nations is about one in thirty births, a dramatic increase from the one in sixty births reported in 1980.[14] This increase is primarily due to the availability of assisted reproductive technology (ART), which allow infertile couples to conceive. Among these couples are those who delay having children and thus experience difficulty conceiving. ART mostly elevates the chance of having fraternal twins, although in vitro fertilization (IVF or implantation of embryos in the uterus) has been associated with an unexpected increase in MZ twinning (albeit to a lesser degree), possibly due to manipulation of the zygote in the laboratory.

Classic twin studies involve comparing behavioral and physical similarities between MZ and DZ twin pairs reared together (MZT and DZT). This simple and elegant technique was first described in 1875 by the British scholar Sir Francis Galton. Galton's work preceded scientific knowledge about the biological bases of twinning, yet he reasoned that twins who looked alike shared all their heredity while those who looked different shared only a portion of their heredity. By comparing the life histories of thirty-five twin pairs in which "similarity at first was close" and twenty twin pairs in which there was "great dissimilarity at first," Galton concluded, "It is, that their history affords means of distinguishing between the effects of tendencies received at birth, and of those that were imposed by the circumstances of their after lives; in other words, between the effects of nature and nurture."[15]

A wealth of twin research has since shown that MZ twins are more alike than DZ twins in height, weight, intelligence, personality, athleticism, social attitudes, job satisfaction, and medical conditions, demonstrating genetic influence on these traits.[16] Virtually all measured human characteristics show some degree of genetic influence.

Another powerful way to study twins involves comparing the behaviors of MZ and DZ twins reared in separate families (MZA and DZA, with *A* standing for "apart"). These rare pairs are extremely valuable research subjects because of their shared genes (100 percent and 50 percent on average, respectively) and their exposure to different influences within their respective families and communities. Growing up apart, without the influence of the other twin and without being subject to the same family circumstances, these twins offer scientists sensitive tests of the relative contributions of genes and environments to behavioral and physical traits. In fact, the MZA intraclass correlation (a statistic expressing the degree of twin resemblance that varies from −1.0 to 1.0) directly expresses just how much variation among people is explained by genetic factors.

I must point out, however, that the shared environment of twins growing up together has little effect on their similarity. Evidence to support this conclusion comes from studies showing that the degree of resemblance between MZA and MZT (*T* standing for "together") twins across most traits is quite similar[17] and that twins treated alike are not more behaviorally alike than twins treated differently.[18] Unfortunately, critics of twin research continue to raise objections even while they are not supported by the data. Studying twins reared apart is one approach to addressing their concerns.

TWINS REARED APART

I spent nine years, from 1982 to 1991, working with participants in the Minnesota Study of Twins Reared Apart (MISTRA), which was directed by Professor Thomas J. Bouchard Jr. at the University of Minnesota in Minneapolis. Many reared-apart twins are unaware of having been born a twin, information that is often not known until they reach adulthood.

The participants I studied learned about their twinship in many different ways, such as being told by their rearing parents, by gaining access to birth records, or by accidentally being confused for someone else. All of their stories are worth telling, but I have selected a choice few.

MZA twins Jack Yufe and Oskar Stohr, born in Port of Spain, Trinidad, in 1933, were separated when they were six months of age when their parents' relationship failed.[19] Jack was raised Jewish by his father in Trinidad, while Oskar was raised Catholic by his mother in Nazi Germany. Both learned as children that they had a twin brother, but the concept of twinship did not mean much to them at that time. When they were teenagers, Jack and Oskar began sending each other letters, many quite endearing. "My dear brother," Oskar began; "Your loving brother," Jack ended. Their first meeting in Germany in 1954 when they were twenty-one did not go well because of their sharply diverging political and historical views. They had no contact with one another after that until 1980 when they were forty-six and Jack's then-wife Ona learned about the MISTRA. Jack wrote to Oskar to ask him to participate and he agreed. When the twins were assessed in Minnesota, they began a love-hate relationship that lasted until Oskar's death in 1997. Oskar's passing was very disturbing to Jack, who did not attend his twin brother's funeral because Jack himself was the living reminder of the husband, father, and grandfather whom Oskar's family missed terribly.

An intriguing aspect of Jack and Oskar's story is that each twin knew that had their rearing situations been reversed, each would have become the person whose opinions and ideas he abhorred. These twins illustrate philosopher Dale Wright's view that the self-understanding that grounds our identity is subject to contingencies that are context dependent.[20]

MZA twin Nora Laster was three months old when she was adopted from South Korea by an American couple living in Washington, DC.[21] Her birth parents had had two daughters and could not afford to raise two more, nor could they afford the extra hospital care required by Nora, the lighter-birth-weight twin. Therefore, her mother decided to place Nora in an orphanage. Nora's biological father was working in Liberia at that time and did not know his wife had delivered twins. A year later Nora's birth parents returned to the orphanage to try to reclaim her, or actually to buy her back, but it was too late.

Nora, as a nineteen-year-old college sophomore, began searching for her biological family. Her adoption papers indicated that she had two older siblings, but there was no mention of a twin. Nora contacted the Holt agency in Korea and two weeks later received an e-mail message telling her that she was from a family of four children, two daughters and twins. She was puzzled and wondered if she was a fifth child, but reading further she learned that she was one of the twins. "I was dumbfounded. I could not speak. I wondered if we were identical or fraternal and what it would have been like to have grown up together. I wondered if we had a 'twin connection.' I decided I wanted to see Korea and meet my birth family." In 2008 Nora decided to study in Korea, and there she met her identical twin sister Chun Hei. Their first meeting took place in a taxicab in Seoul that Chun Hei had taken to the university where Nora was waiting. The twins could not really converse because they did not speak the same language, but they could not stop staring at one another. The taxi took them to the central train station, where they boarded a train to their birth parents' home in Busan. They fell asleep on the train holding hands.

Thirty-one-year-old Mark Newman and Jerry Levey were living about sixty miles apart in different New Jersey cities.[22] Both twins were volunteer firefighters, but only Jerry attended the 1985 Volunteer Fireman's Convention in Wildwood, New Jersey. One of Mark's friends, Captain Jimmy Tedesco, could not stop staring at Jerry and finally approached him to ask about his birthday, his family, and whether he had been adopted. Convinced that Mark and Jerry were identical twins, Tedesco arranged to bring them together, telling Mark that they were visiting another firehouse to inspect equipment. When the six-foot, four-inch brothers stood face-to-face and removed their hats, Mark asked, "What's my bald head doing on his shoulders?" Their party lasted for hours.

I wish the Internet had been available to the public when I was working on the MISTRA because it has made finding family members much easier and quicker than in the past.[23] I recently heard from Hanan Hardy, a thirty-five-year-old woman from Washington, DC. She had no idea she was a twin until her identical twin sister Hasania, who lives in Morocco, contacted her on Facebook. That day, Hanan learned that she was a twin *and* that she was adopted. These are just a few examples of the different ways people discover they are reared-apart twins and how they eventually meet.

Most twins are initially stunned, then overjoyed, to learn that they have a twin brother or sister. Some twins, most of whom are adoptees like Nora, begin searching for their biological parents and discover along the way that they have a twin. In most cases, news of being a twin causes them to refocus their search to locate the twin, whose identity becomes more important than that of the parents. Many twins, like Nora, become consumed with finding their twin, a process that can require spending large sums of money on traveling, obtaining documents, even hiring private investigators. These decisions signal the importance of the twin relationship in people's lives.

TWIN RELATIONS

Social closeness refers to the concern, trust, and caring people have for others in their lives, as well as to the enjoyment of those relationships.[24] Research shows that the bond between MZ twins may be the closest of human social connections—certainly the death of an MZ twin is generally the most devastating of losses for the surviving co-twin. DZ twins are not as close as MZ twins, on average, but there is overlap: some MZ twins are not very close, and some DZ twins are.

The bases of the bonds between twins have been debated, but the twins' perceptions of the many traits they share are probably the force driving them together. My late thesis advisor at the University of Chicago, Daniel G. Freedman, put it best by suggesting that recognition of common features may foster a "sense of 'we' between ourselves and our fellow tribesmen. Recognition of this sense triggers a series of emotions whose net effect is tribal unity and the increased chance for altruism."[25] In 2003, I conducted a study showing that MZA twins feel closer to and more familiar with one another than DZA twins, both when they meet and subsequently. I believe that the MZA twins' perceptions of their behavioral and physical similarities explain these social relationship differences between the two types of reunited twins. DZA twins are less alike than MZA twins and are likely to be aware of their differences.

This reasoning can also help us understand why both MZA and DZA twins feel closer to one another than they do to the unrelated siblings with whom they were reared since childhood. The twins' feelings do not imply dislike or rejection of their adoptive siblings but rather an easier rapport with and greater attraction to the twin with whom they have more in common.

Meeting a twin is a major, and generally positive, life-changing event that the reunited Minnesota twins enjoyed talking about. Many of the twins acquired in-laws, nieces, and nephews whom they had never known existed. All of them gained insight into their medical histories, such as the possible genetic origins of their dental disease or tendencies toward weight gain, conditions they may have formerly attributed to inconsistent flossing or occasional overeating. The Minnesota twins, most of whom were adopted, also learned what it is like to resemble someone physically and behaviorally. Many twins said that the missing pieces from their lives were finally filled in.

Some people feel that something is missing from their lives, perhaps a satisfying relationship, a professional goal, or a sense of purpose. It has been found that some adoptees, even those from loving families, experience an inner emptiness or isolation[26] variously linked to their behavioral or physical differences from their family members or their desire to know the origins of their outgoing personalities or artistic talents. I believe that when twins meet one another, their questions finally find answers, closing the gaps in their life stories. They were not pining for a long-lost twin, because there is no scientific proof that intrauterine knowledge of twinship exists. They just wanted the same information that most other people have about their lives.

There is a special class of separated twins for whom reunions are not joyous occasions but are devastating, traumatic, and unwelcome events. These are the twins, like Delia and Begoña, who are switched at birth.

SWITCHED AT BIRTH

Some people will remember the 1988 comedy film, *Big Business*, starring actresses Lily Tomlin and Bette Midler. Tomlin and Midler play members of identical switched-at-birth twin sets, both named Sadie and Rose, born in the 1940s. Two families, one rich and one poor, deliver identical twin girls at the same time, but a senile nurse named Nanny inadvertently switches the first-born twins. The twins finally meet forty years later in conjunction with a big business deal. It seems an improbable premise because only seven switched-at-birth twin pairs have been identified, but the film's plot mirrors actual events in such twins' extraordinary life stories. Some identical twins find one another because they look alike and are confused by people who know one or both of them. However, identical twins who don't look exactly alike because of differences in weight or hairstyle and fraternal twins who may not resemble each other at all might never meet. Even look-alike twins whose paths fail to cross may never learn the truth about their birth. Every one of the seven switched-at-birth twin pairs of which I am aware came to light because the twins looked very much alike and were mistaken for one another from time to time.

It is impossible to know how often newborn infant twins are separated and go home with the wrong set of parents because only the discovered cases are reported. In this regard, identical twins have a clear advantage over switched-at-birth fraternal twins because their matched appearance causes the confusion that ultimately leads to their reunion. Non-twin infants have also been switched at birth, but these events may stay hidden forever because these unrelated children probably do not look at all alike. Nevertheless, switched-at-birth non-twins have been identified, mostly because someone remembered something unusual about the birth or hospital staff and reexamined their records.

Non-twins Kay Qualis and DeeAnn Shafer were unintentionally switched in an Oregon Hospital in 1953. A neighbor who knew both of their mothers told Kay's brother that his mother, Marjorie, had told the nurses that the baby she was given to take home was not hers, but the staff had ignored her concerns. Rumors of a mix-up circulated among some family members for years until DNA testing confirmed who the real relatives were. Kay and DeeAnn celebrated their next birthday together, at age fifty-seven, and are friendly. However, as Kay commented, "I'm trying to move forward [and] look at the positive. You can't look back. It just drives you crazy."[27]

Two baby boys in Argentina's Entre Rios province were inadvertently switched at birth, but both couples decided to keep the child they had been given because of the deep attachments they had developed toward their sons.[28] The children, born on August 16, 1999, were five years old when the mistake was discovered. The hospital realized its mistake soon after the delivery, but it amended the records rather than informing the families. Each family claimed $34,000 from the state for moral damages (pain and suffering), but the sum was reduced to $500 because the babies were not switched back. A Spanish newspaper article written about the Las Palmas twins in July 2008 identified ten pairs of non-twin infants who had been inadvertently switched in Spain over the past twenty years, and in all cases DNA tests had allowed the babies to be returned quickly to their biological families.[29]

These brief news clips suggest that hospital mistakes are accepted and that people go on with their lives, but they are misleading. These short stories hardly capture the emotional turbulence, anger, and self-doubt that accompany such news. Only two book-length accounts of switched-at-birth infants are available. One is by Madeleine Joye, the mother of switched-at-birth twins Paul and Philippe, whom I will discuss in the next chapter.[30] The other is by Frederick George, who at fifty-seven learned he had been accidentally exchanged with another infant, Jim Churchman, during Christmas 1946. "I grew up with a nagging feeling of somehow not belonging," he wrote.[31]

A graduate school friend of mine comes from a family of eight children. When I told her of my plans for this book in the summer 2010 at a conference in Madison, Wisconsin, her face took on a serious expression. She confessed to me that her parents and siblings suspected that one of her brothers had been switched with another infant at the hospital. "He never looked or behaved like one of us," she said. Her brother did not get along with the other members of the family and had been estranged from them for years.

Like the brief news clips, the few theatrical treatments of switched twins also overlook the real-life consequences of these events. Shakespeare's *Comedy of Errors* conveys the hilarity that comes from the confusion created by identical individuals being approached by people they do not know and being rejected by people they think they do know. In the play, two sets of identical male twins are born on the same day, one set to the merchant Egon and another set to a poor family whom Egon purchases as slaves for his sons. A shipwreck separates the true twins, placing one member from each pair together while sending the two mismatched sets down different paths. Errors, misperceptions, and confusion follow until the two true pairs are reunited. The play ends happily, but it is, after all, a play.

Shakespeare knew a great deal about twins, having fathered an opposite-sex twin pair, Judith and Hamnet. His personal connection to twins was probably responsible for his mismatched twin characters Antipholus (of Syracuse) and slave Dromio (of Syracuse), and Antipholus (of Ephesus) and slave Dromio (of Ephesus) in *Comedy of Errors*, as well as the separated male-female twins Sebastian and Viola in *Twelfth Night*.[32] What Shakespeare did not realize is that his mismatched twin pairs in *Comedy of Errors* were really virtual twins, unusual siblings who are of considerable scientific interest because of their shared age and non-shared genes.

VIRTUAL TWINS AND OTHER UNUSUAL PAIRINGS

Most reared-apart twins are separated either because they are born to unmarried mothers, their mother dies during childbirth, or their family cannot afford to raise two infants. But there are twins whose separation is unintentional, traceable to human error by nurses or foster care workers responsible for newborn care. Accidental "switching" of one twin with a non-twin infant sends two children home with the wrong parents. These events conspire to create highly unusual and scientifically informative kinships. Unrelated parent-child pairs and unrelated non-twin sibling sets are produced in the process, as they would be even when non-twin infants are switched. However, switched-at-birth twins generate an additional exotic array of extraordinary relationships, namely twins raised apart, "singleton twins," and alleged fraternal twins, or what I call *virtual twins*.

Virtual twins (VTs) are an especially interesting twinlike group, and I have now studied over 140 such pairs. Virtual twins are same-age unrelated children reared together since infancy. They come about mostly in two ways—couples may adopt two same-age children at the same time, or they may adopt one infant who is close in age to a biological child in the family. Some unusual VT pairs I have studied were created when (a) one child was adopted and the other was conceived by a surrogate mother whose egg was fertilized using the father's sperm and (b) one child was adopted and the other was gestated by the mother following embryo donation.

The fascinating aspect of virtual twins is that they replay twinship but without the genetic link. In fact, virtual twins are the reverse of identical twins reared apart—virtual twins share their environments but not their genes, whereas identical twins reared apart share their genes but not their environments.[33] Virtual twins are valuable participants in psychological research because they tell us how much growing up together affects behavioral resemblance. I have discovered that virtual twin children are much less alike in general intelligence and decision making than identical twins and fraternal twins, demonstrating that a shared family environment has little effect on how similar siblings turn out in terms of these measures.

Parents raising virtual twins create them knowingly but not always intentionally. Sometimes two infants become available for adoption when only one was requested, and families unexpectedly find themselves with a virtual pair. Other times parents seek adoption when their attempts at conception fail, only to find that a surprise pregnancy coincides with the availability of an adoptee. In fact, two families in my study include an adoptee and an artificially conceived triplet set, generating three virtual twin pairs each. Regardless of how these scenarios play out, both the parents and the children are fully aware of the relationship of each child to the other children and to other family members. The children's differences in appearance and behavior largely reflect their different sets of genes and are expected and accepted by everyone who knows them. People on the street may ask if the children are twins, but most parents deny this except when they tire of explaining their children's true relationship.

Events responsible for twins being switched at birth also unintentionally—*but unknowingly*—create a virtual twin pair from one twin and the unrelated infant with whom the co-twin was exchanged. These virtual twins differ importantly from "ordinary" virtual twins (who are hardly ordinary) because they and their parents *believe* they are fraternal twins. The belief that their children truly belong together overwhelms parents' perceptions of the "twins'" differences, which can seem extreme even for fraternal twins. Such differences might include skin color and temperament, as in Begoña and Beatriz's case. The behavioral and physical traits of some of these virtual twin pairs, such as Paul and Philippe, Mari and Samantha (Tairí), and especially Begoña and Beatriz (whose story is the focus of this book) differ dramatically. I describe all these virtual twins' differences in the next chapter.

Some parents are baffled by their fraternal twins' extraordinary differences, even when the parents know that the genetic hand each of us is dealt could have caused them. However, the possibility that twins might be switched at birth never occurs to most parents, including those of Begoña and Beatriz. Instead, they rationalize the unusual traits they see in one of their twin children—a dark-skinned child in a light-skinned family must be due to distant relatives on the father's side, or a blond-haired child in a dark-haired family surely comes from intermarriage on the mother's side. The faith that most people place in hospitals, doctors, and healthcare workers prevents them from considering the unthinkable possibility that a "baby switch" took place.

This book is about families caught by unwelcome surprises, news of twins switched at birth, which changed everything they knew and believed about who they were and who their children were. These rare separated twins also raise issues and questions of universal significance, four of which I will address throughout this book.

ISSUES AND QUESTIONS

Imaginary twins switched at birth are clever literary devices, as in Shakespeare's plays. But in real life they raise issues and questions of universal societal significance that have implications for everyone, not just twins. The first issue concerns maternity certainty, or the process by which mothers know whether or not a newborn infant truly belongs to them. This seems so simple, and most people would say that, of course, they know. But *how* they know is not so easily answered. Unfortunately, modern-day deliveries in understaffed hospitals have made newborn identity an uncomfortable concern for some mothers. Ordinary finger-printing of mothers and babies or attaching name bracelets to both helps, but neither procedure guarantees correct identification because human mistakes can get in the way. I will take a look at the fascinating science behind child identity from both maternal and paternal perspectives.

Neither Delia and Begoña's nor Beatriz's mother ever suspected that their nurses had given them the wrong infant to take home. The fact that neither mother doubted her relationship to her child made the truth even more difficult for them to accept.

A second societal concern involves the shock, disbelief, pain, and reluctant acceptance that the Canary Islands twins and their families experienced. The vital connection between parents and their young children is widely recognized, but the loss of this bond in adulthood has received little attention. Perhaps this is because our personal identities—who we are and where we came from; our sense of ourselves as continuous and connected—are in place by the time we reach adulthood. That may be true, but identities can be shattered, as they were for Delia, Begoña, and Beatriz—as well as for their mothers and fathers and their brothers and sisters.

Adoption is society's wonderful answer to people's desire to raise children when having biological children may not be an option. Adoption is also an excellent alternative for families who are unable to care for the babies they deliver. In my ongoing study of young reared-apart twins from China, a country that has followed a one-child policy since 1980,[34] most families adopted because of fertility problems (44 percent), but others did so because of their desire for another child (33 percent), the previous loss of a child (11 percent), humanitarian reasons (6 percent), or other circumstances (6 percent). However, these parents knowingly adopted these infants whose biological families purposefully relinquished them for adoption. At the same time, none of the families knew at the time of adoption that their child was part of a twin pair, although some suspected this due to their baby's resemblance to another.[35]

The parent-child relationship for Delia (the single twin) and for Beatriz (the unrelated twin) was the same as that between adoptive parents and their children—adoptive parents and children share their family environments, but they do not share genes. In contrast, the parents of the switched-at-birth twins did not give up their children, nor did they decide to raise someone else's child. Their lawsuits were largely intended to call attention to their suffering as a way of preventing other families from suffering their horrendous experience.

A third issue I will address concerns the conversion of psychological and emotional damages (e.g., loss of intimate association) into monetary compensation, a problem that has occupied attorneys representing plaintiffs in wrongful death and custody cases. This is a particularly difficult issue in switched-at-birth twin cases that involve unintentional separation. As I indicated, there have been only a few such cases involving identical twins, and none were examined with reference to the issues outlined above. The twins' attorneys and the Las Palmas judge gave the twin's situation considerable thought. As I will explain, Delia, Begoña, and Beatriz's situation was complex because Spain's judicial system made it unlikely that the twins and their families would receive generous awards.

It is also possible to examine the legal and moral aspects of biological and nonbiological parent-child association, issues posing formidable challenges for lawyers, philosophers, and ethicists. These are topics I will consider in a later chapter.

Throughout this book I will also address a fourth issue, namely the relative effects of genes and environments on intelligence, personality, habits, and health. As I noted, switched-at-birth twins offer scientists extraordinary research situations for assessing these effects, although the small number of cases precludes definitive answers. Nevertheless, what we learn from these cases can be viewed against the backdrop of the wealth of available twin studies.

Most parents believe that they significantly shape their children's behaviors, but research conducted throughout the last thirty years has revised this view. We now know that genetic effects are pervasive, influencing most behaviors, and that a shared environment contributes only modestly to behavioral development. Moreover, even these modest effects are seen mostly during childhood. This does not mean that environment does not matter—instead, the individual experiences people have apart from their families, such as taking an exotic vacation, learning to speak a foreign language, or starting a significant relationship, seem to matter more. And as Professor Bouchard stated in the preface to this book, children require a nurturing home environment to develop normally.

Parents of switched-at-birth twins are the new "experts" in the child development field. Delia and Beatriz's mother was baffled by the behavioral differences between her supposed fraternal pair—one studious and neat, the other not studious and casual. Delia's two unrelated siblings, Gara and Julia, had trouble understanding why Delia was so different from them. Everyone in these families agreed that a common environment does not play as big a role in shaping behavior as they had previously thought.

Twinning rates are rising, drawing needed attention to twins' special rearing and family circumstances. The experiences of switched-at-birth twins—growing up apart, learning the truth, and restoring their shattered identities—are more special than most.

2

SWITCHED AT BIRTH

This story contains the ingredients of a family
drama combined with a detective thriller.
—DAVID KLEIN, GENETICIST[1]

PAUL AND PHILIPPE—AND ERNSTLI

Amram Scheinfeld's classic book, *Twins and Supertwins* (1967),[2]
contains intriguing bits of twin-related information of interest
to scholars and to general readers. Scheinfeld's fourth chapter introduces
the story of three young boys, switched-at-birth twins (Paul and
Philippe Joye) and a non-twin "twin" (Ernstli Vatter) from the town of
Fribourg, Switzerland. Scheinfeld's reference to this case is brief, mostly
a description of the blood-typing and skin-grafting procedures used to
determine the seven-year-old boys' true relatedness to one another. Few
details surrounding the discovery of the switch, as well as the psychological consequences and emotional impact on the children and their families, were provided by Scheinfeld's text.

I recalled Scheinfeld's description of this case when the Las Palmas
story broke and became just as captivated by learning what had really
happened to the Fribourg twins. I discovered an informative and heartbreaking 1954 book, *He Was Not My Son,* written by the twins' mother,

Madeleine Joye.[3] Her story was first publicized in the United States in *Reader's Digest* (1951),[4] with book excerpts having appeared in *McCall's Magazine* (1954)[5] and in popular European publications such as France's *Paris Match* (1955) and Italy's *Gioia* (1956).[6] I also found scientific reports published by the geneticists Sir Archibald McIndoe from East Grinstead in West Sussex County, England, and by Professors Albert Franceschetti, Frederic Bamatter, and David Klein from Geneva, who managed the medical testing of the three children. The medical assessment was part of a judicial investigation into the case assigned to the physicians by Fribourg's justice of the peace. I wondered if any of the three brothers, who at the time of this writing would be nearly seventy years old, were still living. I found that one was.

Paul and Philippe—and Ernstli

Paul and Philippe's Family (Joye)	*Ernstli's Family (Vatter)*
Mother . . . . . Madeleine Joye	Mother . . . . . . Berthe Vatter
Father . . . . . . Philippe Sr.	Father . . . . Deceased
Twin . . . . Philippe	Single twin . . . Ernstli*
Non-twin . . . Paul	Sister . . . . Rose-Marie

*Ernstli, who was originally named Ernest Gottlob Vatter, chose the name Charles after he was returned to his biological family. Charles was the name of one of his uncles, and Ernstli said he chose the uncle's name because "I think he loves me."[7]

Identical twins, Philippe and Paul Joye, were born on July 4, 1941, in the Hôpital de la Miséricorde in Fribourg. Another male infant, Ernstli Vatter, was also born on that day in that clinic. The next morning, Mme. Joye was told by her nurse that her midwife had made a mistake in recording the birth weight of one of her twins—Paul, she thought, weighed twenty ounces more than originally indicated on his chart. In actuality, the true twin weighed 2,470 grams (5.45 pounds), but his weight "changed" in the records to 3,180 grams (7.01 pounds), the non-twin's weight after the accidental switch. The old entry, the erasure, and the new entry were clearly visible on the hospital chart when it was reexamined years later. But at the time Mme. Joye was happy that one of her twin sons was so robust and healthy. She forgot about the confusion over the birth weight until six years had passed, when the possibility of a switch loomed large. The significance of this information then was nearly impossible for her to bear. Mme. Joye was horrified to learn that the twelve newborns cared for at the clinic were identified by a label placed at the foot of their cribs. "Why do they put bands on chickens and not on newly born children?" she protested.[8]

Philippe and Ernstli (named Paul by his nonbiological rearing family) were raised as fraternal twins by Madeleine and Philippe Joye Sr., while Paul (named Ernstli by his nonbiological rearing family) was raised as a singleton by widower Mme. Vatter. In truth, Philippe and Paul were unknowingly raised as virtual twins, or same-age unrelated siblings. Ernstli had an older sister Rose-Marie, also unrelated to him, while the "twins" were the only children in their family. Philippe and Paul spoke only French, while Ernstli spoke only German. Both mothers were housewives and completely devoted to their sons. Phillipe Sr. made a good living as technical director of a film factory, whereas Mme. Vatter's husband, who died when Ernstli was three, left her extremely well off. Vatter had run a shop selling grain and seeds to the Cathedral of Fribourg. Ernstli's mother could provide him with toys, candies, and excursions that his biological family could not afford to the same degree. She also had a car.

Mme. Joye, a slim, dark-haired woman, is pictured on the back cover of her 1954 book with her husband, Philippe Sr. She is seated on a sofa, smiling with her hands folded, while her husband looks at her admiringly. The picture is at great odds with the story Mme. Joye had at last revealed.

Mme. Joye relished the striking physical and behavioral differences between her two sons. She celebrated Paul's irresistible charm and venturesome spirit in her moving memoir, based largely upon diaries she had maintained since the twins' birth and before she learned of the switch.[9] Paul was an "adventure yarn," so different from her true twin son Philippe, whom she called the "sentimental love story." When the "twins" were five, Mme. Joye took them to the barber, who commented on the boys' strikingly different appearance. She replied, "I'm very pleased, for I shouldn't like to have two children who had the same eyes, the same voices, the same faults, and the same illnesses. They would bore me."[10]

Mme. Joye did not disguise her favoritism for Paul, whom she did not realize until the switch was discovered was not her biological son. Seeing her infants in their cribs, she observed, "There was Paul, the beautiful comforting Paul, with his round cheeks, his plump body and happy air. . . . The other was Philippe, the gray, bony unfortunate one."[11] She saw qualities in herself that she shared with Paul but not with Philippe. "[Paul] has my brown eyes, the same shape of head and the same skin, always a little sunburnt. We also have several traits of character in common."[12] Mme. Joye was aware that "[Philippe] is also very jealous of the love I bestow on Paul."[13] When the children were six, Paul asked, "Mamam, who do you love best—Philippe or me? I replied instinctively without hesitation. You, Paul, but what I'm telling you is a secret and you mustn't tell anybody, especially Philippe."[14]

It was by chance that the three children were enrolled in the same German school when they turned five. The school was a half-hour's walk from the Joye's home, but the couple chose this school for their "twins" so they would learn German. Immediately, teachers, pupils, and the people of Fribourg started noticing Philippe and Ernstli's striking physical resemblance, but the idea that the children had been switched never occurred to anyone. In fact, many people in the town found the two boys' resemblance amusing. Then something happened at the annual June 1947 Fête Dieu (a celebration where those receiving first communion are honored) that made Philippe Sr., the "twins" father, think otherwise. At his wife's insistence, Philippe Sr. brought his camera to photograph their son's "double," the child named Ernstli. Philippe, Paul, and Ernstli were part of their school's procession, which stopped to pray and sing before the altars erected for the occasion across the town. When Philippe Sr. saw Ernstli, he was shocked by the similarities between his twin son and this other boy.

In a conversation with Ernstli's mother, Mme. Vatter, who also attended the parade, Philippe Sr. learned the date, time, and place of Ernstli's birth—exactly the same as that of his own sons. And he observed that Ernstli had the same height, smile, gestures, and gentle manner as Philippe. The twins also shared a dental anomaly, the absence of their two central inferior incisor teeth.[15] Soon after the parade, when Mme. Joye began to seriously suspect that Ernstli was one of her twin sons, she approached him at school, spoke with him, and then pulled down his lower lip. She saw the same "wretched, irregular teeth" and absence of two lower incisors she had seen in Philippe.[16] That moment was a terrible turning point for Mme. Joye because in her mind, it left little doubt that a switch had occurred. Hypodontia has been estimated to occur in 0.4% to 0.9% of European populations, but the twins' particular anomaly was even less frequent because most cases involve missing upper teeth.[17]

Mme. Joye could not ignore the implications of this rare shared dental trait and was compelled to seek medical proof of the boys' true relationship. But Mme. Vatter resisted this process for months, refusing to consider the possibility of a switch. The Joyes sought the assistance of the magistrate, who ordered that medical tests be conducted to determine the relatedness of the three boys. Mme. Vatter, working through her own attorneys, still refused to allow the examinations to go forward. Then, according to an October 1947 note in Mme. Joye's diary, Mme. Vatter changed her mind. "I shall probably never know what made her decide," Joye wrote.[18]

The process of establishing the relatedness and zygosity (twin type) of Philippe and Ernstli is chronicled in a fascinating series of papers by the aforementioned genetics team.[19] A series of physical examinations lasting twelve days included fingerprints, electrocardiograms, electroen-cephalograms, skeletal x-rays, and seventy-three body size measures. Charles's 2011 autobiography, *Medical Chronicle of an Ordinary Patient and The Clan of Charles Joye vs The Clan of Sigmoid Metastasis*, offers an insightful account of his childhood experience as a switched twin, as well as his later battle with lung cancer. He recalled that he, Philippe, and Paul had a great time at the Cantonal Hospital in Geneva where the testing took place, and they charmed the staff into decorating a Christmas tree and providing presents for them. Every measured trait showed a far greater resemblance between the boys reared apart (Philippe and Ernstli) than the boys reared together (Philippe and Paul). Philippe and Ernstli, but not Paul, also displayed a rare form of red-green color blindness or Daltonism (now called deuteranopia), a trait carried on the X chromosome.

The twins' case was complicated by the fact that the three children in question had the same blood type (A_1 and MN). However, the recent discovery by Landsteiner and Wiener in 1940 of the Rhesus (Rh) blood group was significant in this case, as shown in figure 2.1. Rh-typing revealed that Paul could not have been born to his legal mother (Mme. Joye) and could not have been the identical brother of his alleged twin (Philippe).[20] Mme. Joye's Rh subgroups were D,CC,ee, and Paul's Rh subgroups were dd,cc,ee. The finding that Mme. Joye had two CC genes (dominant) and Paul had two cc genes (recessive) proved that Paul was someone else's son because Mme. Joye could only transmit a dominant C gene to a child. In contrast, Philippe and Ernstli's Rh subgroups were D,Cc,Ee, consistent with their being Mme. Joye's children.

The Rh subgroups suggested, but could not prove, that Paul was not the biological son of his rearing father (Philippe Sr.). Philippe Sr. had Rh subgroups D,cc,Ee, so he could have transmitted c and e to Paul, who was dd,cc,ee. However, Philippe Sr. was also type D, so his underlying genotype could have been either DD or Dd. Because the d gene is relatively less frequent in the population,[21] he was most likely DD, in which case he could not have fathered Paul. The P blood group system was more informative because both M. and Mme. Joye were type pp, whereas Paul was type P, indicating that Paul could not have been conceived by the couple.

Paul's Rh subgroups were compatible with those of Mme. Vatter, so her maternity could not be disproved on that basis (see figure 2.1). Comparing blood groups between parents and children can rule out a biological connection if the groups do not match, but they cannot confirm a biological connection if they do match. Simply put, unrelated people may have common blood groups, especially if certain types occur frequently in a given population. For example, 37.4 percent of people living in the United States have type O+ blood,[22] but a type O+ female is not necessarily the mother of a type O+ child. It was also impossible to use the Rh subgroups to determine if Ernstli could have been the biological child of his rearing father because M. Vatter was deceased.

A final, conclusive procedure involved reciprocal skin grafts; this was the first time the technique had been used to establish personal identity. A skin graft is a patch of skin that is surgically removed from one part of the body and attached to another part of the body.[23] Reciprocal skin grafts typically involve exchanging skin from different parts of the body, such as from the forearm and abdomen in a study of patients with systemic sclerosis (connective tissue disease).[24] However, in this case, reciprocal skin grafts meant attaching skin taken from one boy to another. The grafts between Philippe and Ernstli healed perfectly, while those between Philippe and Paul showed necrosis (dead tissue). The results of the skin grafts were considered definitive proof that Philippe and Ernstli were MZ twins.

Analysis of multiple blood groups can establish MZ twinning with virtually 100 percent certainty, but the skin graft was considered the

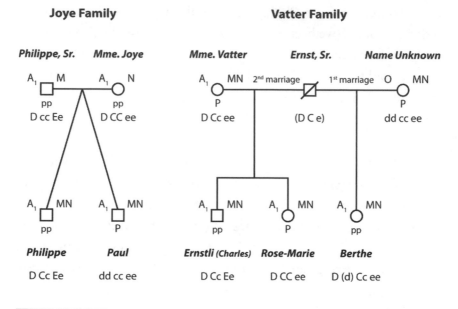

Joye Family   **Vatter Family**

Philippe, Sr.   *Mme. Joye*   *Mme. Vatter*   *Ernst, Sr.*   *Name Unknown*

A₁ □ M   A₁ ○ N   A₁ ○ MN   2ⁿᵈ marriage � 1ˢᵗ marriage O ○ MN
pp   pp   P   P
D cc Ee   D CC ee   D Cc ee   (D C e)   dd cc ee

A₁ □ MN   A₁ □ MN   A₁ □ MN   A₁ ○ MN   A₁ ○ MN
pp   P   pp   P   pp
Philippe   *Paul*   *Ernstli (Charles)* *Rose-Marie*   *Berthe*

D Cc Ee   dd cc ee   D Cc Ee   D CC ee   D (d) Cc ee

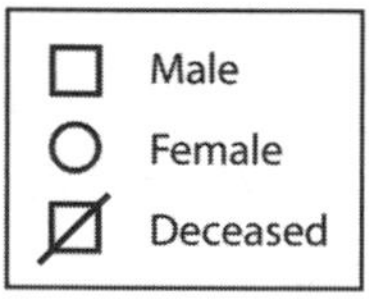

□	Male
○	Female
⊠	Deceased

Fig. 2.1. Rh blood group factors for the members of the Joye and Vatter families show that Paul could not have been Mme. Joye's son. Adapted from Albert Franceschetti, Frederic Baumatter, and David Klein, 1948.[25]

Fig. 2.2 a–e (facing page).
(a) Philippe (top) and Ernstli (bottom) show the same rare dental anomaly that is absent in Paul (middle), involving the absence of the two central inferior incisor teeth. The congenital lack of one to six teeth is known as hypodontia.[26]
(b) Radiographs of the boys' hands show missing radial carpal bones in Ernstli (left) and Philippe (right) but not in Paul (middle).
(c) Paul (left) and Philippe in the Joye household.
(d) Philippe (left) and Charles (right) in the garden surrounding the Joye home.
(e) Charles and Philippe vacationing near Kingsbridge, England.
Teeth and hands reprinted by permission of Elsevier Journals.[27]
First two childhood photographs courtesy of Charles Joye's family.
Third childhood photograph reprinted by permission of the *Daily Express/ZUMA Press.*

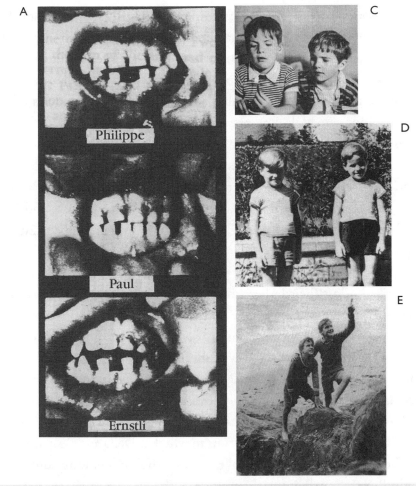

A Philippe

Paul

Ernstli

C

D

E

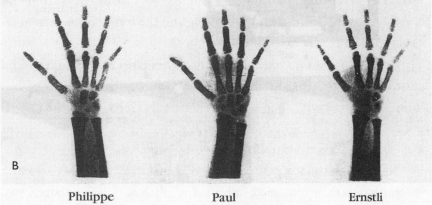

B Philippe Paul Ernstli

experimentum crucis (critical experiment) in this case.[28] It established the "absolute genetic proof" that Philippe and Paul were monozygotic or identical twins.[29] It is possible, albeit very rare, for nonidentical or dizygotic twins, or even unrelated individuals, to show agreement across multiple blood groups, especially if the population frequencies of the blood groups are high. Philippe and Ernstli's successful skin grafts were present upon examination ten months later.

The medical papers written after these procedures include wonderful photographs and charts created during the investigation.[30] Images of the boys' teeth and hands are shown in figures 2.2a and 2.2b, and pictures of the boys themselves are shown in figures 2.2c, 2.2d, and 2.2e.

Ernstli's lack of a rearing father reminded me that Begoña and Beatriz also lost their father when they were six years old, twenty-two years before the switch was detected. Therefore, their situation also precluded a test of whether each sister was the biological daughter of both of their rearing parents. However, in 2002 and 2003, establishing that Begoña and Beatriz were unrelated sisters and Delia and Begoña were the true MZ twins, respectively, was accomplished easily by modern DNA testing. And while the twins and their families waited for the results, there was never any worry as to whether Delia and Beatriz would be "returned" to their biological families—the women were adults, and only Beatriz was living at home.[31] But the Joyes and the Vatters did worry because their children were young and the future of their families was in the justice's hands.

The genetics team concluded without hesitation that Philippe and Ernstli were MZ twins and that a baby switch had inadvertently placed Philippe together with Paul. The physicians also recognized the importance of making the right decision with regard to the future placement of the boys, but they did not offer their opinion.

On June 19, 1948, a judge determined that Paul and Ernstli were to be returned to their biological families on July 1 of that year, barely two weeks away. The children were only seven years old, making the exchange emotionally excruciating for the small boys. Some think that the advantages and disadvantages of removing them from their loving homes at such a young age can still be debated, but others (like myself) think otherwise. I believe Paul and Ernstli should have remained with the families who raised them. The parent-child bond is very strong by age seven, so visitation and/or joint custody would have been an emotionally easier and more realistic choice for everyone, especially since the families lived in the same town. The twins, Philippe and Charles (formerly Ernestli), eventually adjusted to their new circumstances, but the process was especially painful for Ernstli (Charles) who spoke no French and was very attached to Mme. Vatter, who doted on him. Ernstli was also unaccustomed to sharing his parents with another child his age and suffered from having to share his belongings with a brother. But having a father in Philippe Sr. was a real attraction for him and helped ease his adjustment. The reunited twins also enjoyed the media attention and perks that went with it, such as fancy meals and interesting trips, in which Paul did not take part.

Less is known of how Paul coped with his new home because Mme. Vatter severed ties between the two families. In a 1990 autobiographical essay, David Klein, one of the geneticists who helped determine the relatedness of the three boys, reported that Mme. Vatter, already a widow, was devastated by the loss of the boy she adored and was psychologically unable to provide the same love and care to a boy who was unfamiliar to her. Consequently, Paul was raised in a series of boarding schools and foster homes. As for Mme. Joye, I believe that writing the book was her only reprieve because Paul stayed close as long as she had a pen in hand.

Mme. Joye's memoir gives the impression that she failed to fully comprehend the consequences of the medical studies she pressed so hard to obtain. It is likely that her immediate desire to know the truth blinded her to the fact that she might be giving up a son whom she loved. She may have persuaded herself that a relationship with Paul would still be possible, but it wasn't. Mme. Joye's actions also reveal the power and pull of biological connections, as well as the ease with which a mother can fall utterly in love with a child she raises from birth. She never got over losing Paul, and Mme. Vatter never forgot about Ernstli.

When Paul was eighteen, he visited the Joye home. There was some discussion of taking him in as a third brother, but it was not a workable plan. Philippe Sr. and his wife had moved on, and everyone had new problems of his or her own. Paul was abandoned yet a second time. Philippe and Paul saw each other as strangers even though they had been "twins" for the first seven years of their lives. Philippe still stayed in contact with Paul, whom he affectionately called his "false brother," describing him as a friend.[32]

In October 2008 I found the real twin Phillipe Joye, the subject of this discussion, living in Geneva. While searching for him, however, I first found a different and younger Philippe Joye, a specialist in electrical computer science and a professor at Fribourg's University of Applied Science of Western Switzerland. The younger Philippe, age forty-six, is unrelated to the switched-at-birth twins case, but he knew it well. He had met the older twin Philippe in 1992 while working for the Swiss Engineering and Architects Association (SIA), of which the twin Philippe was a key member. He also told me there are two other Philippe Joyes in the region and that one of them had run-ins with the law.[33] This created a strange situation for both the younger computer specialist Philippe and the older twin Philippe.

My finding the wrong person with the right name proved to be useful. The unrelated younger Philippe said the twin Philippe was "a real great person" and sent me a link to his website. Twin Philippe answered my message right away but could not speak at the time because he was caring for his ailing father. Eventually we spoke by telephone.

At age sixty-nine, the real twin Philippe Joye is a well-known architect and patron of the arts living in Geneva, Switzerland. He was married and divorced and has two sons, a daughter, and three grandchildren. Philippe is the only one of the three brothers who is still alive. His identical twin brother Charles (Ernestli), famous for his work in shopping center design, passed away in 2008 from cancer. Charles was also married and had a son, two daughters, and four grandchildren. Charles's business associate Neil Mitchenall, who works in property consultancy, called Charles a multitalented person, adding that "his brother is no fool, either."

Philippe was often seen at Geneva's University Hospital during his twin brother's treatment. According to Charles, "[Philippe], who manifested to me an unrelenting attachment, was one of my most faithful visitors. . . . There is not a day without a phone call from Philippe."[34]

Paul, the unrelated youngster raised with Philippe for seven years, passed away suddenly at age forty-five from cancer, probably brought on by excessive smoking. Paul had married, raised children, and become a postal worker. Philippe did not tell me about his relationship with Paul after the exchange, although he had maintained some form of contact, as indicated earlier.

The professional career paths chosen by the twins and the service-related job chosen by Paul are important differences between the twins and non-twin. Studies of job satisfaction and work values using twins reared apart and together have indicated genetic influence on these measures.[35] Of course, Philippe and Charles's similar personalities and temperaments were obvious even before they were reunited. Both twins were gentle and well behaved and had the same desire for intellectual success. Mme. Joye was once asked to list the ways in which Philippe and Paul were alike after living as presumed fraternal twins for seven years. She replied, "A categorical negative—in no way at all."

Philippe and I spoke several times by telephone between 2008 and 2009. At first he was willing to share his thoughts about his unusual life story. I arranged to visit him in Geneva in September 2009 after I had completed my work in the Canary Islands—he offered to show me his childhood home in Fribourg and the German school he had attended with his brothers. Philippe thought it might also be possible for me to meet Paul's sister, Rose-Marie, who was six years older, as well as some others in his family who remembered what had happened. But the plan fell apart days before I'd planned to arrive. Ultimately, Philippe's family members refused to revisit this painful episode. In an emotional e-mail message, Philippe explained that switching two boys back at age seven had been a terrible blow from which no one had recovered. He still found it incredible that no one could realistically assess the advantages and disadvantages of giving the boys back, weeping as he wrote these words to me. I was disappointed, but I understood.[36]

Mme. Joye probably did what most people in her situation would have done, which was to press hard for the truth—but it was an agonizing decision because the boys were young enough to be returned. Before medical proof was available, Mme. Joye believed her duty was to act in Paul's best interest, not her own. "Had we the right to keep a child who was not our own on the sole pretext that we loved him like a son and that we were convinced that we had his happiness at heart? Could one in any case be certain that one was acting for the happiness of the child? It was quite possible on the contrary that at twenty Paul would reproach us for having kept him. . . . There were too many unknown quantities in this problem for one to be able, without great danger, to flout natural laws. If Paul were truly [Madame Vatter's] son, he should be returned to her."[37] Two nights before Paul was to be taken to his new home, Mme. Joye wrote, "We wanted it like this and we thought we were doing our duty. Today I don't know which is true. I no longer know if it was really necessary to act as we did, and that is terrible."[38]

There are parallels between the events affecting Philippe and Charles (Ernstli), the twins Brent and George, whom I discuss below, and the Canary Islands twins, whose story I present in full later on. A common concern is whether it was better to learn the truth about the twins or to live contently with a concealed untruth. I am certain the

Joyes and the Vatters would have been happier had the truth never been known. I wonder if Philippe Sr. and Mme. Joye sometimes wished the school they had chosen for their children had been closer to home.

Whether twins are children or adults, once a switch becomes known, it significantly shapes the problems and dilemmas families face. It should not be assumed that the situation is easier for adult twins and their families. Switching back was not an issue for Delia and Beatriz because they were adults, but learning they had been born into different families severed their connection to a familiar past, leaving them with an uncertain future. This theme (and others) was also evident in a case of switched-at-birth male twins from Ottawa, Canada, named George and Brent. Learning that your grown son is not your son, and that a child you adopted years ago was destined for another family, has its own legal headaches and emotional heartaches.

GEORGE AND MARCUS—AND BRENT

George and Marcus—and Brent

George and Marcus's Family (Holmes)	Brent's Family (Tremblay)
Mother . . . . Laura	Mother . . . . Carroll
Father . . . . Randy	Father . . . . Jim
Twin . . . . George	Single twin . . . . Brent
Non-twin . . . . Marcus	Adopted brother. . . Wade
Biological sister . . . . Jessica	

I was visiting my parents in New York the night ABC aired an extraordinary segment of *Prime Time Live* called "My Three Sons." Events completely paralleled the story of Philippe, Paul, and Ernstli, at least in

Fig. 2.3. Reared-apart identical twins Brent (left) and George, with George's unrelated brother, Marcus. Photo by Wayne Cuddington, reprinted by permission of the *Ottawa Citizen*, April 5, 2000.

the beginning. The program documented the accidental switching of an identical infant male twin (Brent) with an unrelated infant (Marcus), sending false fraternal twins (George and Marcus) home with one family and one identical twin (Brent) to parents awaiting their adoptive baby boy. The switch occurred in 1971 when the children were two months old. The true twins met by chance at Ottawa's Carlton University when they were twenty years old because both were members of the Strategy Club, a group that shared interests in board games, cards, and chess. Brent was a student at Carlton; George was not, but he attended club meetings anyway. Someone who knew George thought she saw him on campus, but when she realized the person she was seeing wasn't George, she arranged for the two look-alikes to meet. George, Brent, and Marcus are shown in figure 2.3.

The ABC program aired on April 7, 1994. I was no longer working on separated twins in Minnesota, but I was studying virtual twins in

California. I was stunned by the human drama and scientific richness posed by the unusual situation faced by the two families. It was then that I realized George and Marcus formed a unique virtual twin pair, different from the type I had been studying, because George and Marcus and their parents had always believed they were twins. In my other virtual twin cases, the parents knew the true relationship of their children. I telephoned my colleague Dr. Thomas J. Bouchard Jr., the director of the Minnesota Study of Twins Reared Apart, and learned that all three brothers had been scheduled to visit his laboratory. George and Brent were the only pair of twins studied in Minnesota who had been separated under such circumstances. I regretted no longer being part of the Minnesota twin project but found ways to study George and Brent on my own. I visited Brent's family in Ottawa in 2002 and communicated with the twins by telephone and e-mail.

In George and Brent's case, an apparent succession of oversights by social workers and foster parents was responsible for the accidental switching.[39] The twins' mother and father, Laura and Randy, were unmarried when Laura delivered the twins, so they decided to place their children in the temporary care of the Children's Aid Society of Ottawa (CAS). The CAS provides community services, including foster care for up to one year, to protect children from abuse and neglect.[40] Marcus was placed there, as well, until he could be adopted. Soon, all three boys were sent to the same foster family. But their elderly foster parents were unable to manage three infants, so they made arrangements to move the twins to a different home. It was at this juncture that the right records accompanied the wrong babies to their second home. According to one source, the babies' ankle bracelets were temporarily removed and incorrectly replaced. According to another source, the elderly foster mother associated each child with his favorite stuffed animal, identifying each in this way. Perhaps one infant dropped his toy or grabbed his neighbor's, effectively deciding their fates.[41]

The twins' parents married and, as planned, returned to the Children's Aid Society to reclaim their children two months later. They were delighted with their fraternal twin sons and added a daughter, Jessica, to their family several years later. Across town, another set of parents, Jim and Carroll, also discovered the pleasures of parenthood with their single infant. Nobody knew that a child they were calling their own belonged elsewhere.

In the years to follow, had anyone paid greater attention to the odd events and strange coincidences that occurred to George and Brent, the truth might have come out earlier than it did. Perhaps the delay was a good thing, however, because it prevented the trauma caused by uprooting young children, as had happened to Paul and Ernstli. One afternoon, the twins' younger sister, Jessica, spotted Brent on a bus, but he didn't speak to her—she assumed that "George" was too embarrassed to be seen with his younger sister. There was also the night that the twins' parents attended a concert and noticed "their son" was there, too. They assumed his failure to acknowledge their presence reflected the self-consciousness of a teenager being seen with his family on a Saturday night. Had the parents or sister pursued these events, they would have realized that Brent, not George, had been riding the bus and enjoying the concert. But these occurrences went unmentioned until the twins' chance meeting at the Strategy Club in 1992.

Brent and George became fast friends for about a year, delighting in their common interests, such as weird movies, sports statistics, and grunge music. They had similar mannerisms and voice qualities. When they finally discussed their early childhoods, it became increasingly clear that they were identical twins, a possibility they hadn't really considered. The fact that this possibility did not present itself to them by surprise, but instead dawned on them gradually as they became friends, should have made the trauma of DNA confirmation easier to bear. It did not.

It may be surprising that it took Brent and George so long to figure out what appears so obvious in hindsight. Interestingly, twins reared together accentuate their differences, while twins reared apart accentuate their similarities. Brent and George were not exceptional in this regard, although unlike most other separated twins, their meeting was not in the context of a twins' reunion. Having a long-lost twin is not something most people think about. Even when others insist that we "look just like someone else," the tendency is to discount such claims as chance. Delia and Begoña did so even when others were so struck by their physical resemblance to someone else. George had no reason to doubt that Marcus was his twin brother, especially because Marcus coincidentally looked a lot like their father.

Brent and George surprised both sets of parents by walking into the other's home unannounced. George's grandmother had no idea that the young man giving her a hug was not George, and Brent's mother was completely fooled when George showed up for dinner wearing Brent's clothes. But the jokes wore off quickly, and both sets of parents were seriously shaken when they realized the deeper implications of the situation. DNA tests eventually proved that George and Brent were the real twins, and Marcus was an unrelated and unintended member of his family. The emotional aftershocks escalated, but Laura and Randy never abandoned Marcus, insisting that he would always be their son. And like Mme. Joye, Laura did not see her newly found son as a son, even though he looked exactly like the other child she'd raised. Parents' attachment to a child comes from continuous care and interaction, and she had enjoyed neither with Brent.

The two families filed a lawsuit against Ottawa's Children's Aid Society, a case that continued for years. The terms of the settlement remain undisclosed, but the rank ordering of each person's compensation is generally known. The twins' parents were compensated most generously for having missed the opportunity to raise their biological son. The judge decided that this hardship outweighed the distress that Brent's family underwent because they were destined to receive an adoptive child. The twins and Marcus were compensated for the loss of family connections, but Marcus received a greater award than Brent.

The families' attorney, Arthur Cogan, justified the size of Marcus's compensation by his sudden loss of a biological connection, although Cogan was also sympathetic to Brent's suffering. The twins' biological sister, Jessica, and Brent's adoptive brother, Wade, received modest compensation for the trauma they endured. Brent's adoptive mother was unhappy with this outcome. In her unpublished diaries, she claimed that Brent deserved the most in compensatory damages because he always believed his biological family had rejected him.[42] Of course, deciding whose loss was "worth more" is a complex task, and there is no single solution.

The friendship that Brent and George established so readily was remarkable. Perhaps they came together easily because they met as friends, not as switched-at-birth twins. Their early relationship flourished free from any emotional turmoil on the part of their parents, who did not yet know. However, by 2002 George and Brent's relationship had unraveled. George changed in ways that Brent did not. Perhaps this is because Brent had struggled within a restrictive family environment that did not match his easygoing temperament; when he met George's more relaxed family he fit right in. When I spoke to the twins in 2005, George had cut his hair and secured a full-time job, while Brent had kept his hair long and bounced from one job to another. Perhaps George felt that Brent mirrored what he believed were his less desirable traits and tried to distance himself from the person he once was or thought he could become again.

George and Brent enjoyed a lot of quality time together. Early in their relationship, George said, "You would not find two people more in sync than Brent and me."[43] I hoped they would reconcile some day because there was so much potential there for great friendship and understanding, and it turned out that they did. I learned this in September 2010 when I contacted Brent's mother, Carroll, to see if Brent would participate in a reared-apart twins documentary being planned by a cable television station in the United States. Carroll said that Brent and George had reconnected during the summer of 2009 and had been drinking coffee and watching sports together. In February 2009 Brent became a commissioner, a security professional, working in one of Ottawa's government buildings. He earned high marks on the qualifying exam, was accepted for the job, cut his shoulder-length hair, and began working twelve-hour shifts. According to Carroll, "Brent turned his life around. Now he and George have something to talk about."[44]

Actually, Brent and George always had something to talk about, but for a while their lives were out of sync. Sometimes one twin gets ahead of the other, but the one who is behind usually catches up.

KASIA AND NINA—AND EDYTA

Once I discovered the Canary Islands twins, other switched-at-birth pairs started to surface. Perhaps I was more aware of such events, paying greater attention to relevant twin news, or maybe reports of one switched-at-birth pair encouraged others to come forward. These stories piqued journalists' interest and ultimately my interest as well. In April 2009 I read about another court case, which had settled after seven years, involving twenty-five-year-old identical female twins from Warsaw, Poland. In October 2010 I mentioned this case to California State University, Fullerton graduate student Michael Mikulewicz from Poland, who remembered it had been covered widely by the Polish press.

Kasia and Nina's Family (Ofmański)	*Edyta's Family (Wierzbicki)*
Mother ..... Elzbieta	Mother .... Halina
Father ...... Andrzej	Father .... Aleksander
Twin .... Kasia	Single twin .... Edyta
Non-twin ... Nina	Older brother ..... Martin

During the night of December 15, 1983, Polish identical twins, Kasia and Nina Ofmańska, and another newborn girl, Edyta Wierzbicka, were born prematurely in different maternity clinics in Warsaw.[45] Kasia and Nina (Edyta) were the first and only children in their family, while Edyta (Nina) was the second child in her family. Edyta's brother, Martin, was three years older than her; he had been born after another infant who had died. According to the twins' father, Andrzej Ofmański, whom I interviewed by telephone on October 23, 2010, while he was on his yacht, he and his wife, Elzbieta, had not been told initially whether their twins were identical or fraternal. In fact, Elzbieta developed pneumonia while she was in the hospital and hardly saw her babies, who were transferred immediately to incubators.

At first all three babies went home with the right parents, but that was about to change. Two weeks after their birth, the true twins, Kasia and Edyta, and Nina ended up in the Saskiej Kępie Clinic after developing lung infections from the cold temperatures in the hospitals in which they were born. Parental contact during the infants' intensive treatment was limited to "looking at them through a window."[46] Kasia came home after one month, and Nina came home two weeks later. Ofmański did not know when Edyta had been released to the Wierzbikis, but the switch conceivably could have occurred before Nina's release. Photos of the virtual twins, Kasia and Nina as babies, and all three sisters as young children and adults, are displayed in figure 2.4.

Even though it is uncertain at what point the baby switch occurred, it is easy to see how it happened. Nurses who had penciled in identifying information removed the babies' ID tags while they were bathed. The newborn twins and non-twin infant were housed in the same crowded nursery, increasing the chances of human error.

The truth about the twins first became known in June 2000 when Emilia, a primary school friend of Kasia, gave seventeen-year-old Kasia the phone number of her "double," who lived on the other side of Warsaw. This was not the first time the twins had been confused for one another.[47]

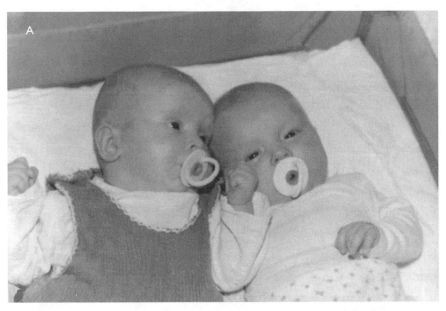

Fig. 2.4. (a) Virtual twins Kasia (right) and Nina (left) as six-month-old infants. (b) Kasia and Nina at age four. (c) Edyta, Kasia, and Nina at age eight (courtesy of Andrzej Ofmański). (d) Kasia displaying photographs of herself (left), her identical twin Edyta, and her sister Nina (reprinted by permission of Janet Skarzynski/AFP/Getty Images). This picture was taken in 2005, five years after the twins' reunion.

In March of that year a young man whom Edyta did not know came up to her at a concert and kissed her. Jacek Hugo-Bader, the first journalist to interview the twins, called this "strange and shocking."[48] Kasia's friends were surprised to see her at the Barbicon[49] alongside teenagers wearing black leather jackets and army boots, but she denied being there.

Elzbieta overheard the twins' first telephone conversation.[50] Kasia was asking someone about dates of birth and exclaiming how much their voices sounded the same. Elzbieta listened more closely. She heard something about "different maternity hospitals," information that was reassuring, but when she heard about a "right foot deformity," she became anxious. One of her newborn twins had been diagnosed with a clubfoot, but the condition had apparently cleared up by the time she went home from the second hospital. Perhaps a touch of concern triggered by the babies' differences, but disregarded for years, suddenly returned. Kasia refused to give her mother Edyta's telephone number.

The twins met for the first time by Zygmunt's Column, which is situated in Warsaw's Castle Square.[51] Andrzej said they decided to keep their relationship secret for two months because they were afraid of their parents' reactions. When Kasia finally told her father about Edyta and the possible switch, Andrzej was angry. "I did not believe it and I told her never to mention it again. I thought she was being a crazy teenager," he told me. A week later, Kasia invited Edyta to meet her mother, Elzbieta, and the sight of this girl who looked exactly like her own daughter sent Elzbieta into a deep depression that required medication for some time.[52] When Andrzej met Edyta a week later, he was shocked at the discovery and "angry at the doctors [who were responsible]."

I asked Andrzej to describe his first meeting with Edyta. "I noticed that she didn't know what to call [my wife and me], so I immediately suggested she call us by our first names, and that is what broke the ice." The family had dinner and talked about their relatives, jobs, hobbies, and vacations. But already [Edyta] was treated by my wife and me as our own child. The moment I saw her . . . well, she was just my daughter."

Andrzej told me he had "*never* suspected that Nina was not his daughter." In fact, when the girls came home the second time, one of their grandmothers remarked that Kasia resembled her father and Nina resembled her mother. By then, a doctor in the Saskiej Kępie Clinic had examined the twins and had told Elzbieta that they were not identical. Even when Andrzej could not tell the twins apart when they came home the first time, Elzbieta always could.

Andrzej said that once a switch was suspected, it was Nina who insisted that DNA tests be done, although there was little doubt that a switch had occurred. The DNA test results, completed in January 2001, showed a 99.99 percent probability that Elzbieta had given birth to Edyta and Halina (Wierzbicka) had given birth to Nina.[53] Nina, knowing she was unrelated to the mother and father who had raised her, cried herself to sleep each night, causing Andrzej unbearable pain as he walked past her room. Andrzej was close to Nina and described her to me as "a very emotional, modest, and timid girl."

Edyta's parents, Halina and Aleksander Wierzbicki, were also in shock over the discovery, causing Halina to emphasize any small difference between the twins as possible evidence against their twinship.[54] Some of the parents sought counseling, and Aleksander started drinking occasionally due to the loss of his relationship with his daughter Edyta, who severed relations with both him and his wife.[55] Edyta told the press why she could not get along with her parents: "It's because we have different blood. . . . I thought I fought with them because I matured. On the other hand, Nina fits perfectly with them."[56] The families sued the hospital for 100,000 zlotys, equivalent to US$33,000. The case settled in April 2009.

The Warsaw twins' case had warning signs that went unheeded. As I indicated, one of the twins (the original Nina) was born with a right clubfoot, a minor deformity of which her parents were aware when she entered the Saskiej Kępie Clinic at two weeks of age for lung treatment. However, when she was released, the condition had miraculously disappeared! The physiotherapist assigned to administer Nina's massage treatment did not detect a problem because he was examining the wrong infant. "Nina" had also gained a considerable amount of weight, an improvement that pleased her parents enormously. At the same time, the supposed non-twin child, Edyta, "acquired" a foot problem after her hospital stay, something her mother and father, Halina and Aleksander, might have examined more closely. But according to the twins' mother, Elzbieta, "You have to remember that those were Communist times. You didn't ask too many questions of hospitals in those days."[57] Regardless, some questions need answers. Interestingly, both Kasia's and Edyta's parents had told their daughters about the respective "disappearance" and "appearance" of the foot problem, further convincing the two girls that they were twins when they first met.

If the twins' parents didn't ask the right questions, they certainly made the right observations. The Ofmańskis were struck by the fact that Kasia and Nina grew more and more dissimilar over time. Kasia was an outgoing girl with a zest for skiing and sailing, while Nina was an introvert who preferred staying home and playing with dolls. But fraternal twins (and full siblings) often show different behavioral patterns, owing partly to their different genes. This is well known, so there was no reason for anyone to question the twins' differences. But old observations assumed new significance following the discovery. Andrzej recalled, "My wife reminded me later, after we found out about all this, that when Nina was ten or twelve she kept saying, 'Mommy, something is wrong because I don't look like you or dad.' She walked around saying that as if she sensed something [wasn't right]. She was insistent about it. . . . We treated it as a little child's invention."

In contrast with the false twins, the real twins Kasia and Edyta had a long list of similarities. Their smiles, their walks (leaning slightly forward), and their school grades were the same. Kasia and Edyta even had the same moles on their hands. Andrzej also told me that both twins paint, wear the same outfits, and enjoy pork roast with prunes.

The two families are friendly and celebrated the twins' first birthday together when they turned eighteen. However, the twins were estranged from one another at the time of this writing. Nonetheless, their lives are inextricably intertwined as they and their parents imagine a childhood and a life that might have been but can never be. In fact, Edyta severed ties with everyone in both families, but Andrzej could not say exactly why—he suspects that she did not know how to cope with the discovery and its aftermath. Elzbieta deeply regrets that one of her twin daughters was home for only a few days, then taken away for seventeen years. Elzbieta still suffers considerably because, according to Andrzej, she has been belittled for not knowing her own child. Elzbieta said that people don't understand why she and her husband didn't realize that "Nina wasn't Nina," but she explained that the baby was placed in an incubator immediately after birth.[58]

The media attention the case received exacerbated everyone's personal difficulties. The Internet included unkind comments from people who faulted the families for taking legal action. However, some people responded with compassion, while others suspected that their own children had been swapped and wondered what they should do.

I spoke briefly by telephone with Kasia in September 2009, but she found the situation too difficult to discuss and her limited English made it difficult for us to talk. Like Philippe Joye, she and her family have been traumatized by the upheaval in their lives and the media attention that disrupted their privacy. I sent her my e-mail address, but she never responded. Then, in August 2010, I received a request from Dr. Cezary Zekanowski of the Medical Research Center of the Polish Academy of Sciences for a twin research paper I had written on such diverse topics as athletic talent, leukemia, and unusual twins.[59] I sent him the paper, asking him if he would kindly call the Ofmański and Wierzbicki families to determine if interviews with any family members might be possible. The Wierzbickis, who no longer have contact with Edyta, declined, but Andrzej Ofmański was willing to talk to me. Andrzej told me he represents all four parents and is not shy about speaking out. He is an interior and theatrical set designer for film and television and is comfortable with the media.

Andrzej said the two families have been accused of filing a lawsuit simply for financial gain, but he insisted, "It is not about the money. We had to make things right. People in Poland don't have a tradition of suing hospitals, and it was hard to find an attorney. But [our case] is breaking barriers."[60] The Ministry of Health tried to persuade the court that the babies had been swapped outside the hospital, but Andrzej procured documentation showing that the doctors were at fault. In fact, the doctor responsible for the three infants' treatment in the second hospital testified that other baby switches had probably occurred.

Like the parents of the other switched-at-birth twins, the Ofmańskis and the Wierzbickis did not willingly relinquish their children for adoption; their children were taken from them, even if unintentionally. Their emotional reactions mimic those of families mourning the loss of a child that was supposed to be. It's common knowledge that families sue doctors and hospitals for medical negligence leading to the death of a child. The "care-taking negligence" of the nursing staff in this case seems to justify compensation to the two families.

Kasia, Edyta, and Nina were seventeen when they learned the truth, an age at which "switching back" was not an option. Andrzej Ofmański said he wished the mistake had never been discovered. "I'd have preferred to continue living as we did before, without knowing."[61] Andrzej also said, "If only the mistake had been discovered when they were little." If Andrzej understood English, I would have sent him Mme Joye's book so he would realize that baby switches are painful even when young children are involved.

Mistakes discovered when twins are toddlers can also lead to lifetimes of unhappiness and regret, as shown by a "double-twin-switching" case in Puerto Rico. The mistake in that case was caught (somewhat) in time, or so I thought at first.

Mari Tairí and Samantha—and Tairí Mari and Jennifer,
or
Mari Tairí and Tairí Mari—and Jennifer and Samantha

Mari Tairí and Tairí Mari's Family (Hernández)	Jennifer and Samantha's Family (Hernández)
Mother . . . . Dulce	Mother . . . . Rosaura
Father . . . . Juan	Father . . . . Unknown
Twin . . . . Mari Tairí	Twin . . . . Jennifer
Non-twin . . . . . . Tairí Mari (really Samantha)	Non-twin . . . . Samantha (really Tairí Mari)
Aunt . . . . Gloria	

> This is not the kind of case they teach you in law school.
> HAROLD D. VICENTE, ATTORNEY[62]

Lexis-Nexis, the computerized search engine containing US statutes, laws, and case opinions dating back to the 1770s, seemed like a good resource for finding other switched-at-birth twin cases that made it as far as the courts. The case I found involved two simultaneous switches, just like the two fictional Sadie and Rose pairs from the film *Big Business*. The difference was that *Big Business* was a comedy, whereas this Puerto Rican situation was a tragedy in ways that distinguish it from all the others. I discovered the unusual case of identical twins Tairí Mari and Mari Tairí and fraternal twins Samantha and Jennifer in September 2008, shortly after I discovered the Canary Islands twins.

On September 3, 1985, physicians at the University Hospital in the Rio Piedras Medical Center of Puerto Rico delivered two sets of twin girls, one MZ and one DZ, to two different women.[63] The mothers, Dulce Hernández Ramos and Rosaura Hernández Morales, had the same first family name (Hernández), and it was this information alone that was used to match babies with their mothers.[64] Today, everyone thinks this practice may have contributed to the mistake in this case, but no one knows for certain. In 2010, I located Dulce and her family through her attorney, Harold D. Vicente. I was unable to speak with Rosaura and her family, despite having contacted one of her attorneys, José A. León Landrau. Landrau said that Rosaura and her daughters had decided to close the matter entirely so as to live their lives in privacy. However, I learned a lot about the other Hernández family from Dulce; Dulce's husband, Juan Ramón Flores De León; and Dulce's sister, Gloria, who had had considerable contact with Rosaura and her twins. I [Ramón] also spoke with US District Judge Hector M. Laffitte, who rendered the opinion in this case.[65]

According to Dulce, for whom having twins was an unexpected surprise, mothers spent twenty-four hours in the University Hospital after giving birth, but twins remained under observation for forty-eight hours. She did not hold or touch her infant twins after their birth; she only saw them briefly. But on the second day, the nurses brought Mari Tairí and Tairí Mari for her to hold and breastfeed, which she did that morning, afternoon, and evening. "I found them really alike the day I was discharged," she recalled. In fact, the doctors had told her the girls were identical because there was only one placenta. Single placentas are consistent with, but not proof of, monozygotic twinning (the two placentas of a dizygotic twin pair can fuse to create the appearance of one placenta). In fact, about 30 percent of MZ twins have two placentas and 40 percent of DZ twins have fused placentas, so the number of placentas does not necessarily reflect twin type.[66]

Once Dulce was discharged from the hospital, she and Juan saw their twins only through a glass panel. When they returned to the hospital four days later on September 7 to finally take them home, they noticed that one twin was missing her ID bracelet, possibly because the baby was thin and it had fallen off. But the bracelet was in the crib.

Looking at the girls, Dulce thought there was something unfamiliar about one of the twins.[67] "I told the nurse that the babies didn't look alike. The nurse told me babies usually change suddenly and that the baby was mine. I had never heard about switches, and you always think those hospitals are 100 percent safe. I never thought they had switched them. I was only twenty-one years old. The nurse said I probably had concerns because I was a new mother. She didn't even try to check if there was a mistake." In fact, legal documents say the nurse remarked disparagingly that Dulce was a "primeriza" (first-time mother).[68]

If Dulce had never nursed her twins, she might not have had the reaction she did when the wrong baby was released to her care. "When I first saw Samantha [the baby I named Tairí Mari], at that moment I didn't feel the same love I felt for the other baby. . . . I felt there was something strange." Soon this baby developed severe asthma attacks, requiring hospitalization. Dulce stayed at the hospital with the baby, lying next to her much of the time. "I began to love her more and more and to feel deeply sorry for her until I eventually got used to it." Perhaps Dulce was trying to compensate for feeling differently toward this twin.

Dulce's husband Juan had a similar experience. Juan was a new father at age twenty-one, also shocked but completely delighted by the birth of twins. "When I saw a trolley with the two babies, I asked who they belonged to, and the nurse answered Hernández, Dulce. I asked the nurse which one of the two was mine and she answered that both of them were mine. I began jumping for joy." He and Dulce were told that the twins were identical, but when he finally saw them, they did not look identical. "Somehow they scoffed at us because we were young parents. [The nurse] said there were twins who looked alike and some that didn't. I never thought they had switched the babies."[69]

Juan accepted the nurse's reasoning and was happy that the dark-haired twin (Mari Tairí) resembled his wife and the light-haired twin (Tairí Mari, who was really Samantha) resembled him. It turned out that Samantha and her twin sister Jennifer were born to a fair-skinned mother and Black father, but the twins were both fairly light skinned. Like the other parents whose babies were switched, Juan and Dulce mentally reviewed their family pedigrees to convince themselves that the different-looking child was really theirs. Juan's mother, while Caucasian, appeared to be of mixed origin, and everyone said Samantha looked like her father and grandmother.

A year and a half went by before Dulce's sister Gloria (the twins' aunt) figured out that one of her young nieces was someone else's twin.[70] The discovery was made in a hospital waiting room in a two-part scenario told to me by Gloria and Dulce. On April 10, 1987, one of Dulce's sisters (either Zoraida or Marilyn according to Gloria) took one of the nineteen-month-old twins to the Public Hospital of Guaynabo for vaccinations. There, Rosaura, the other twins' mother, saw the child and seemed to think she was hers—Rosaura seemed to want to take the child but then apologized, saying she had a daughter who looked just like her. When Dulce heard this story, she immediately remembered that a woman in the hospital had given birth to twins the day after she had. Gloria said not to worry and offered to follow up on this incident. But it is easy to see how unsettling this event would be to Dulce, who had experienced initial doubts over one twin daughter's identity.

The actual switch was discovered by the twins' three-year-old cousin Yarimar, a point that is inexplicably missing from the articles and documents I've reviewed. Gloria, Zoraida, and Marilyn took young Yarimar with them when they returned to the hospital waiting room, expecting Rosaura to show up with her twins. Rosaura did arrive accompanied by the twin she had named Jennifer—in reality this girl was Tairí Mari, the dark-haired twin of Mari Tairí. Yarimar happened to spot the child and mistook her for her cousin Mari. According to Dulce, who heard the story from Gloria, "The child told her mother 'Mari is here.' [My sister] told her daughter that was impossible because Dulce is home with the twins. The child kept insisting that Mari was there, but her mother didn't give it much importance. Gloria said they had to check, and when she approached the baby, she realized she was identical to my daughter Mari Tairí. At that moment, the baby made a gesture that the other twin also used to do, and that gesture impressed Gloria the most. She thought [the two girls] did everything in the same way."

Gloria approached Rosaura. "We asked Rosaura when and where she had given birth. We asked her some other things related to the twins.

Fig. 2.5. Dulce and Juan Hernández with identical twins Mari and Tairí (above) and Rosaura Hernández with fraternal twins Jennifer and Samantha (below). The switched twins were returned to their biological families at age two. Reprinted by permission of the *Weekly World News*.

We asked her if her daughter had a twin sister with blonde curly hair, and she said yes. Every detail matched up. I told her I thought the twins had been switched. We took her address and followed her home to be sure she lived where she said she did."[71] Rosaura, a single mother with four daughters besides the twins, lived in the Jardines de Guaynabo public housing project. Juan told me that these residences are subsidized by the state and can be situated in dangerous neighborhoods. Judge Laffitte remembered this case immediately when I spoke with him, calling it "exceptional—it seemed strange, sending a twin from a wealthy family back to a housing project."[72]

Later in the day that Yarimar saw a girl she thought was "Mari Tairí," the two families arranged to meet at Rosaura's apartment. Dulce had called Juan at work to tell him to meet them there. At first Juan told Dulce not to go because it might not be safe, but she insisted. When they arrived, each girl was immediately attracted to her real twin, reacting as though staring into a mirror. Juan remembers that Rosaura kept laughing, possibly from nerves, but it bothered him because it was inappropriate to the situation. Blood tests eventually confirmed that Mari Tairí and Tairí Mari were identical twins and that Jennifer and Samantha, who looked very much alike, were fraternal twins. Pictures of the two twin pairs and their mothers are shown in figure 2.5.

The baby exchange took place gradually over the following six months and became final on September 17, 1987, just days after the twins turned two. Dulce insisted on a slow transition to ease everyone's adjustment. In fact, Dulce and Juan cared for all four girls on several occasions and would have kept all four, or at least their own whom they hadn't raised (the real Tairí Mari, called Samantha) and the one they had raised (the real Samantha, called Tairí Mari) if at all possible. But when Rosaura filed a lawsuit, Dulce was told she could no longer have the real Samantha in her home. "My older sisters took the baby to the room and I left crying. . . . I felt as if I were giving my baby away as a present. It was a horrible, shocking experience, and I felt I was doing a very bad thing. Samantha would not stop crying. She kept grabbing my leg as if to say 'You can't leave me here.'"[73] Dulce visited the child every three days after that but was told to limit her visits to every three weeks because Samantha was not bonding with her biological mother. "We went to visit the child three months after that. When I saw her, she turned her face away, and the sensation was just horrible. . . . Shortly afterwards, she greeted me and sat next to me. It was a very difficult time." Gloria was also there on that day. "It was as if [Samantha] had stabbed a knife in our hearts."[74]

Rosaura presented a very different picture in the press, claiming, "When Dulce left Samantha here it was as if she had spent her whole life here. And when Tairí Mari comes over to visit she doesn't want to go home afterward."[75]

In contrast with Rosaura's opinion, Dulce claimed that Tairí Mari, formerly Jennifer, made a wonderful adjustment to her new home. "[Tairí] behaved as if she had always been living with me." In a 1990 interview in the *San Juan Star* newspaper, Dulce admitted that Tairí can be "distrustful and insecure."[76] She would not stay with anyone unfamiliar unless her mother; Aunt Gloria; or twin sister, Mari, were there, too. This is understandable—at age four and a half children cannot fully articulate their feelings, but they can connect events in what they see as a causal way, even if their thinking does not seem rational to adults. Being in a new location might have signaled a permanent relocation in Tairí's young mind—once she left Rosaura's apartment, she did not return except for visits. Having her mother, aunt, and sister nearby probably made her feel more secure.

Juan saw that the real identical twins had an "inexplicable bonding." He explained that Tairí immediately copied what Mari did. Mari had a habit of sucking her middle and ring fingers. She would then take a bit of cotton and pretend it was a moustache, rubbing it with her index and little fingers. Tairí used to suck only one finger, but she began to suck two like her sister. "She got used to Mari really quickly." Some people might think her behavior implied that identical twins are alike simply because they mimic one another, but that is not necessarily so. More likely, Tairí found it easy to act like her sister because she was like her to begin with. After all, it was the twins' similar gestures that caught Gloria's eye before the twins met.

Lawsuits were filed separately by both families. Juan and Dulce's complaint was filed by Juan's father, Pablo De León López, because he was living in Saint Croix, which made him eligible to file in US federal court; in Puerto Rico Juan and Dulce could only have filed in a local court. The case has been settled at the time of this writing.

The difficulties did not end once the babies were switched back. Dulce lost a great deal of weight, dropping to between eighty and eighty-five pounds from ninety-two. She began having panic attacks. Juan also experienced considerable stress, and the couple eventually divorced; each has since remarried. Juan resigned from his job, not realizing he was jeopardizing the family's medical plan, a decision that caused Dulce even greater upset. Everyone, including the four girls, received counseling. In a telephone interview Juan said, "I have to say you are lucky to hear this story because I don't usually talk about it with anyone." During the proceedings, his psychologist encouraged him to move forward, meaning he should forget the events of the past. "I tried to forget everything that happened. . . . Somehow the pain was still there, but it was softer." He said he would have been happier not knowing the truth—"No one likes to hear that their child has been switched. That's like saying your child has been killed. I haven't been able to overcome it."[77]

Juan believed the entire event would have been more painful if it had happened when the twins were older. That is difficult to judge. In the other cases, it was too late to return the older twins like Kasia and Edyta, Brent and George, and the Canary Islands twins Delia and Begoña. I believe that it is impossible and unproductive to assess hypothetical outcomes in these cases because each is unique. Families learning the truth when their twins are children cannot anticipate the effects of learning the truth about switched twins when the twins are adults and vice versa.

Fig. 2.6. (a) Tairí (right) and Mari (left) at age eight with their younger sister Karla (courtesy of Tairí Mari De León Hernández) and (b) Tairí at age twenty-four in California (courtesy of Iris Blandón-Gitlin).

Outside events can also intervene, as Juan and Dulce's second cata-
strophe shows. About one month after the exchange took place, Mari,
the twin Juan and Dulce had raised from birth, began vomiting everything she ate. Doctors eventually determined that Mari had a brain
tumor, and she had to spend weeks in the hospital for surgery and
chemotherapy. Dulce prayed that the twins would have some time
together at home and at school to get to know one another, and they did
until the fourth grade, when nine-year-old Mari relapsed. Mari suffered
a brain hemorrhage that proved fatal. Juan had to tell Tairí that her twin
had passed away, and Jennifer, who had been raised in Rosaura's home
with Tairí (as Samantha) for a year and a half, fainted at the funeral
thinking the deceased was Tairí.[78]

I spoke with Tairí Mari in February 2010 and met her in June 2010
when she came to southern California to visit the California State University, Fullerton campus; she was considering the school for her graduate
studies. Tairí is a charming and beautiful twenty-four-year-old. She holds
a bachelor's degree in information technology and several academic and
nonacademic honors. She also danced part-time in a televised children's
production while looking for work and planning for her education.

Tairí stayed in California for six days during which time a Spanish-
speaking colleague, Dr. Iris Blandón-Gitlin, and I listened to Tairí's
extraordinary life story, introduced her to students, and took her to Dis-
neyland. A photograph of Tairí Mari and Mari Tairí at age eight is
shown in figure 2.6 alongside a photograph of Tairí as an adult enjoying
California.

Tairí had an interesting perspective on what had happened to her
and her family. She remembers virtually nothing about the time she
spent in Rosaura's apartment as Jennifer's twin.[79] This is not surprising
because autobiographical memory does not emerge until close to age
three.[80] However, Tairí does remember the four girls playing together
when they were a little older, always in the pairs in which they were initially raised. Tairí's present suffering comes from seeing her parents, Juan

and Dulce, suffer and from the loss of her twin sister Mari Tairí. She believes it would have been far worse for her had the switch occurred later in life because she would have returned to a home without a twin after having lived life with a twin, albeit a false one. Tairí also wonders about the nature of her relationship with Rosaura, the mother who raised her for the first year and a half of her life. According to Tairí, Rosaura never reached out to her during the visits following the exchange, whereas Dulce and Juan felt a deep attachment to Samantha and stayed in touch with her as much as possible. Samantha still calls Dulce her "mum" and has told her sons that Dulce is their grandmother. She calls Dulce on Christmas and Mother's Day.

Tairí still feels like a twin and gains strength from the short, wonderful relationship she shared with Mari. She is very moved when she sees other twins. Her thoughts on fraternal twins are strikingly different from those of most people, but they are fully understandable: "When I see fraternal twins, I always ask myself if they have been switched. I try to have a look at their parents. They could be fraternal twins, but there could also have been a mistake." Tairí and her mother are planning to write a book further describing their perspectives on the switch and its aftermath.

Tairí has emerged relatively unscathed from the mix-up that happened twenty-five years ago. Her young age shielded her from memories of her first home and her entry into her second home. Dulce and Juan are the only parents she ever knew, and she became the eldest of six children when her mother remarried. Samantha and Jennifer did not fare as well, even though they were also reunited as toddlers. Gloria described Samantha as a confused teenager who would run away from high school and misbehave, but she admitted she didn't know that for sure. Gloria tried to help Samantha by taking her to a center that assists people trying to return to school and get their lives back in order, but that attempt failed. Samantha became pregnant when she was fifteen or sixteen and has two sons, but Gloria knows nothing of her whereabouts.

"[Samantha] changes her cell phone number constantly. For many years she spent Christmas at home, but last year we couldn't reach her. We're waiting for her call."[81] Less is known of Jennifer, probably because she was never raised with Juan and Dulce. Juan told me he believes she is in Santo Domingo.[82]

The press was eager for the twins' story, and Tairí brought a large packet of newspaper stories with her when she came to California. Articles appeared in the *Weekly World News*, the *Ocala Star Banner*, and in other publications around the world, such as Spain's *¡Hola!* (*Hello!*) magazine. All four twins had appeared on the well-known Puerto Rican television show *Carmen Jovet: Controversial* when they were about five. Juan and Dulce were invited to appear on *The Cristina Show*, which broadcasts from Florida, but Juan declined this offer. "I never wanted to do TV because it was too painful." He changed his telephone number many times to avoid contacts from the press.[83]

The intense public interest in switched-at-birth pairs is worth exploring as a topic all its own. For me, the best way to approach this has been to ask myself why I and so many others find these particular life stories so compelling, given their disturbing and devastating effects. The scientific significance of switched-at-birth twins is only a partial explanation as to why these stories attract us as they do. And scientific information alone would not command the public's interest. Instead, I believe the human aspects of these events are what truly engage us. Identical twins are intrinsically interesting as a human situation—the idea that two people can look and behave so much alike runs counter to our belief in and appreciation of the uniqueness of each individual. Identical twins are also separate individuals, but they are really like variations on a common theme, capturing this quality better than any other possible pairing of people. Identical twins also convey an extraordinary sense of connection, acceptance, and understanding of one another, making their relationship one that most people envy.

Identical twins' attraction for us is present only when we see them together. When identical twins are separated and grow up apart, we are struck by the unfairness of such an unfortunate turn of events—especially when people such as hospital workers, who are entrusted with protecting the twins' best interests, create the error. Newborn infants lack control over who takes them home, and most new parents trust the hospital staff to do their job competently. Everyone knows that "mistakes happen," but some mistakes have profound consequences that can never be undone. Family relationships assume primary importance in virtually every culture, and when events prevent the development of these relationships, everyone suffers.

I suspect most people who give up their babies for adoption do so to benefit the child, but parting with a baby can be emotionally heartbreaking. Twins in the Korean-born pairs I have studied were separated because their families could not afford to raise two children, but their parents suffered just the same. When the decision to part with a child is unknowingly taken out of the parents' hands, as it was in every case from Fribourg to Las Palmas, the level of personal suffering can be worse. Perhaps the twins' eventual reunions are what we, the observers, find pleasing—the idea that life may be restored to what it was intended to be. But of course the reunions never make up for the twins' solitary years. Or maybe the twins' incredible stories draw us in much the same way as great novels and films that present unthinkable, but plausible, plots. Learning about switched-at-birth twins lets us momentarily experience these families' suffering, but when we close the book or leave the theater, we return more gratefully to our own parents, siblings, and children. Perhaps the fascination comes from the fact that these stories heighten our private fears, making us wonder if we are who we think we are and if our children are who they are supposed to be.

Earlier, I mentioned that news of switched-at-birth twins brings out media stories of new pairs. When the story of the Canary Islands twins was released in May 2008, a second case that had also occurred in Las Palmas was discovered and publicized later that month.[84] The case attracted less attention because the families did not pursue legal proceedings. In 1973, identical male twins Marcos and Matías were born at the same Las Palmas hospital as Delia and Begoña—the Hospital Nuestra Señora el Pino. Marcos was accidentally exchanged with another male infant and grew up happily in a family that he always considered his own.[85] As a salesperson, he encountered his twin brother when he visited a company where his twin was employed, and their striking physical resemblance told them all they needed to know. Marcos is now in his midthirties and married with one child.

Marcos and Matías kept their relationship secret to avoid upsetting their families. Sadly, they were separated a final time when Matías was killed in a car accident. The switch, unknown to their families at that time, was ultimately discovered by the twins' biological sister who, by chance, spotted Marcos on a Las Palmas street and realized he looked exactly like her deceased brother. It is difficult to imagine how she felt seeing the image of a brother who was no longer alive. DNA tests determined that Marcos was not the son of his rearing parents but the son of Matías's parents. Rosa Reyes, who worked in the hospital's gynecological unit for twenty-seven years, recalled that infant identification was rudimentary in those years compared with current procedures.[86]

Interestingly, Marcos and Delia had known each other long before Delia even knew that she was a twin. Perhaps this is not so surprising because Marcos and Delia were the same age and Las Palmas is a relatively small city.

The separated Canary Islands twins, Delia and Begoña, are among the latest additions to the list of switched-at-birth twin pairs. Many of their family members wish the truth had never been revealed. Their individual experiences and beliefs explain why these parents and siblings prefer fiction to reality. The twins still struggle with the truth, but they have both shown greater acceptance of their situation than have the others. My own discovery of their case and why I thought it was significant are explored next.

3

CROSSING PATHS

On Monday, June 2, 2008, I received the all-important e-mail message from psychologist Payam Heidary. Heidary's message, sent the night before, read: "Hi, Nancy—Hope you are doing well. Here is another interesting 'twin' news article. What do you think? Have you seen this?" The link led me to an article posted on Yahoo! titled "Twin, Separated at Birth, Sues for Mix-Up."[1] The story was brief:

A Spanish twin, separated from her family for 28 years, is suing the Canary Islands for a mix-up at the maternity hospital which led to her being taken home by the wrong mother, media reported Wednesday. The woman discovered she had an identical twin when she was mistaken for someone else in a shop in 2001. The two sisters, who were not named, found they were born in the same hospital in 1973 around the same time and a DNA test subsequently showed they were identical twins. "In 1973 there were two assistants and one supervisor for 60 babies," Densi Calero, who worked in the maternity unit of the clinic at the time, told local radio. "It's not impossible to imagine something like this could happen." The woman is suing the Canary Islands health services for 3 million euros ($4.7 million) for emotional trauma, *El Pais* newspaper reported. "I wish I'd never found out about it," her lawyer quoted her as saying. Her sister was brought up alongside another girl, believing they were twins.

This was only the third such case I knew of at the time, the other two involving Swiss twins Philippe and Charles and Canadian twins Brent and George. I sent a reply to Heidary: "Many thanks! I had not heard about this one!" and e-mailed the link to my colleague Professor Bouchard from the Minnesota Study of Twins Reared Apart. Bouchard immediately replied, "Sounds like a fascinating pair. The two non-twins brought up as twins would also be incredibly interesting. Any chance you could study them?" Bouchard wrote exactly what I was thinking. The timing was perfect because I was planning a yearlong academic leave from California State University, Fullerton that would begin in fall 2009 and I was looking for an interesting project. My "year" away ended up lasting twice as long.

The Yahoo! story made no mention of the twins' attorneys, but it would be important for me to work through them to gain access to the twins. I suspected that the twins and their families were being harassed by the press and might not wish to speak to anyone, even a professor with an academic interest in their story, but I hoped that their lawyers would support my request and make the necessary introductions. I was also interested in gaining the lawyers' perspectives on this case and on the court proceedings that were ongoing at the time.

Other Internet coverage of this story indicated that Sebastian Socorro Perdomo, of the law firm Socorro Ley & Asociados in Las Palmas, was representing Delia, the twin who had been raised apart from her biological family and co-twin. I sent Socorro a message through his office website offering to assist him in this case, while requesting interviews with him and the twins. I received a reply quickly on June 5 in which Socorro agreed to collaborate with me as long as the twins' identities were kept confidential. I also learned that another attorney, José Antonio Rodríguez Peregrina of the law firm R. Peregrina Abogados, also in Las Palmas, was representing Begoña and Beatriz, the twin and non-twin raised as fraternal twins, and their mother Laura. Peregrina had also been hired later by Delia's parents, Débora and Juan. Peregrina, too, was willing to speak with me and to have me interview his clients.

Family relationships are complex and overlapping in switched-at-birth twin cases. The names of the twins' family members have been disguised to protect their privacy, as per the request of the twins and their attorneys. However, I received permission to use the twins' and non-twin sister's real first names because they had already been released publicly.

Begoña and Beatriz's family		*Delia's Family*	
Mother	Laura	Mother	Débora
Father	Fernando*	Father	Juan
Twin	Begoña	Single twin	Delia
Non-twin	Beatriz	Sister-1	Gara
Sister-1	María	Sister-2	Julia
Brother-1	Miguel	Niece	Elena
Brother-2	José	Attorney (Delia)	S. Socorro
Attorney	J. Peregrina	Attorney (parents)	J. Peregrina

*Deceased

I interviewed all the individuals listed above except for the twins' siblings: María, Miguel, and José. José, now age twenty-seven, has Down syndrome, so an interview would have been difficult. (The chance of having a Down syndrome infant increases with maternal age, especially after forty;[2] José was Laura and Fernando's last child, delivered when Laura was forty-three.) Miguel, now thirty-three, married and living on another island, has distanced himself from what happened to his sisters. According to Laura, "Miguel doesn't want to see Delia. It breaks his heart to think that someone separated Delia from him. He saw a picture of her on the Internet, and he suffered terribly." The twins' older sister, María, now a forty-two-year-old married woman and mother living in Las Palmas, was unavailable at the time. Still, I filled several notebooks and digital tape recorders with information that captures the event at the Las Arenas shopping mall that brought Delia and Begoña together.

The twins' story forces us to think, not only about who we are, but about who we might have become had we grown up in a family other than our own, all because of a nurse's mistake. As indicated previously, twin and adoption studies show that shared genes generally matter more than shared environments when it comes to behavioral resemblance between biological relatives, living either together or apart, in intelligence, personality, and religious interests.[3] However, the unique or non-shared experiences we have apart from our family members also have an impact on behavior. For example, a child visiting Japan as part of a semester abroad may develop an interest in Asian culture that siblings would not share. Estimates of genetic influence on general intelligence range from 50 to 70 percent, while genetic influence on most other behavioral traits, such as personality, attitudes, and interests, is about 50 percent. This means that genetic factors explain 50 percent of the individual differences in extraversion or religiosity among people in a population, while the other 50 percent are explained by nongenetic factors.

Knowing that shared environments have little impact on behavior after childhood and especially adolescence helps us understand why identical twins raised apart, like Philippe and Charles, Brent and George, and Delia and Begoña, can be similar in surprising ways. Behavior geneticists (twin, family, and adoption researchers studying the genetic and environmental bases of behavior) believe this is explained by active gene-environment correlation, a process by which people select opportunities and experiences compatible with their genetically influenced traits. Tall, strong people might gravitate toward sports activities, while the more artistically inclined might prefer visiting museums. In other words, we create our own environments to a large extent, and it works the same way with twins reared apart. For example, identical reared-apart British twins Bridget and Dorothy, who participated in the Minnesota Study of Twins Reared Apart in 1979, were given different educational experiences by their rearing parents.[4] One twin's home was rich with books and other stimulating material, while the other twin's was not. However, the less advantaged twin's genes "guided" her toward intellectually interesting experiences. She discovered books at her local library, and both twins independently became avid readers of historical novels written by the same author.

This does not imply that parental influence does not matter—sensitive parenting means being attentive to and supportive of the needs, desires, and talents of each child.[5] Parents can help their shy children feel more socially at ease or encourage their outspoken children to try listening to others. These parents probably cannot convert a shy child into an extroverted one or an outspoken child into a quiet type, but parents can have moderating effects on children's behaviors. Parents with sufficient resources can more easily provide desirable opportunities for their children than parents who are less well off, although some children are able to seek out interesting experiences on their own. Of course, when parents are unresponsive or abusive to their children, they can inhibit their children's abilities and confidence.

Delia and Begoña were raised in very different homes, one (Delia) in a rural area with two younger sisters and the other (Begoña) in an urban area with an older sister, a "twin" sister, and two younger brothers. Begoña, therefore, enjoyed greater exposure to Las Palmas's cultural and educational opportunities than did Delia. Begoña also resembled her family members physically, whereas Delia did not. Begoña lost her father when she was a young child, while Delia grew up with both unrelated parents. As I listened to their stories and studied their questionnaires, I discovered striking similarities and surprising differences between them.

The three sisters—Delia, Begoña, and Beatriz, age thirty-six when we met—described their life events simply and honestly. Their last seven years since the discovery show that an event from the past, once revealed, can shatter identities and destroy lives. But there is a bigger picture, and it's not all negative, because the twins' experiences affirm the universal significance of family relations and underline the importance of knowing who you are.

The twins' circumstances also exposed serious problems in news reporting, mother-infant identification, and legal procedure. These issues may sound familiar because they also affected the progress and outcomes of the other switched-at-birth twin cases described earlier. The fact that infants are still inadvertently separated from their mothers means we need to pay closer attention to what the Canary Islands twins have to tell us. I will introduce the sisters and their parents below and provide greater detail about their lives in the chapter that follows.

THE THREE SISTERS

Beatriz

Of the three sisters, I met Beatriz first, in Peregrina's office, on September 14, 2009.[6] She was waiting in the reception area when I arrived with my interpreter, Jessica. Beatriz's dark hair was short and curly and held in place with a wide, white hair band. She wore a yellow T-shirt with a short jean skirt. A black Holly Boop bag hung from her shoulder, while white high-heeled mules adorned her feet. "My sisters liked dressing well and using makeup, but I have never been like that," she said. Beatriz's comment was the first indication that she had always felt different from her parents and sisters.

Beatriz was living with her mother at the time of our interview. Beatriz owned a house, but once news of the switch broke, the presence of journalists waiting outside her door forced her to return to her mother's home. Beatriz didn't enjoy studying and had left school at sixteen. At age seventeen, she began working in the local tomato fields; then she cleaned houses and worked in a hotel in the southern part of the island. She was back to cleaning houses in the city when I met her. Beatriz was unmarried at the time but had been with the same boyfriend for the past seven years; her prior relationships had been short-term.

Beatriz seemed a little nervous at first, but she relaxed over the course of our interview. She was a very likable and caring young woman. Her part of the story added a remarkable dimension to the events as I knew them. She, as well as her sister Begoña, had been mistaken for "someone else's sister" whenever they visited certain areas in the northern part of the island. "People on the street used to tell me I looked like Gara, Delia's sister." Beatriz knew she did not physically resemble her family. When she first met Delia at the mall, "I just felt . . . I felt. . . ." She could not find the words to express her feelings.

Begoña

Begoña arrived in Peregrina's office the next day, a striking contrast to her non-twin sister, Beatriz.[7] Her hair was arranged in smooth layers that fell neatly around her shoulders. She wore black pants and a black jersey embellished with shiny beads. Her slightly asymmetrical watch bore the label DKNY, and she wore dangling earrings with a pearl/rhinestone setting. Begoña had left high school at age sixteen and had cleaned houses before working as a shop assistant and then a nanny. In 2008, at age thirty-five, she began studying to obtain her high school diploma, and in 2010 she planned to take the university entrance examination. Begoña told me she hopes to study law someday. When we met, she was the chambermaid supervisor at a hotel at Las Palmas's Las Canteras beach. Begoña owns her own home but is still paying the mortgage. She was single when we met but had had three boyfriends at different times.

Like Beatriz, Begoña spoke hesitantly at first but seemed relaxed by the end of our conversation. She admitted that when she first met Delia, she had harbored slight doubts about whether or not she and Delia were twins, but her doubts had faded fast to the point that the DNA test did not seem necessary. "Before the [DNA] test I was sure about the results. . . . We needed that test done to go to court. The situation was unfair."

Begoña invited my interpreter, Jessica, and me to her house the next Saturday, and we agreed to come. I had a great time that day—but I wished that Delia had been there so I could have seen the twins together.

Delia

Delia was the last sister I met, and for a while I was worried that I might not meet her at all during my stay.[8] Just one week before I was scheduled to leave for Las Palmas, Socorro's assistant Carolina e-mailed to say that Delia was getting married. She and her new husband were planning a honeymoon and would not be returning to the area again until the first week in October. I was crestfallen—I was scheduled to fly out of Las Palmas on September 23, then travel by train to Geneva, Switzerland, to meet Philippe Joye (the visit Joye eventually cancelled). Fortunately for me, Delia's situation in Las Palmas somehow changed; Delia would be married in a small ceremony on September 11, returning in time for me to meet her on September 21, two days before I would leave the island.

Delia was a little over two inches taller than Begoña and was heavier when I met her because of her medications. She looked less like Begoña than I had expected, but she was not feeling well that day, which most likely affected her appearance. Still, I could see that her facial contours matched Begoña's closely. Delia seemed quite comfortable during the interview and spoke easily and without hesitation. I asked her to tell me about the meeting at the shopping mall. "I was so shocked that I couldn't think. I didn't say anything when I got home because I was scared of my family's reaction." At one point during our conversation Begoña called Delia, and I was dying to know what they talked about, but I didn't ask. I mostly wondered to what extent they were communicating like old familiar friends. Had I understood Spanish, I might have caught half the conversation.

THE SHOPPING MALL

The events that led to their reunion, as I heard about them directly from the twins, differ somewhat from those reported in the press. Their meeting happened because of Begoña's two trips to the Las Arenas shopping mall, just outside the center of Las Palmas. The press did not report that Beatriz was with her on the second visit.

In December 2001, Begoña had purchased a T-shirt from Stradivarius, a popular fashion chain for teens and young adults located in the mall. The shop sells embossed tops, jeans, jackets, belts, bags, and other items and has branch stores all over Spain. A shop assistant, Clarisa, thinking she recognized her friend Delia, approached Begoña to say hello. But Clarisa saw Begoña, not Delia. Begoña didn't know Clarisa and left the store without returning the greeting. Puzzled, Clarisa told her mother she had seen Delia but that Delia had ignored her. Clarisa's mother telephoned Delia to find out why she had been so unfriendly to her daughter but learned that Delia hadn't been to the mall that afternoon.

Several days later Begoña returned to Stradivarius, this time with Beatriz, to exchange the T-shirt for a larger size. They were in the fitting room when Clarisa appeared again. Begoña asked her if another T-shirt was available, but Clarisa just stared at her. Clarisa then turned to Beatriz and asked her why "Delia" wouldn't speak to her. Beatriz replied, "Her name is Begoña, and I'm her twin sister." Clarisa jokingly suggested, "Begoña's twin sister is in another town," referring to Delia. Clarisa also commented that Beatriz looked just like Delia's younger sister, Gara. Maybe Clarisa suspected a baby switch or maybe she was just amazed by what she was seeing, but either way, this time she asked Begoña for her telephone number so they could stay in touch. Clarisa's mother called Delia that afternoon, and a meeting involving all the sisters was arranged.

At this point, neither Delia, Begoña, nor Beatriz was especially concerned about what might happen at this meeting. All three believed that the mistaken identities were most likely coincidence. Nevertheless, curiosity prompted Delia to meet her look-alike—it turned out that Delia had been confused for someone named Begoña on two previous occasions. By contrast, Begoña was "slightly suspicious" because she, her family, and her friends were all keenly aware of the striking physical and behavioral differences between Beatriz and herself, and Clarisa had been adamant about the physical similarities between the sisters in these two families. Begoña had also been confused on other occasions for someone named Delia. "But it was still not important," Begoña insisted.

The meeting took place later that day, at half past seven in the evening, at a coffee shop on the top level of the Las Arenas mall. This convenient spot offers marginal food and great views, but neither concerned the six people assembled at that moment—Delia; a friend of Delia's; Begoña; Beatriz; their youngest brother, José; and a friend of Begoña's. Clarisa wasn't there. Delia and her friend arrived first and waited. Begoña's friend came before the other three, purposefully sent as "a spy to check things out." When Delia finally saw Begoña it was a huge shock—"I saw myself walking—I have a weird walk, and I thought I was the only one who walked that way." Begoña was uncomfortable at the time. "My first impression was that it's not true, she doesn't look like me—but maybe I didn't want to think it was happening. Maybe we look alike, but we're not identical."

Over the next two to three hours they compared their hair, their hands, their ears, their feet, and their nails, and everything matched perfectly. Delia wasn't completely convinced that she and Begoña were twins, but, she admitted, "something strange had happened." Begoña grew more and more uncomfortable as everyone discovered a growing list of similarities between Delia and herself, especially the way they gestured. The two of them realized that they push their food away when eating with a fork or spoon and fold their lips over their teeth when they get anxious. No wonder Clarisa claimed that they were "as alike as two drops of water" (*son dos gotas de agua*)—this phrase appeared in many articles written about the twins. Begoña also worried about her sister Beatriz and how Beatriz would react if they turned out not to be twins—or even sisters.

During the course of the meeting, Delia told the others she had been diagnosed with leukemia when she was sixteen years old. This revelation made Begoña afraid of her increasingly likely genetic connection to Delia. Begoña did not believe any of her family members had suffered from leukemia, although Beatriz said that they did; the twins' father, a heavy smoker, had died from lung cancer. But something else was nagging at Begoña. Delia had started chemotherapy sometime after her cancer diagnosis, and the treatments took place every Thursday at 11:00 AM—precisely the time each week when Begoña felt feverish and developed a sore throat. Her symptoms always subsided the next day.

I am more impressed by the twins' similar behaviors and mannerisms than I am by Begoña's ailments that seemed to coincide with Delia's treatment. Begoña's feverish feeling and scratchy throat, which would have occurred about twelve years earlier, cannot be documented and could have many explanations. Perhaps Begoña had contracted an infection or was reacting to something she had eaten. It is understandable that Begoña attached a special significance to her symptoms once she learned the timing of Delia's treatment, but the basis of her symptoms can be questioned.

Delia and Begoña did not meet again for an entire year. Knowing how excited most reared apart twins are to meet, I found this surprising at first. But theirs was not an ordinary meeting because the happiness and well-being of so many parents, brothers, and sisters depended on whether Delia and Begoña were truly twins or just extraordinary lookalikes. Begoña and Beatriz decided to keep their meeting secret from the rest of their families so as not to upset them. Begoña also told me that her decision to keep silent was important because Beatriz began suffering a great deal, worried that her family would reject her were she not truly Begoña's twin. Then Delia sent Begoña a text message on January

15, 2002, to wish her a happy birthday. Things changed after that, and when I went to Las Palmas I learned how.

LAS PALMAS, IN GRAN CANARIA

I left Los Angeles on September 9, 2009, and arrived in Barcelona for a two-day stay before taking the three-and-a-half-hour flight to Las Palmas on September 12. My Las Palmas hotel, besides being conveniently located between the two attorneys' offices, was adjacent to the offices of *La Provinica*, a Canary Islands newspaper that had covered the twins' story since its May 2008 release. I thought this was a great break because I was interested in meeting two of the reporters, Delia Jiminez and Miguel Ayala, whose articles about the twins I had read. Ayala had also written about the other switched Canary Islands twins, Marcos and Matías.

I was not expected in Peregrina's office until Monday, September 14, so I arranged to visit Las Palmas's exquisite Botanical Gardens on Sunday, September 13. My hosts were molecular biologist Ruth Jaén-Molina, who worked at the gardens studying the origin and evolution of the Macaronesian flora; her husband Ryan; and their four-year-old son, Joaquim. I had been "introduced" to Ruth over the Internet while searching for an interpreter. Ruth, who had a twin brother Ivan, had an excellent command of English, having studied the molecular biology of plant life at the University of Texas. However, I chose to work with Jessica because of her professional credentials and experience as an interpreter and translator. Jessica was also flexible with respect to her availability, a crucial qualification because the twins, their families, and their attorneys had obligations that affected our scheduling.

Jessica's flexibility proved to be more important than I had anticipated. On one occasion, we met Delia's two sisters at a morgue following their cousin's suicide and then took a taxi to my hotel and conducted our interviews in the lobby until nearly 11:30 PM. Another time, we traveled several hours to Delia's home in a remote village outside the city. And one day, Jessica and I took a chance at finding the judge who had ruled in the twins' case, and we succeeded. I never knew for sure with whom we would speak or when—aside from two scheduled sessions with Peregrina and Socorro on September 14 and 15, respectively. Each day was unplanned, and we had to be prepared to speak with whomever was available. We conducted many of our interviews in Peregrina's office, but Jessica's cell phone could ring at any time with a new appointment.

When I arrived in Las Palmas, the twins' case had been heard in the administrative court (*tribunal del contencioso administrivo*). This is the body of Spain's judiciary system that decides conflicts between the Public Administration (in this case, the Canary Islands Health Service or Servicio Canario de Salud) and the people. The judge's award in March 2009 to the families of a total of 900,000 euros (US$1,195,460, based on 2009 exchange rates) was far less than the 3 million euros (US$3,984,870) the lawyers had requested. At this stage in the legal process, both Peregrina and Socorro, who had filed appeals, believed that my input as a specialist in twin research would help their case. They wanted popular opinion on the side of the twins because, as they explained, what the Las Palmas public thinks can significantly impact the rulings in such cases. Much more information about the twins' lawsuit is provided in chapter 7.

Interestingly, the two attorneys had met in advance of my arrival and had decided that I was not to talk to the press while I was in Las Palmas. They worried that interviews I might do would allow journalists to discover the identity of the twins, who they felt had suffered enough from the media's intrusion into their lives. Even if I did not mention the twins' names, I might be followed to the attorneys' offices or to the twins' homes, and the lawyers warned that journalists were known to track telephone calls. I was happy to comply with these conditions, although perplexed when they were later reversed, a circumstance to be discussed later.

The twins first met with their attorneys in 2004. But before they hired their lawyers and filed their complaints, the twins' parents had to know the full extent of what had happened. There is no satisfactory way to tell mothers and fathers they have been raising someone else's child for twenty-eight years, but the ways in which these parents learned the truth could not have been more difficult for them.

TELLING THEIR PARENTS

It was Delia's birthday message to Begoña in January 2002 that ultimately led Laura to discover what her daughters had been keeping from her. When Begoña read the text message to Beatriz—"Delia has just sent me a message to wish me a happy birthday"—she was overheard by one of their cousins. Begoña explained, "My cousin asked me who Delia was, and I told her the whole story. My cousin, who is also a mother, told me she wouldn't like her daughter to hide such a thing from her." Regardless, Begoña said nothing to Laura until one day, without warning, Beatriz told her mother about the meeting at the Las Arenas Mall. "I usually don't measure my words, and I just talk without thinking. I told her 'Mum, I'm not your daughter. The real twin is someone else.' Then my mum began crying. She didn't want to listen to anymore. She thought I was kidding. After that I went to my mum and told her that it was just a lie. And we didn't talk anymore about it that day." But Laura went to Begoña and asked her if what Beatriz had said was true. "At first, we decided to deny it, but eventually we told her it was true," Begoña said. When I spoke with Laura on September 15 in Peregrina's office, she told me she "went mad."

Laura was a sweet and somewhat reserved woman who was sixty-nine years of age at the time of our interview. She wore a white peasant blouse, black slacks, and black and white pearls around her neck. Her brown hair was cut short and fashionably styled. Laura had attended school until the age of thirteen, when she left to work in the canneries. She was a working housewife until the death of her husband, a police officer, when the twins were seventeen. After his death, she began working in the tomato fields and then at a factory. Laura seemed ill at ease when we met, not fully understanding my interest in her case, but she knew I was writing a book and that her cooperation during the interview might help the legal appeal. She cried softly at times as she took us through the seemingly ordinary events leading to the day that Beatriz broke the news to her.

The twins were a surprise, she told us, detected by ultrasound just prior to their delivery. When they were born, the doctor told her that her infant daughters were identical twins, but she hardly saw them because their low birth weight demanded immediate medical attention. Laura herself had experienced delivery complications—she had hemorrhaged and required a blood transfusion. When Laura was discharged from the hospital five days after the twins' birth, she took five-and-a-half pound, blonde-haired Begoña home with her; her other twin still weighed less than four pounds and had to remain in the hospital for three more months. During this time, Laura made frequent visits to the hospital to see her second twin, never realizing she was visiting the wrong baby. She assumed that Beatriz's dark hair came from her husband's side of the family. "I always thought she was my real daughter, and I raised her, of course, for almost thirty years."

The twins' father, Fernando, died when the twins were six, but I asked Laura how he might have reacted to the news of their separation. "I think he would have gone crazy," she said. "His feelings [for Begoña and Beatriz] were the same."

Delia's mother, Débora, discovered the truth in a far more public way, *seven years* after the twins' meeting at Las Arenas.[9] She remembered that it was a Monday. Débora was at home with her daughter Julia, who was employed as a babysitter for her niece Elena (Débora's grandchild) while the little girl's mother (Débora's other daughter Gara) was at work.

It was the middle of the day, and Débora had just finished cleaning the house and was watching the news on Television Canaria, or maybe on Canal (Channel) 9 or Canal 7—she could not recall. "They were talking about my town, and they had taken a picture of the front of my house while I was shaking out a blanket. When I saw the front of my house on TV, I realized I was part of this case. I had an attack. I fainted." Julia told me that the reporter mentioned the year 1973. "So, my mother said she had given birth that same year, and that the baby had gone directly to the incubator. [My mother] began doubting and saying that Delia was definitely the baby that had been switched."

I met Débora in Peregrina's office in the afternoon of September 15, several hours after I had met with Laura. Débora was a small woman of fifty-five years, with dark curly hair that framed her face. She wore a red blouse with puffy sleeves over a shiny flower print skirt. She confessed, "I don't want to meet people. I don't use makeup anymore, and I don't dye my hair." Her mood was alternately sad and angry, but she graciously shared her thoughts on what had happened to her and her family over the past year. What struck me most when I first saw Débora was that her skin coloring and the shape of her nose were the same as Beatriz's, the daughter she hadn't raised.

By this time, Débora and Juan had met Beatriz several times. Interestingly, they both believed that Beatriz resembled Juan and the paternal side of the family, but I thought Beatriz looked more like her mother. I have found that someone meeting family members for the first time is often better at detecting physical similarities among them than relatives and friends who know them well. I see few facial similarities between my twin sister Anne and me, but people who know only one of us often say we look like sisters when they see our pictures or see us together for the first time. I do, however, recognize certain expressions we share, such as staring very intently when we are focused on something.

Like his wife, Débora's husband, Juan, learned about the switch suddenly and unexpectedly.[10] He came home from work the day his wife had watched the news on TV and found Débora crying inconsolably. Eventually he learned why. "I didn't know what to believe," Juan admitted. "Then a friend of mine advised me to look for a lawyer. The year of the switch coincided with Delia's birth date." He looked very sad. "I have lost half my life with this case. I loved Delia a lot. I love them all."

Juan and Débora had married when he was twenty-one and she was seventeen, but they had been childhood neighbors since youth. Débora was Juan's first and only girlfriend. Juan's parents were poor, forcing him to leave school when he was ten to begin working. When I met him, he was in the construction industry, assisting in putting up buildings but not actually building them himself. He was a pleasant and friendly person who was shaken to his roots by the news he had heard almost exactly a year earlier. Jessica, my translator, noted that Juan had a distinctive speech pattern, as did Beatriz, the daughter Juan did not raise; Delia, the daughter Juan had raised from birth, did not.

After two days in Las Palmas, I felt exhilarated because I had already met Begoña, Beatriz, their mother, and both of Delia's parents. A meeting with the court-appointed psychiatrist was scheduled for the following day, and I was hoping to meet Delia early the following week. Jessica and I also had long sessions with both attorneys during which we posed questions about their involvement in the case, the emotional state of their clients, the social significance of the situation, and their hope for outcomes. Full appreciation of this case required understanding the legal approach to the twins' claims and the judicial system that might or might not rule in their favor.

THE CASE IN CONTEXT

José Antonio Rodríguez Peregrina's law firm, R. Peregrina Abogados, is comprised of three attorneys who handle cases involving family law, administrative-adjudicative proceedings, commercial law, and civil procedures. The firm was housed in a tastefully appointed suite of offices on the second floor of 30 Calle Luis Doreste Silva (the Picasso Building). The walls were painted a soft blue tone, and a large flat-screen television in the reception area delivered the news continuously. Peregrina's office, one of the larger rooms, was packed with law books and academic diplomas, including his 1988 certificate from Granada University's law program. Lawyers in Spain complete a five-year university education that allows them to practice law. Peregrina also holds a master's degree from the University of Las Palmas.

Jessica and I arrived for our first visit to Peregrina's office on September 14.[11] Peregrina introduced us to his wife, Noelia Vigil Torres, who offered us the use of an office and computer during my stay. Noelia was originally from Peru, and since coming to Las Palmas in 1999, she had been studying English and conducting legal research for her husband.

Peregrina sat at his desk in the center of his office making calls to arrange our appointments with his clients, the court-appointed psychiatrist, and Delia's two sisters. He seemed to enjoy this organizational role, and we learned that he could be very helpful in this capacity. Peregrina even revealed the identity of the judge assigned to this case, María Olimpia del Rosario Palenzuela, and gave us her address, adding, "Please don't say I gave you her name." I was surprised by his secrecy, but it seemed that not everyone knew of her involvement in this case. I imagine that she did not want to be pressured by people holding different opinions about how it should be settled.

Peregrina admitted that he was busy that morning, but he was willing to give us more time later that day. He also warned me against talking to the press, an issue that likewise concerned his wife. Noelia talked a great deal about the insensitivity shown toward their clients by many members of the press. "[The twins and their mother] are really good people. We didn't want the press involved because our clients wished to remain anonymous. The unfortunate side of their media exposure was the focus on their identity, rather than on their suffering.

Journalists have offered them a lot of money for their story, but they want to lead normal lives. The Spanish 'gutter press' would run the story for several weeks to satisfy people's morbid need to know the details, then forget about them. . . . Information about the case is posted on our website, along with people's comments. Some say the case is very sad; others say there are more important problems for the social services to worry about."

We saw Peregrina again at 6:00 PM in his conference room. He spoke at length about his legal work, his clients, the status of this case, and the inner workings of Spain's judicial system.

The sisters, Begoña and Beatriz, had approached Peregrina for assistance because one of their cousins was his former client. Peregrina accepted their case and filed a complaint several months later against the health service to force it to admit its mistake and provide compensation. "The first time I heard about the case, I found it extremely interesting from both a legal and humanistic point of view. It is also one of my top cases in terms of its unusual nature, and it is number one in terms of the courage [Begoña, Beatriz, and Laura] had in order to face their problem and reveal the truth publicly." Peregrina explained that people in Spain are convinced that other switched-at-birth twin and non-twin cases have occurred, but none of them have been legally documented. "We have to bear in mind the context. In Spain there could have been similar cases that nobody dared to report because of the politics. We lived in a dictatorship in which there was obedience and fear of bringing such cases against a government service. The situation changed with the democracy, but older people kept their way of thinking—I'm talking about [the twins'] parents, for example. There are not many instances of people bringing cases against the government services because the practice and culture of doing so didn't exist before. The government was untouchable. In 1978, Spain had already changed [to a democracy], but a lot of older people have remained the same [in their way of thinking]."

I thought about the Polish twins, Kasia and Edyta, and Kasia's unrelated "twin sister," Nina, and how their lives were damaged by a mistake that might have been corrected if not for a political system that silenced its citizens. Had the Ofmańskis felt free to ask the nurses about Nina's weight gain, or had the Wierzbickis questioned the doctors about Edyta's foot deformity, the traumas that emerged seventeen years later might have been prevented.

Ten previous switched-at-birth cases have been reported in Spain, but none involved twins. These incidents involved babies born after 1978, the year Spain became a democratic nation under King Juan Carlos, who succeeded the dictator Franco after his death three years prior. Perhaps these younger mothers felt freer to question their health professionals when they believed that the baby they had been given belonged to someone else. Details of these cases, published in 2008 in the Spanish newspaper *El Pais* by journalist Mónica López Ferrado[12] and summarized in table 3.1, were known only through the media. None of these families had filed complaints against the health services, explaining why Peregrina and Socorro had no legal precedent with which to work. Information on some of these cases is more complete than on others.

It is curious that none of these families filed legal proceedings against the hospitals that delivered their babies. Perhaps the legacy of Spain's dictatorship explains their reticence. More likely, it was because most of the babies were returned to their birth families before deep parental attachments developed with the wrong families. It is also likely that the parents were relieved to have been reunited with their correct infants and preferred to get on with their lives despite their emotional upset. In every switched-at-birth twin case, except for the male twins Marcos and Matías in Las Palmas, lawsuits were filed, probably because the twins were one-and-a-half years of age and older. By then, the parents had developed strong affectional ties to their children. When switching is discovered later, simply switching back is not an option, but the situations are just as complex and alarming.

TABLE 3.1

Year of Birth:	Location:	Circumstances:
1980	Zaragoza	Two babies born two hours apart were taken from the nursery for vaccinations and returned to the wrong cribs. One family noticed the mistake when the infants were brought home, and the babies were returned.
1993	Valladolid	Two babies were exchanged because incorrect information was entered on the mothers' wristbands. The error was detected when the babies rejected the breast milk of the mother to whom each was given.
1993	Madrid	Two babies were exchanged in the neonatal unit of a private clinic.
1997	Guipuzcoa	Babies given the same name were exchanged and spent several days with the wrong mother. One mother was released from the hospital, while the other mother remained there recovering from a caesarean section. She had reason to doubt that the infant given to her was really hers, and the hospital agreed. DNA tests determined that the babies had been exchanged, and they were subsequently returned.
1999	Tarragona	Two babies were exchanged in the neonatal unit, and the families were notified nineteen days later.
2001	Baza	Nurses presented two mothers with the wrong child, an error that went undetected for an extended period of time.
2002	Granada	A baby boy and baby girl were inadvertently exchanged. Parents realized the mistake when they took the babies home and changed their diapers.
2004	Valencia	Two infant girls were exchanged when their identification bracelets slipped off their wrists. One mother noticed the mistake while breastfeeding the child.
2004	Madrid	Two babies were exchanged, an error that was detected when one mother was home and the other mother was about to be discharged.
2005	Ciudad Real	An exchange of babies occurred in the hospital.

Peregrina claimed that damages needed to be recovered for pain and suffering caused by growing up without a twin sister (Begoña), growing up in a family with which one has no biological connection (Beatriz), and for raising someone else's child (Laura). He wanted to draw a crucial distinction between physical damages sustained in an accident and emotional damages sustained in the present case. Spain uses a preexisting scale to award compensation commensurate with physical suffering in traffic accidents only, based on age and severity. The scale can be used by analogy in other situations. Peregrina hoped to go beyond this scale with the help of psychologists' assessment of his clients. "We don't have a tradition of huge compensation in Spanish courts. It's not like in the USA where compensation can be in the multimillions. Pain and suffering are not well valued in Spain, and there is no legal tradition [behind it]. Even so, I expected much higher compensation . . . but I'm pessimistic about getting much more money [on appeal]. . . . We hope that the High Court of Justice will reconsider the case. At least we want our case to have equal status with one in Seville in which a mother lost custody of her child due to alleged abandonment. . . . [That case] was compensated with 1,200,000 odd euros [approximately US$1.6 million as of October 2010]. That is the highest compensation that has been given. . . . For example, in a case of death in a traffic accident, the compensation can be around 180,000 to 200,000 euros [approximately US$250,000 to US$280,000]. If death, which is the biggest loss, is estimated in that amount, you cannot expect a lot for moral damage."

Moral damage is a complex concept with diverse meanings both internationally and nationally.[13] I will discuss it in greater detail in the context of the lawsuit in a later chapter.

Peregrina knew his clients had suffered a great deal. "Maybe Beatriz is affected the most. Begoña has a stronger personality, although she is also affected. The relationship between Laura and Beatriz is excellent—Laura never suspected a thing, but finding out Beatriz wasn't her daughter hasn't changed anything between them." Peregrina also said that Begoña and

Laura were satisfied with the money awarded to them [in March 2009], but Beatriz felt "excluded" because Delia received higher compensation than she did. After all, both Beatriz and Delia had been raised in the wrong families. I believe Delia's loss of both her twin relationship *and* her ideal bone marrow donor influenced the judge's decision.

Peregrina's derogation of the press was matched by his harsh words for the physician who conducted the first round of DNA tests. DNA testing took place in several stages, the first one involving Begoña, Beatriz, and Laura. The tests established that Beatriz and Laura were not mother and daughter and, consequently, that Begoña and Beatriz were not related. Delia delayed having her DNA tested for a few years because she was afraid of the truth, but when her relationship with her rearing family worsened, she changed her mind. Begoña said she understood Delia's decision to wait. Delia also knew that DNA testing was needed for a lawsuit. The test determined that Delia and Begoña were identical twins with over 99.99 percent probability.

According to Peregrina, there was a "breach of professional discretion" because the physician performing the tests agreed to an interview with the press and nearly revealed the results once the family had been told. While at the doctor's office, Laura recalled sitting next to a journalist who appeared to be eavesdropping on her conversation with Begoña. The journalist subsequently revealed in the press that Delia was Laura's daughter, which attracted other reporters to her home. Laura blamed the physician in charge. "It was all [his] fault. He spoke up when giving us the results so the journalist would hear them." What the journalist overlooked was Laura's reaction to the news. "The doctor said 'Beatriz is not your daughter.' I felt terrible," she said. In an ideal world, had the press been genuinely interested in helping these families, reporters would have allowed the families to grieve privately and possibly approach them for interviews at a later time. The families wanted to share their story, but in a matter as sensitive as this one, they were right to want to do so on their terms.

DNA tests were later performed to determine whether or not Beatriz was Débora and Juan's biological daughter, and the probability of her being so was high. Until those results were known, it was possible that she belonged to another couple in what would have been a three-way swap. This time a more discreet laboratory was chosen, and it was there that everyone finally learned the truth about their family ties. The results took twenty-two days to process, but Beatriz's biological father Juan didn't need to wait. "I already knew Beatriz was my daughter because she looked exactly like me." Débora couldn't stop crying. Peregrina filed a complaint on behalf of Débora and Juan early in 2009, expecting that it would not be settled for some time. In fact, the case was heard in court in January 2011. At the time of this writing, a decision was still pending.[14]

The news coverage of this case is unconscionable on one level but understandable on another. What is unconscionable is the fact that the twins and their families were simply going about their lives when they were caught up in a situation that they had never anticipated. They depended on help from lawyers and doctors, but the act of reaching out to these professionals raised the risk of placing themselves under the relentless gaze of the public eye. Everyone I spoke with agreed that someone leaked the story to the press, but no one knows who it was. The only families not pursued by the press—the parents of the switched male twins from the Canary Islands—did not file lawsuits. Newspaper coverage of that case amounted to a single article in *La Provinica*, a Canary Islands publication with a circulation of 33,414.[15]

The news coverage of this case is also understandable because of its human interest and the societal issues and legal consequences surrounding babies switched at birth. Furthermore, baby switches can happen to anyone, so families expecting a new child or grandchild would pay special attention to these reports. I also believe that if this case had involved the switching of two non-twin babies, it might not have become as well-known as it did. The twin angle added a dramatic element that was hard to resist, as happened with the previous cases. I am not excusing the conduct of the journalists who upset the twins; I am trying to understand it. The public was interested in the twins' story and the journalists wanted to satisfy that interest, but they overlooked the real emotions of real people. Of course, newspapers want to make sales, and the twins' story kept readers riveted for months. As with any case of private matters made public, the twins might have been more cooperative in revealing their story had the journalists given them privacy and shown them respect.

The Society of Professional Journalists' code of ethics is embraced by journalists on a voluntary basis.[16] Under the section titled "Minimize Harm," it is recommended that journalists "recognize that private people have a greater right to control information about themselves than do public officials and others who seek power, influence or attention. Only an overriding public need can justify intrusion into anyone's privacy." Some journalists may have used the twins' story to warn prospective parents of the possibility of baby switching. But coming to their home, filming their neighborhood, and reporting sensitive DNA findings cannot be condoned.

A dramatized version of the twins' lives, *Mi Gemela Es Hija Unica* (*My Sister Is an Only Child*) appeared on the Spanish station Tele 5 and was not helpful. The twins' lawsuit was intended to prevent further suffering, as well as to assuage their own. Socorro, Delia's attorney on the other side of Las Palmas, was also wary of the press.

Sebastian Socorro Perdomo's office, Socorro & Ley Asociados, was located on Dr. Verneau, 1, in Las Palmas's old section Triana Vegueta. Socorro had earned his degree from the University of Las Palmas and had been in practice for eighteen years at the time of our interview.[17] His two-person firm specializes in civil, criminal, and administrative proceedings. Despite the building's historical setting, the office interior was very contemporary with glass partitions, modern artwork, and state-of-the-art technology. An unusual painting of dyads and triads of brightly colored female figures hung on a wall of the reception area, perhaps a portent or consequence of what Socorro called his "top one case." Socorro was a dashing figure, fashionably dressed with an engaging presence. He welcomed Jessica and me into the conference area located in the center of his suite—a space offering little privacy. A statue of a reclining female nude was displayed on the conference table.

Our first meeting with Socorro took place on September 15, the day after I met with Peregrina. Socorro had worked on the case for about five years. He explained his introduction to this case, his legal approach to its resolution, and the press's negative effects on his client, Delia. Our second meeting, on September 22, the day before I left Las Palmas, had a different focus, to be described later.

"When [Delia] came for the first time to talk to me about the case, I couldn't believe it," Socorro told us. "I had never heard of anything similar." He accepted the case because it was "interesting and important," and it appeared that everything was in place for its success, especially because the DNA tests had been completed by that time. Knowing his client had limited finances, Socorro decided to set the fees once they had succeeded with the trial, enabling her to collect the money. He saw his objective as acquiring compensation, not ameliorating the damage, because in his view doing so was impossible. Like Peregrina, Socorro was operating in the absence of legal precedent and had to think creatively. His reasoning about what constituted appropriate compensation in this case was fascinating and brilliant.

"I searched for other types of compensation set by the Supreme Court [of Spain]. I decided to compare [Delia's situation] to that of people deprived unjustly of freedom. That is the case of, for example, a person who is imprisoned and found not guilty afterwards. We used the same criteria because we understood [Delia] had been deprived of freedom, the freedom of having a relationship with her relatives. . . . There were the difficulties of finding out she had been living with a family that wasn't her biological one, not having shared a childhood and adolescence with her twin sister, the loss of counting on her sister during the difficult process of dealing with cancer, facing an autotransplant because they couldn't find a bone marrow donor when she had a perfect 'photocopy,' and not being able to meet her biological father. For [Delia], it was as if the past was suddenly erased and she only had an uncertain future. These were the factors we took into account."

Socorro told us that the day after the twins' case appeared on television, the males' switched-at-birth case appeared in the local newspaper *La Provincia*. But Socorro cited a personal element to the women's story that kept it newsworthy—it generated public alarm. "People began to feel that those born [during the early 1970s] should undergo a DNA test to see if their siblings were biological. The means used by hospitals [for mother-infant identification] were not appropriate." Socorro did not elaborate on this point, but I remembered Peregrina saying that newborn records must have the baby's footprint and the mother's fingerprint—and one mother's fingerprint was missing from one baby's record. It is uncertain if this omission was responsible for the switch, but Peregrina told me that a nurse working in the hospital's nursery in 1973, the year the twins were born, called the conditions "disastrous." Only two assistants and one supervisor were responsible for sixty babies."[18]

One day Socorro listened to a message left on his answering machine. It was from a former university classmate who called to give him her support on this case and to tell him something similar had happened to her in 2004. In her case, however, the mistake was discovered the next day. "It means [baby switching] isn't a common situation, but it still happens," Socorro concluded. But we really do not know how often baby switches occur. Perhaps babies are exchanged more often than we think, but the rarity of discovery makes us think they are not.

Socorro was stunned by the media attention his case received. "I got calls from New York and London. It was a Kafkaesque week. All the existing media in Spain came, and they were angry because I was supposed to be on a TV show, which was a lie. They offered me astronomical amounts of money. . . . A journalist from *La Provinica* called me, telling me she had an important piece of information and that she was willing to make the names public by herself if we didn't agree to an interview. It was coercion. We decided that since the news was going to be published, we should control the information in order to avoid the use of it against our interests. I don't know who gave the information to the journalists in the first instance, but the case had already been in the courts for three years. Many people work in the court, many civil servants, and, in fact, it usually happens in Spain that cases get easily published in the newspapers."

Socorro said I surprised him—"but not really." He welcomed collaboration with someone in twin research who showed serious interest in this case. It seemed that I was the only nonjournalist who had contacted him, something I found surprising because I was certain the case would have been of great interest to my twin studies colleagues. Socorro also said he hadn't consulted with experts because there was no precedent. He was, however, aware that Delia was suffering greatly. As indicated, Delia had initially delayed doing a DNA test because she feared the disastrous effects the results would have on her family. But her anxiety did not disappear, and she knew the DNA test had to be done. Socorro suggested that Delia see a psychiatrist, and she did until the fees became unmanageable and she could no longer afford to.

Eventually, all three sisters and Laura were examined by a court-appointed psychiatrist, Dr. Angel Trujillo Cabas, who acted as a legal expert. Jessica and I were scheduled to see him on September 16 at his office in the Hospital Universitario de Gran Canaria.

Despite the lack of precedent, I was surprised that a specialist in twin studies was not involved in this case. Prior to my arrival in Las Palmas, Socorro had suggested that I testify via video, an idea that was abandoned following the judge's March 2009 decision. He'd hoped that my opinion on the case would help convince the court that Delia had suffered severe moral and physical damages, explained largely by her lost twinship and not being reared by her biological family. But on that September day in his office he believed I could be the "cornerstone" when determining the damage on appeal. "It is important for Peregrina and me that [you] appear on TV. This is not the right moment because the media are trying to take a picture of the twins together. If you appear now maybe you won't be able to interview them." Socorro emphasized that by swaying public opinion I could have some influence on the court, but this would have to be done after I left Las Palmas. I was comfortable with this decision, and I did not want to do anything to jeopardize my standing with the twins and their families.

4

TRAUMATIC TRUTHS—I

Researchers like myself are in privileged positions because we get to know people very well in short periods of time. This situation is similar to the open, often honest interactions that can develop between people seated together on planes and trains. Travel companions we do not know but happen to meet on a leg of our journeys are not part of our daily lives, so what we say to them, we feel, cannot come back to haunt us. These insightful strangers can sometimes settle a difficult problem or issue for us because they bring a fresh perspective. Like familiar strangers, research participants also reveal information about themselves that they would hesitate to share with family and friends for fear of judgment, embarrassment, or recrimination. But trust and respect on the part of those being studied, and knowledge and interest on the part of those doing the studying, solidify the researcher-participant relationship. Both parties know they can gain a great deal from this fruitful partnership, secure in the knowledge that the two worlds will not cross paths.

I have interviewed hundreds of twins and parents of twins. My being one part of a twin pair has been an invaluable asset in this process because the twins, their families, and I share something of tremendous importance. Our intimate connection to all things twinlike lets us express thoughts and feelings without fear and be understood without explanation. I shared the anticipation of Brittany L. a twenty-four-year-old reared-apart twin who was meeting her twin sister for the first time in September 2010. I understood Cathy G.'s distress when her high-achieving teenage twin sons were accused of cheating on a standardized test because of their similar answers to free-response questions. I also felt Linda McGee's grief and pain when her twin sister Brenda perished in the World Trade Tower attack in 2001. I could describe many more such happy, frustrating, and heartbreaking twin events—all of which I understood without explanation.

Delia, Begoña, and Beatriz and their families presented a unique challenge for me because we could not communicate with one another directly—they spoke only Spanish, and I speak only English. But they supported my purpose, which was to understand the behavioral, societal, and legal aspects of their situation. With the help of a skilled and sensitive interpreter, Jessica, who initiated direct communication and explained the purpose of my research, the researcher-participant relationships I had hoped for were, for the most part, realized.

I will tell the families' detailed stories as I learned them from the different people I interviewed, in the order in which I met them. This linear approach best preserves the research process by creating a timeline for the revelation of new information and insights and the occurrence of surprise events. My twelve days in Las Palmas were largely unplanned, adding excitement and uncertainty to this undertaking. There were some unexpected successes and memorable moments I might otherwise have missed had my schedule been structured in advance. Meeting Beatriz, the unrelated sister, was one of them—the press largely ignored her story, probably because she was not one of the twins.

MONDAY, SEPTEMBER 14

Beatriz

When Beatriz was twelve, she realized there were fundamental differences between her and the rest of her family.[1] "We didn't look alike, and I always felt like the ugly duckling in my house." Beatriz's hair and coloring are darker than those of her parents and siblings, so she stood out from them. Her contrasting appearance was hardly a secret—her mother used to tell her she looked like her great-grandmother. "They always compared me to distant family and used to tell me I didn't look like Begoña or any of them." Beatriz showed us a picture of her biological parents and her biological sister Gara, the one whom everyone said Beatriz resembled when she traveled across the north part of the island. "I used to tell people my name is Beatriz, but they still called me Gara. We look alike."

The population of the Canary Islands includes a blend of people of North African and European ancestry. The islands were originally inhabited by the Guanches, who were typically tall, muscular, and blond. How the Guanches arrived at the islands is debated even today. There was considerable immigration to the Canary Islands from Europe and North Africa during the first half of the fourteenth century, and this diversity is apparent when wandering through the streets of Las Palmas and other parts of the island. This may explain the physical contrast between Beatriz and her rearing family—"They're all light and I'm dark-skinned. Also the shape of my face is different"—as well as the plausibility of the family's belief that Beatriz resembled distant relatives.

The differences between Beatriz and her rearing family were not limited to appearance but extended to her thoughts and actions. "My character was so different. . . . I felt out of place." The impromptu Las Arenas mall reunion no doubt intensified her feelings. For Beatriz, recalling that day was to relive her sense of loneliness and upset at the situation. She felt that she and Delia had "clashed" with each other and that Delia saw Beatriz as having replaced her in her biological family, making her life difficult. She felt isolated and alone when she saw Begoña and Delia together. "I couldn't stop staring at them. They talked and laughed the same way. I started thinking about who I really was. I asked myself, 'Who am I, then?' I felt so strange. My relationship with Begoña has always been great, and when I suddenly found someone that looked exactly like her, I was afraid I would lose her." But like most fraternal twins, Beatriz and Begoña had had separate friends and had performed differently at school. Beatriz repeated a grade when she was six years old, which separated the twins academically. In contrast, most identical twins share their friends and achieve similar success at school.[2]

Beatriz took us back to the moment the DNA tests were completed. "I think the results weren't ready for fifteen days. I felt a bit anxious waiting . . . but I already knew what they were going to tell me. My mother and Begoña went to the hospital to pick them up. I was at my mother's house that day so Begoña told me the news. [My mum] wasn't my biological mother, but Begoña was her biological daughter. . . . [My mother and Begoña] hugged me and told me nothing was going to change."

Beatriz reminded me of Marcus, George's twin of twenty years whose perceived family ties and personal identity vanished in a day. Fortunately, both Beatriz and Marcus had rearing families who loved and supported them. In Beatriz and her mother's case, fear of rejection went both ways. According to Beatriz, "When my mother learned I wasn't her real daughter, she thought I would reject her. Our mother treated Begoña and me the same way—everything stayed normal. I thought things would change [between us], but they didn't. I thought my sisters would reject me since I belonged to another biological family. I sensed they were rejecting me, but that was just my own interpretation. They began worrying about me too much, and I felt stressed out. They called me all the time. . . . I began to feel depressed, and I didn't feel like talking to my family. I began asking myself why [the hospital] had done this to me—after so many years, they tell you that you belong to a different family."

The physical and behavioral differences between Beatriz and her family suddenly made sense, but that knowledge provided them with little comfort. Beatriz held a special place in her family that she began to question once the DNA findings were known. "I feel like I was the oldest sister. The four of us were brought up together. We're actually five [siblings], but my oldest sister [María] moved out, and the rest of my brothers and sisters have always asked me for things as if I were a second mother. My mum always asks me what to cook for lunch and things like that. Our relationship remains the same, but my mum is afraid I will leave and move out with the other family. But what do I do now with the other family, being thirty-six years old?"

In wondering what to do with the "other" family, Beatriz asked an important question. Finding out an as adult that you were switched at birth is no easier to bear than if you were a child hearing the same news. Some people might assume that discovering the truth as an adult is easier, reasoning that personal identity is established by adulthood and so pain and suffering on the part of the affected individuals dates only to the time the mistake was discovered. But this thinking ignores the nature and progression of life events before news of the switch. For example, Beatriz was aware of her different physical appearance well before the mistake was confirmed and sometimes felt like an outsider in her family because of it. One could argue that seven-year-old Ernstli had an easier time than Beatriz because he eventually adjusted to his new home, albeit after many confusing moments and tearful nights. I would argue that the uniqueness of each switched-at-birth twin case precludes the rank ordering of these cases as to the degree of emotional upset experienced by the different family members. However, the consequences differ depending on when the mistake is discovered—or if the twins are infants, children, or adults.

Beatriz told me about the first time Delia visited their home. "Our house was opened to Delia. I don't remember the exact date when she came to our house, but I think it was many months after the first meeting at Las Arenas. I cannot tell you for sure. But when Delia came to our home, my mother was astonished. I'm an open-minded person, so I felt happy for my family at that moment because I wasn't thinking about myself and the consequences of that new situation." Beatriz next described a type of detail that mystifies the general public but that researchers studying reared-apart identical twins try to understand from a more scientific perspective. "Delia's lipstick was the same as my mother's. My mother loves red for lips even though she's so light, and Delia had the same taste. When we saw her red lips with some lipstick outside the corner of her lips—like my mother does when she uses makeup—we felt amazed."

Their same choice of red lipstick and its application are striking details, but even more so because they are not coincidence. The clothes and makeup we choose are partial functions of our facial features, skin tone, and color preferences, all of which are genetically influenced to some degree.[3] Therefore, it is not surprising that Delia and her mother enhanced their appearance in similar ways. Both Delia and her biological mother, Laura, had pale skin, and while some light-skinned people might choose subdued lipstick shades to downplay their fairness, both women preferred to accentuate it. The small bit of coloring beyond the corner of their lips could reflect an attempt to alter the contours of the mouth in a desired way or could simply result from the same unsteady hand. My explanations are speculative, but observing similar dress, makeup, and demeanor in identical twins and other close relatives living apart offers a new source of hypotheses that may ultimately explain behavior more accurately than we can do now.

"My mother, Laura, said she [now] had six children [not five] . . . but Delia's house wasn't opened for me." Beatriz also told me about her first few meetings with her biological parents, Débora and Juan, and her sisters Gara and Julia. "At first I enjoyed the mystery of finding out if they looked like me. I was excited about meeting them and comparing myself to them. But when I met them for real and realized how things were, I began to distance myself from them. I get along with Gara; she's really different from Delia and Julia. She's more like me. Gara's like my twin sister. There is a difference of nine months between her and me. The way she behaves and thinks is similar. . . . She liked being home with her family, too. But now I don't talk to any of them, not even Gara." (The sisters' age difference is actually fifteen months.)

Beatriz's first meeting with her biological family took place about one year before a DNA test confirmed that she was Débora and Juan's daughter. But she had seen her parents on TV before then. Delia had told Begoña that her parents used to dance at Canal (Channel) 25, the set of the *Don Francisco Show*, on which couples are taped dancing for a later television broadcast. Begoña had seen pictures of Débora and Juan, so when she and Beatriz watched the show, she could point them out on the screen. The first meeting between Beatriz and her biological parents took place at Canal 25.

Beatriz, Begoña, their female cousin, and Beatriz's best friend went to Canal 25 together. Beatriz recalled, "We didn't speak during the first meeting, but Débora was looking at Begoña and me all the time. Nothing special happened. When Delia's mother and father saw Begoña, they had to sit down. They began crying because Begoña looked exactly like Delia. Juan invited Begoña to dance." The twins' lawyer Peregrina didn't know about this meeting until later. He told me, "The first time they met it happened out of curiosity, but in the laboratory they became aware of the truth."

Peregrina arranged the family's second meeting, which took place at the DNA-testing laboratory. Peregrina accompanied Beatriz to the lab that day. "He asked me if I wanted to see them, so I decided to stay. At the beginning I [debated] whether to stay or to leave, but I finally stayed. . . . Delia's mother and father began crying. I wanted to meet Gara because everybody said she looked like me. So instead of going to their village, which was a bit far, we decided to meet at Canal 25. That's how maybe I appeared on TV. We greeted, kissed, and kept on staring at each other." But Beatriz wasn't happy.

"I felt like a puppet. I was the center of attention—everybody wanted to meet me. My biological parents wanted to show me to all their friends, and I felt pressured . . . so after that we began to grow apart. That happened a year ago [in 2008]. After thirty-five years they wanted to [treat] me as if I were a two-year-old girl, but I was already an adult. And I think Julia is jealous of me . . . maybe she thinks I want to take her parents away from her. I didn't want to take anything from anyone; I just wanted to know to which family I belonged." I was surprised that Débora and Juan were so public in their reunion with Beatriz because they were clearly outraged that Clarisa, who had mistaken Begoña for Delia at the shopping mall, hadn't talked to them first about reuniting the twins. Perhaps they didn't see Beatriz as their adult daughter but as their young child whom they were starting to know for the first time.

One perspective says that traumatic truths are better known than unknown because past experiences can be properly assessed and future decisions can be accurately informed. But some life events may not fit into this tidy framework, and knowing which ones do and do not may come only from personal experience. Beatriz told us, "Before all this happened, I felt good about my life in general, both my working life and my family life. I've always been a healthy person, but I suffered from a facial paralysis on the left side of my face because of the stress [of this situation]. I still feel that facial muscle when I get stressed. I also have some stomach problems due to the fact that I've become a heavy smoker and I've been drinking a lot of coffee lately because of all these problems. Even if my family loves me, I have wished many times this had never happened. I am still worried about having problems with my family. Now it's a bit too late to stop everything, so I prefer to know the truth."

Begoña and Beatriz had each been confused for other people before and had thought of those incidents as coincidental and not worth following up. Perhaps it was shop assistant Clarisa's insistence that Begoña and Beatriz looked so much like Delia and Gara, respectively, that persuaded them to meet. Had they disregarded Clarisa, their lives might have continued as before and stayed that way. Or perhaps there would have been another odd encounter. Beatriz thinks that fate placed her in the family that raised her. Perhaps fate also led her to her family of birth.

Beatriz returned to work, and Jessica and I agreed to meet later that night for our session with Peregrina. I realized I knew more about Beatriz's situation than anyone outside her family, possibly even her lawyer. She struck me as feeling rootless—-grateful that her family was supportive, but also questioning their love for her. Based on my interviews with the other members of her rearing family, I am certain Beatriz had no reason to doubt them, but she was sad and confused. Her beliefs about herself were very different from what she had always supposed was true. She had always known that she was not like her parents and siblings, but upon hearing news of the DNA tests, she knew the difficult reason why. And she was no longer a twin. Not being a twin did not bother Beatriz, however, because being so different from Begoña, she had never felt like one. I understand that to some degree because of the differences between my twin sister and me. But our joint birthday parties and other shared events like getting a library card, going to college, and having a legal drink reinforced our twinship on many levels. Having those memories altered by new knowledge would be devastating.

There were only two nurses in attendance at the Nuestra Señora del Pino Hospital's newborn nursery, and one of them was responsible for switching Delia and Beatriz. That nurse was never identified; the day the switch occurred is unknown, making it unlikely the hospital could ever identify which nurse was responsible. Wandering back to my hotel, I wondered if she was out there reading the newspapers and grappling with the guilt she surely must have felt. Perhaps she preferred to remain silent, knowing that anything she said or did could not make amends.

Later that night, after meeting with Peregrina, Jessica and I walked over to the hospital where the twins had been born. This impressive-looking building, located at the top of hilly Calle Angel Guimerá, is no longer a maternity hospital but a center for the elderly. The newer Hos-

Fig. 4.1. The former Nuestra Señora del Pino Hospital where the twins and Beatriz were born. Courtesy of Nancy L. Segal

pital Universitario Materno Infantil is located on the scenic Avenida Marítima Del Norte. There were several maternity hospitals in Gran Canaria in 1973 when the twins and Beatriz were born, but there were no maternity facilities in Beatriz's parents' town; families living there traveled 13.5 miles (22 kilometers) to Las Palmas to deliver their babies.[4] We tried to enter the building to visit the former nursery, but the security guard prevented us from doing so. I was still glad that I saw the old hospital because it helped to place the events of 1973 in my mind's eye. The next morning we interviewed Laura, the mother whose twin babies had been delivered there.

TUESDAY, SEPTEMBER 15

Laura

"The doctor told me my babies were identical.[5] Then they took the babies to the incubator and switched them. The three babies were in the same incubator." Laura now knows that the baby she was given three months after her discharge from the hospital wasn't hers. "I was a bit doubtful, but I finally thought maybe the baby looked like my husband or his parents because she was quite dark haired. The real twins were blonde."

Perhaps Laura doubted that the twins were identical as the doctor had told her—or perhaps she recalled feeling the slightest doubt as to whether the second twin was really hers and wished she had acted on that doubt. But she insisted that "even [when she was] growing up, I always thought [Beatriz] was my real daughter."

Laura remembered the day Begoña came home and told her the truth. "When I found out about the switch, I went crazy. I didn't want to think about it, but I couldn't stop thinking about it for three months. I told Begoña that we had to do the DNA tests. For the next three months I couldn't believe that the situation was actually happening to me. I felt oppressed, and I still feel like that. I'm going to doctors. I went to a psychologist who also treated Begoña and Delia."

Laura appeared to be a mother who was missing two of her children. She had raised Beatriz as her daughter since Beatriz was an infant, then discovered she had not given birth to her. This did not mean that Laura loved Beatriz any less—after all, the love and care that parents provide their children, whether biological or nonbiological, are the basis of their bond. But Beatriz belonged to a different set of parents, so the biological connection that Laura had perceived was gone. "Sometimes Beatriz thinks I treat her differently because she isn't my biological daughter. I usually tell her she's my daughter because I brought her up."

Once the switch was discovered, Laura also faced the realization that she had not been part of the important developmental events in Delia's life. Laura had missed Delia's formative years. She didn't know how she did on her first day of school or whether she was a happy teenager and adult. But she felt as if she had known her all along, possibly because Delia was so much like Begoña and the rest of Laura's family. "Delia walks and talks like me. I felt that Delia was my daughter at first sight. I feel I'm her mother—I have the same feelings for Delia and Begoña. The first time Delia learned I was her mother, Beatriz and Begoña were there. I sat at the entrance with Delia and Begoña next to me, and Beatriz on one side. I told Delia I hadn't lost a daughter but I had actually gained two."

It struck me how differently Laura and Mme. Joye, Paul and Philippe's mother, had reacted to the twin child they hadn't raised. Laura felt an immediate connection to Delia, whereas Mme. Joye did not feel that Ernstli was her son, despite his physical resemblance to Philippe, the twin child she did raise. This is understandable because Ernstli spoke only German and he cried constantly for the mother who raised him. Moreover, Mme. Joye felt a special affinity for Paul, the boy who was not her son, even seeing her own character traits in him and not in his brother. Mme. Joye came to love Ernstli, renamed Charles, and would have happily raised all three boys if she had had the opportunity. Of course, that was never possible.

I asked Laura to describe her relationship with Delia. (I also wondered how Delia saw her relationship with Laura, but that was a question I would ask Delia.) She said, "I think Delia sees me as a mother. She always kisses and hugs me as if I were. And she invited me to her house. I call her sometimes and I buy her Christmas presents. Last Saturday I went to Delia's hen [bachelorette] party. Delia's aunt asked me a lot of questions and took a lot of pictures of Delia and Begoña. Delia's mother didn't go to the wedding—only one of her aunts did."

Laura continued, "I felt sorry for Delia. I know Delia learned of [the switch] years after looking for a donor. If I had known all this before, we could have given her our bone marrow. Begoña was very affected by this." Laura was also aware of the similarities between Delia and Begoña. She mentioned their gestures and the way they ate. "They're quite refined the way they wipe their mouths [after eating]. They both like studying. Begoña wants to attend university now, although she didn't want to study when she was a child. Beatriz doesn't like studying, and her way of speaking differs from Delia's and Begoña's. Begoña is impressed with how much genes impact behavior."

According to Laura, Delia and Begoña have developed a relationship of which Beatriz is not a part. "Delia called Begoña almost every day. Beatriz has nothing to do with the other two." Exacerbating Beatriz's distress was an act on the part of Beatriz's biological mother, Débora. Débora called Laura to discuss changing Beatriz's last name. "How did she think to do that kind of thing? It also hurts my feelings. . . . When Beatriz first learned the truth, she spent time locked up at home feeling depressed. I had to go to a psychologist with her."

Laura was upset with the press and with the people producing a television drama based on their story. But she believed the lawsuit was important to set a precedent to prevent other families from suffering. Her emotional distress was not over. "I feel so terrible—I'd rather have not known the truth."

I knew I could not take pictures of the twins or their family members as per our prior agreement. But I was curious to see pictures of Begoña and Delia having met Beatriz and Laura. We arranged to meet Laura and her daughter Beatriz at their home the following Monday morning, September 21, so that I could see the family photos. Most mothers carry photos of their children in their wallets, something I know from having attended so many Mothers of Twins Club workshops. Mothers of twins are especially proud to show their children to other people who express interest. Laura told me she always carried pictures of her daughters with her, but she didn't have a picture of Delia. "I hadn't thought about carrying a picture of Delia with me." She searched through her bag, not finding pictures of either of her twin daughters.

Then she found one. "I don't have any picture of Beatriz with me. I have one of Begoña because she put it there herself. She put it there a month ago. I don't know why she did it." I was surprised that Laura did not have pictures of her daughters with her since she said she always carried their pictures. Perhaps she had recently changed purses or perhaps these pictures had become painful reminders of how her life had changed.

Had Laura not had a picture of Begoña, it wouldn't have mattered because we were meeting Begoña very shortly, at 11:30 in Peregrina's office. But having seen the photograph, I was better prepared for the physical differences I would witness between the two women who had grown up as twins.

Begoña

Begoña is the outgoing, confident, and cool-headed sister of the pair in which she was raised, possibly because her genetic proclivities predispose her in these directions, but also because she came from a home where people were like her. Begoña had been greatly upset by the switch and continued to suffer, but her experience differed from that of her mother and sister. We talked first about the three times she had been mistaken for a girl named "Delia." In some ways I was surprised these incidents did not occur more often.[6]

Las Palmas has been ranked as the ninth largest city in Spain[7] with a population of 381,847 as of 2009 and a population of 354,863 in 2001 when the twins discovered one another.[8] Half of the inhabitants of Gran Canaria live there.[9] Begoña had lived in Las Palmas all her life, while Delia had visited the city from time to time. The island is not geographically that small, at 794 square miles (2,057 square kilometers),[10] but because the biological twins (Begoña and Delia) and biological sisters (Beatriz and Gara) were the same age and sex, they were likely to frequent similar places and events, such as schools, concerts, discotheques—and shopping malls. These circumstances would "shrink" the spaces they visited, thereby reducing the number of people with whom they came into contact. Together, these factors would raise the probability of their encountering someone who knew one twin but not the other. It was also possible that, unbeknown to them, the twins' paths crossed closely on some occasions, perhaps when they attended the same film or ate at a favorite restaurant. Begoña occasionally visited Delia's part of the island, a small, historic village thirteen miles outside the city, but more often Delia came to Las Palmas for work. This was not unusual—Delia's lawyer Socorro lived near her and commuted to Las Palmas every day.

The three times Begoña had been mistaken for Delia had taken place in Las Palmas or in a nearby suburb. Begoña was twenty when this happened the first time. A young man at a bus stop approached her and asked, "Are you Delia?" but she didn't recognize him and just said no. Begoña thinks the young man really believed she was Delia and that "Delia" was trying to brush him off. The next time Begoña was mistaken for her twin occurred when she was twenty-seven. Begoña's neighbor, who worked as a waitress at a coffee shop, told Begoña she thought she had seen her at the restaurant, but Begoña hadn't been there; Delia had. "My neighbor told me we even had the same freckles. She wanted to put me in touch with her. I thought maybe we could be alike, but I didn't give it too much importance. People usually say that kind of thing—then you see the real person and you realize you don't look that much alike." The third time Begoña was mistaken for Delia was at the Las Arenas mall, the encounter that resulted in the twins' reunion when they were twenty-eight. They might have met sooner if only the young man or the neighbor had been more insistent that they get to know each other.

Intruding into people's private lives, particularly when they are strangers, is not something most people do. Suggesting that someone has a twin or insinuating that they could have been raised in the wrong family comes across as insensitive and rude by most standards. I once encountered a woman at a theater who bore a striking resemblance to my uncle's wife, whom I knew had been adopted. I gently questioned the woman about her family background, but she became visibly upset, so I stopped. The idea of having firm, secure family relationships disrupted in a minute is alarming to most people. When approaching the woman who resembled my uncle's wife, I had enough doubt that I could easily end our conversation and let it go. And I imagine that the man at the bus stop and the waitress at the café felt the same. But the woman at the mall was serious to a degree that Begoña could not ignore.

Twins in 18 (13.6 percent) of the 137 reared-apart pairs who participated in the Minnesota Study of Twins Reared Apart met as a result of mistaken identity.[11] Genetic testing showed that twins in just one of these pairs, Kerrie and Amy, were fraternal, but they looked enough alike to pass for identical twins. Some of these twins did not know they were twins and were initially skeptical of the possibility that they could be. However, most knew they had been adopted, and because their family histories were often unknown or concealed, they may have been more open to the idea of twinship than Begoña and Beatriz, who were not adopted.

Many of the twins I interviewed in Minnesota said they had been worried about meeting someone who looked just like them, concerned that this would hurt their identity or sense of self. The thought that their physical appearance was no longer unique seemed more threatening to them than the possibility that their habits and behaviors might also be repeated in their twin. Perhaps this is because physical features are the first things we see when meeting someone for the first time, and our first impression matters. Most people (non-twins) never have the experience of "seeing" themselves as others see them and might well find the prospect intimidating. Furthermore, identical twins' matched physical appearance can cause them to be mistaken for one another, making some newly reunited twins uneasy. However, the twins' fears were unfounded because as alike as identical twins are, they are also separate individuals both physically and behaviorally. Most of the Minnesota twins got along famously once they met. Begoña had similar concerns that began when the twins first saw each other. "The first time I saw Delia, I didn't want to believe she was my twin. I realized we looked alike, but I thought not enough for us to be twins. It's difficult to explain. I felt paralyzed. At the same time, I denied what was happening."

Begoña's denial changed over the five years since their first meeting to recognition and acceptance of being an identical twin. "When Delia and I are together, you can see some differences. But if we are apart, we are so alike. Even our gestures are the same. However, you have to bear in mind that Delia suffered from leukemia and that disease has left a mark on her body. For example, Delia is heavier than I am. I've seen pictures of Delia when she was a little girl, and we looked identical." It was also easy to understand the source of Laura's comment about Begoña believing that behavior was genetically influenced. "There aren't any similarities between Beatriz and me, even if we were raised together. We have very different characters—she is more introverted and finds it harder to socialize. She is also the type of person who [prefers] more than one explanation for things. Delia and I share the same opinion about many topics. When I talk to Delia, I know what she's going to answer," Begoña told me.

Our interview shifted to the time one year after the twins' first meeting when Begoña received the "happy birthday" text message from Delia. Begoña was torn between the tensions of her "two" twinships: her lifelong relationship with Beatriz and her new relationship with Delia. Begoña told me, "At this point, I was conscious of the real situation because Beatriz was suffering a lot. Delia and I couldn't have a normal relationship because the situation was complicated. It was so strange to see a person who looked and behaved like me. Delia often came to see me with a different person, so [early on] I felt as if I was on display. . . . But I understood that it was due to people's curiosity."

If Delia seemed more eager to develop a relationship as twins, it was probably because she did not get along as well with her family as she would have liked, nor did she feel she fit in. Her parents and sisters did not hear about the 2001 meeting in Las Arenas until 2008, but Delia began distancing herself from her family before that and eventually moved out. Begoña revealed that before any of this had happened, Delia wondered if she had been adopted because none of her close relatives was a suitable bone marrow donor. However, I did not hear this from Delia.

If Begoña felt reluctant to spend more time with Delia, it was not because they did not get along; it was because of Beatriz. "When I learned Delia was my twin, I felt a mixture of feelings related to Delia and Beatriz. I preferred not to see Delia to avoid Beatriz's suffering. Beatriz had a very bad time and thought [our mother] would reject her and choose Delia instead. Beatriz is a very apprehensive person, and any problem becomes a big deal for her. She is not able to see that this case is nobody's fault and that all of us are just victims. The relationship between my mother, Beatriz, and I has not changed because of this. I don't think my mother has ever favored me, but I know she leans on me."

Parents have different relationships with each of their children, largely based on each individual's personality and abilities. If Laura relied on Begoña for some things, she relied on Beatriz for other things, such as arranging family meals and related activities. I believe this is fair and not favoritism. Fair parenting means being responsive to what each child is good at and therefore usually means treating each child differently.

I asked Begoña to talk about what it was like growing up as a twin, albeit, as it turned out, an unrelated one. Her views did not surprise me, perhaps because as a nonidentical twin myself, I understood. "I wasn't raised as a twin. I was raised as a person who has one more sister. It isn't like my [ten-year-old] identical twin nephews who spend all their time together. I cannot explain how I feel being a twin because I wasn't raised as one." Begoña had probably always answered this way when people asked her about being a twin, but she could not have known how truthfully she spoke.

During our interview, I wondered about Begoña's current views on twinship. "I think if I had grown up with Delia, we would be really close to each other—I can feel it. That's for sure. She's the kind of person you talk to and you realize you know her. Delia understood that we could not have a close relationship because of Beatriz's suffering. I know Delia and I understand each other and reach agreements even if we have different opinions. But Beatriz and I have different ways of thinking, and we don't [always] understand each other. That's basically the big difference between the two [Delia and Beatriz]. I love Beatriz and she's my sister, as different as we might be—it has nothing to do with blood ties. . . . I think Beatriz feels jealous of the special relationship I share with Delia. I can understand how she feels."

The last time the twins had been together was at Delia's hen party, the Saturday before our interview. Begoña explained that they live quite far apart and both have work obligations, so they stay in touch by telephone. "With time we calmed down and our relationship changed. We decided to separate our lives because we were somehow rubbing salt into the wound. Everybody wanted to see us, to find out more about us, and that was causing pain in the people concerned. After some time we went back to our daily routines. Delia moved out of her parents' house and has no relationship with them at present. Delia and I have always had a relationship and we've grown closer, but there is always that [physical] distance. At the beginning we arranged barbeques so we could meet, but with time things got back into a routine. I think I'll always be close to Delia. She is really different from her nonbiological family—she stands out in that house."

As I indicated, Delia was raised in a small village with fewer cultural and educational opportunities than Begoña and Beatriz had in Las Palmas. It's likely that part of Beatriz's difficulty lay in seeing the atmosphere in which she would have grown up if the mistake hadn't happened. Beatriz told me that she found the people of that village "uncommunicative and hard to talk to." She seemed caught between rejecting her biological family's lifestyle and not measuring up to the one in which she was raised. Beatriz reminded me of the twins Oskar and Jack, whose identities were so differently shaped by their separate rearing in Nazi Germany and Trinidad but knew that each would have become the other had their places been reversed. If Beatriz had been raised by

Débora and Juan, she would have only known their way of life. She might have felt more comfortable in their home than the one she was raised in.

Because Begoña was raised as a fraternal twin but didn't feel like one, I asked her again for her concise definition of twinship. She replied, "I think twins have a special tie that links them if you compare them to [non-twin] brothers and sisters. I believe it's a genetic bond. I see Beatriz as a sister, and I obviously see Delia as a twin."

Begoña had a philosophical streak and a practical mind that probably helped her through her crisis. She was not happy about what had happened, but she attempted to come to terms with her situation. "I think things always happen because there's an underlying reason. It's nobody's fault, and we had to know the truth." She also drew a distinction between children who are adopted and children who are misplaced. "I am not discussing adopted children's rights to meet their biological parents. The nature of that [situation] has nothing to do with mine. In my case, each of us should have been raised in our biological family." She sounded a bit like the lawyer she wanted to be.

Begoña had not been back to the Las Arenas shopping mall since the twins met there in 2001. "There are lots of shopping malls," she said. Begoña had run into the shop assistant, Clarisa, who had reunited the twins, but she didn't comment on this chance meeting.

Begoña promised to pick up Jessica and me at my hotel at 10:00 AM the next Saturday for the visit to her home. I looked forward to this get-together because people's homes tell a great deal about who they are and what they like. This second meeting would also let me follow up on certain themes Begoña had raised during our first meeting and to see her in a relaxed atmosphere. Begoña told us to meet her in her car so she would not risk being seen by a journalist.

After a short break following the interview, Jessica and I returned to Peregrina's office to meet Delia's parents, Débora and Juan. We spoke with them separately, Débora first.

Débora

Débora summarized the effects of the switch on her life in the first minutes of our conversation: "I'm always feeling bad . . . thirty-six years. . . . It's not a joke. . . . What can I do?"[12]

Delia was a wanted child. Débora and Juan waited several months before having children, and the pregnancy "worked perfectly." But the baby was born early, after only seven and a half months. After delivery, Débora saw her baby only briefly before the infant was taken to the incubator where she remained for about twenty-five days. Débora had hoped for a girl so she could dress her up, and she got one in Delia. She and Juan and a neighbor went to the hospital every day to see her, but only through a glass partition. Débora sounded bitter: "Delia was always sick. They gave me a sick baby. The doctor told me to put hot water bottles over her legs, otherwise she could die. . . . She was always sick her entire life."

Delia was discharged from the hospital on February 8, 1973. "Nothing was strange when I took her home. Through the glass pane she looked like my husband's family. We didn't suspect anything. It was because of the [TV] cameras I found out [she wasn't mine]. I almost went crazy." Débora had terrible things to say about the media's handling of her very personal situation. "It was a mess. Neighbors wanted to talk to me, and TV [cameras] began to appear. But I don't want to be on TV because I don't want to walk on the street and see people staring and talking about me. . . . I have committed no crime. It's killing me. I just took [the baby] they gave me." She even said that the TV reporters had changed the names of the twins in the broadcast "so that I couldn't find out."

Débora's emotional wounds were still as fresh as if she had discovered the mistake only recently. She had seen a psychologist on four occasions, she said, but added that she no longer went because of the cost and instead unburdened herself by crying. I felt she was in mourning.

"The most important loss is the fact of not having either of them, of losing both [Delia and Beatriz] at the same time. I try to psychologically replace them both with my granddaughter [Elena]." In Débora's mind, Delia rejected her family once she knew she belonged elsewhere. "After finding out the whole story, [Delia] didn't want to go anywhere with me. . . . She was angry all the time because she knew she wasn't my daughter and [was] so incompatible with the rest of us. . . . When I pass her on the street, she goes right by me." Débora sounded hurt and heartbroken as she went on to talk about the financial sacrifices she and Juan had made for Delia's cancer treatment, such as selling their house and their car. The family had moved into Delia's grandparents' home, where they were living at the time of my interviews with them.

Despite her bitterness, Débora was still a mother who loved her daughter, and she wanted to know what I knew about Delia's wedding because she had not been invited. Débora wasn't even sure the wedding had taken place. "If my husband learns about the wedding now, he'll suffer from a heart attack! Delia should have invited us. Why is she doing this to me?" Débora and Juan hope to be compensated for their pain and suffering, although Débora said no money could make up for their loss. She also said she wanted to buy a house of her own.

"I have lost both my daughters," she repeated.

Débora had met Beatriz several times, calling her "a copy of my husband." She had hoped for a relationship with Beatriz but felt rejected by her, too. "I can see she doesn't love me."

At the end of our session, Débora made a simple but provocative statement, one that lawyers and philosophers will no doubt debate for years to come. "Delia's friend [Clarisa, who confused the twins] should have talked to my family first." She was unable to continue.

Juan

Jessica and I interviewed Juan in two locations, first in Peregrina's conference room and then in his secretary's office, because Peregrina eventually needed the conference space.[13] Juan sat at an angle from me the first time and directly across from me the second time and appeared generally at ease. He had dark hair and eyes like those of his wife and daughters. Juan was also well groomed, wearing a tattersall button-down shirt, pressed gray pants, and shiny black shoes. His long answers to my questions sometimes strayed from the topic, making it necessary for Jessica to redirect his responses.

The slight grin on Juan's face as he spoke did not hide the strain he had been under since learning about the switch just over a year earlier. "I loved Delia so much."

There had never been any doubt in Juan's mind that Delia was his daughter. But she was different from his younger children, Gara and Julia. "Delia argued all the time with her sisters. Delia had a car and used to pick up her friends, but she never wanted to go out with her sisters. The other two got along well.

"Delia wanted what her sisters had. Once a neighbor bought a set of perfumes and makeup for Julia, and I had to buy the same thing for Delia because she was jealous." He also talked about Delia's more recent rejections of him and his wife, such as ignoring them in public places. Parents complain about their imperfect children, but they still love them. If that were not so, then Juan would not be suffering as much as he was. "I never thought Delia was different from my other daughters."

At one point Juan told me, "Delia once said I was her father, but Débora was not her mother. She said that before the DNA test. At that moment she didn't even know she was a twin." It is difficult to know how to interpret that statement. Children feeling frustrated by differences between themselves and their parents or by their parents not understanding them sometimes say cruel things they do not mean. It is also possible that Juan forgot the sequence of events; perhaps Delia did know she was a twin by then and was at least trying to spare her father's feelings.

Juan and his wife, Débora, had hired Peregrina as their attorney. "I needed someone to defend me," he said. He also mentioned the large sums he had paid for Delia's cancer treatment, but said again how much he loved her. "Every day I wake up thinking of Delia. I would rather have not known the truth. I'd have preferred to die before finding out."

The two families saw their situations very differently. All three parents suffered greatly upon realizing they had raised someone else's child, but Débora and Juan felt a loss of the daughters Laura believed she had gained. This situation most likely reflects Beatriz's close relationship with Laura and Débora and Juan's distant relationship with Delia, patterns that were in place before the mistake was detected. It did not have to be that way—if Beatriz had been unhappy at home or if Delia had been more contented, the outcomes might have differed.

Everyone I interviewed in Las Palmas felt he or she had the story right. Nevertheless, the stories told thus far clearly reflect the emotional turmoil of the tellers, guaranteeing slight distortions and exaggerations of incidents and conversations. This is not surprising because a large psychological literature shows that people process and remember events very differently.[14] It is also possible to implant false memories, as shown by an experiment ironically titled "Lost in a Shopping Mall."[15] The twenty-four subjects in that study were shown three true memories and one false memory (being lost in a shopping mall) that had been provided by their relatives. Seven subjects initially believed all four memories were true, and several weeks later, five subjects believed the false memory was true when told that one of the four was incorrect.

The members of the two families had undergone various amounts of private and court-appointed psychological assessment and counseling. What transpired is confidential, but on Wednesday, September 16, I met with psychiatrist Dr. Angel Trujillo Cabas and his colleagues, who spoke generally about the case. But first I headed to Peregrina's office to meet Julia, Beatriz's younger biological sister.

5

TRAUMATIC TRUTHS—II

WEDNESDAY, SEPTEMBER 16

Julia

Beatriz's sister Julia waited for Jessica and me in Peregrina's reception area.[1] Almost twenty-seven years old at the time, she had short, wavy, reddish-brown hair that I suspected was tinted slightly, given the darker shades that ran in her family. She wore a turquoise halter top, jeans, and several gold earrings studded with rhinestones. Julia looked a lot like her birth parents, Débora and Juan, but somewhat less like her sister Beatriz than her sister Gara, whom we would meet later. She had taken a one-hour bus ride and taxi from her small village in the north part of the island to Las Palmas to meet us. Unlike her mother and father, Julia was quickly at ease in talking to us about what had happened to her family. She even allowed me to take her picture. Her speech didn't show the distinctive qualities Jessica detected when speaking to Beatriz and Juan.

Julia was born on October 13, 1981, so she was nearly nine years younger than Beatriz. She didn't like studying and had stopped going to school when she was thirteen. "I have never worked [outside my home]," she told us. When we met Julia, she was employed by her sister Gara as a babysitter for her two-and-a-half-year-old niece, Elena, while her sister worked as a cook at a nearby restaurant. Julia knew relatively few details about the Las Arenas meeting, but she had been at home when her mother heard the news about a baby from their village who had been switched at birth.

"The first time I heard [the story], it was on the news. It was about midday, and I had already finished the housework. I was watching TV with my mum at home and they were talking about the year 1973. It was May last year [2008], around the 17th. They talked about our town. So my mother said she had given birth that same year and that the baby had gone directly to the incubator. She began saying that Delia was definitely the baby that had been switched. She knew there had been a lot of problems at that hospital in those years. When I heard the news, I thought about how that family would be feeling—I didn't think it was our family, but my mum did. I heard her grumbling in the dining room and saying she couldn't believe she was the one whose baby had been switched. [Over the years] my mother never expressed any doubt [that Delia was her daughter], so I did not understand why she was suddenly so sure she was not. I stayed at home the whole day and told my father the news of the switched twins when he got home. He was surprised; he didn't know what to think. Our story began at that point."

It struck me how quickly Débora believed that her family was involved even though their names had not been mentioned. The delivery date and place of residence matched, but in their town and local community many babies had been born in 1973 and at the same hospital. Débora said she had never doubted that Delia was hers but she had always known her daughter's appearance and behavior differed considerably from the rest of the family's. What Débora so quickly accepted—the news of the switch and the possibility of a personal connection—seemed unlikely to Begoña, Beatriz, Laura, and nearly everyone else until they met one another. When Débora heard the news, perhaps a sliver of doubt she had silenced over the years, because [a switch] was so unthinkable, returned and was just enough to convince her that Delia was someone else's child.

Julia had never doubted that Delia was her biological sister. "Since we were raised together, it becomes really difficult to suspect that kind of thing [a baby switch]." However, the relationship between the two sisters was often tense, and Julia saw many more similarities between herself and her older sister Gara than with Delia. Gara became Julia's "second mother" when Delia was sick with leukemia. "Delia is quite open with her friends, but inside our house she was completely different. . . . Anything we said made her feel upset. Now I realize some things. Living with [Delia] was a strange thing—she had such a bad temper. I asked myself: Why? Now I understand because she already knew the truth. She always had a bad temper, but it became much worse after she found out. We thought she was behaving that way because of the [cancer]. We thought her change in attitude was lasting too long—after a disease like cancer you can feel bad for a period of time, but not that long. . . . We couldn't have [close feelings]."

Julia didn't know if Delia's September 5 hen party, prior to her September 11 wedding, had actually taken place—she had only heard rumors—but families' emotional ties are not easily severed. "It's difficult to forget you have a sister." Julia knew her parents still recognized Delia as their daughter and had strong feelings for her as such. But like her parents, who felt they had lost two daughters (Delia and Beatriz), Julia felt she had lost two sisters. "I saw Beatriz twice, the first time at the DNA test and the second time in my older sister's house. The first time I saw her, I saw her from the side and thought she looked identical to my sister Gara. I greeted her but didn't talk too much to her. I'm twenty-eight, she's thirty-six, so we have an age difference of eight years. I was too young for her so she preferred to have a close relationship with Gara." This was Julia's understanding; however, we had learned from Beatriz the day before that she and Gara had never established a meaningful connection.

Like her mother, Julia said she believed Clarisa, the shop assistant who had confused Begoña for Delia and instigated their meeting, should have shared her observations with Débora and Juan before arranging the

Las Arenas meeting. However, it isn't clear to me what that would have accomplished. Had Clarisa approached Débora and Juan before bringing the twins together, she could have aroused suspicions that they might have taken seriously—after all, immediately upon hearing the news on TV, Débora believed that the baby involved in the switch was hers. But even if Débora and Juan had regarded Clarisa's story as coincidence, or had asked her not to pursue the matter further, it is unlikely Clarisa would have kept silent. Clarisa was impressed enough with the resemblance between Delia and Begoña, and between Beatriz and Gara, to insist that they meet. Clarisa and her mother brought the twins together the same day that Clarisa had met Begoña for the second time.

Julia told us that she feels everyone's lives have been irreparably damaged by the discovery of the switch. "I'd rather have not known that Delia wasn't my biological sister. Sometimes it's better not to know the truth. You have a way of living, and suddenly your life changes." Julia is not personally involved in her parents' lawsuit, but she hopes they are compensated for their suffering. That would depend, in part, on recommendations from a psychiatrist based upon an extensive evaluation of Débora's and Juan's mental statuses.

I wanted to meet Julia's older sister Gara, who is also Beatriz's younger biological sister. Julia thought this might be difficult because Gara's job as a restaurant cook kept her busy from nine in the morning until seven in the evening, but Julia suggested that meeting the next Sunday evening would be possible. Julia promised to ask her sister if we could at least conduct an interview with her by telephone. However, an unexpected event allowed Jessica and me to spend more than an hour with both Julia and Gara the following night at my hotel.

Later the same morning we'd spoken with Julia, Jessica and I had an appointment at the Canary Islands Health Service at the University Hospital (Servicio Canario de Salud, Hospital Universitario). The hospital was located outside the central area of Las Palmas, about a fifteen-minute drive from Peregrina's office. There, we were introduced to psychiatrist Angel Trujillo Cabas, psychiatrist Casimiro Cabrera Abreu, psychologist Jorge De Vega, and other staff. We were escorted to a medium-sized conference room in the psychiatric wing where we spoke as a group.

Trujillo

The psychiatrists, psychologists, and others introduced themselves before I began my interview with Dr. Trujillo.[2] Given the secrecy surrounding the twins' identities, I was surprised to find myself speaking with Trujillo in the presence of about ten other psychologists and psychiatrists, but everyone seemed interested in this case.

Trujillo, a dark-haired gentleman wearing a white coat, probably in his sixties, was the court-appointed psychiatrist assigned to evaluate Delia, Begoña, Beatriz, and Laura. Trujillo's specific task was to determine whether or not any of the four women showed evidence of a current mental disorder. He did not speak English, so Jessica interviewed him in Spanish and later translated his comments into English. Trujillo explained, "I analyzed the [three sisters'] basic needs[3] and also the indignity of knowing that because of a nurse's error, instead of [Delia] having a life in Las Palmas, she was in [a different place]." Trujillo also documented the different complaints variously voiced by the sisters, such as not having her family's affection and not having a job, but felt he could not compare them among the three. "I pointed [these problems] out to the judge so she would be able to evaluate them. That was my duty." As I indicated, the confidentiality of Trujillo's reports could not be breached, and when he spoke he did so only generally about the case and his findings.

Trujillo said he'd never had such a case before. "When I finished the analysis, I did not consider it a psychiatric case—it is a paradoxical, terrible life situation. I examined the people about seven years after finding they were identical twins and seven years later no mental disorder had taken place." Trujillo did not deny that the twins and Beatriz had suf-

fered emotionally since their discovery of the switch, but he found that
none of them displayed clinical psychiatric symptoms as a result. His
conclusion was instrumental in the resolution of the case and would be
again with respect to the appeal.

Trujillo continued, "Delia's key issue was her parents' rejection and
having to leave her family's house. Her parents rejected her, and she had
to come to Las Palmas. She suffered from rootlessness." In my interviews, both Julia and Débora indicated that Delia had left home on her
own, whereas Delia told me that she felt hurt psychologically and she
had to go.

"Then a series of events related to the twins' relationship began, as
well as to the relationships among the one who wasn't a twin [Beatriz],
the twins' mother [Laura], and Delia's nonbiological mother [Débora].
This series of problems complicated relations among all of them." An
event that Delia told Trujillo "in an angry tone" was that Laura had
accompanied Beatriz to her first meeting with her biological family at
Canal 25. Trujillo said Delia's response to this meeting was that she "had
lost both mothers." Perhaps Delia was jealous of Beatriz at that time, per-
ceiving that both Laura and Débora were focused on Beatriz, not on her.

Trujillo saw similarities and differences between Delia and Begoña.
"The twins not only looked physically alike, but their way of dressing
was similar. They had different lifestyles and different jobs, although of
the same status. They were also both introverted, but I think Begoña is
more assertive than Delia. Delia played the victim role in the process—
she complained about her parents, about being alone, about not having
a family and not having either a biological or legal mother." Trujillo
stressed that each twin faced different issues. "There was a series of
changes in Delia's life. She was the separated twin, whereas Begoña spent
her entire life with her biological mother. I could appreciate that Begoña
was harmed relatively less. Begoña's key issue was finding out there was
an exact copy of her in the world, a double." But Begoña also discovered
she had been raised with an unrelated "twin."

Trujillo's description of the twins as "introverted" still surprises me because neither twin displayed this tendency during my meetings with them. Perhaps they reacted similarly to Trujillo's more formal interview, which occurred within a subdued hospital setting.

The twins also faced a common problem, namely their inability to develop and enjoy their new relationship. According to Trujillo, "They met behind other people's backs. Both mothers pressured them by asking why one had to meet with the other, thinking they didn't love them." Interestingly, Trujillo felt that Delia was the most confident of the three women. In contrast, in Trujillo's view, Beatriz appeared somewhat as a spectator, watching events as they unfolded. "I had the impression that this was the twins' problem and Beatriz kept out of the situation. She seemed to suffer less." Based on my interviews with Beatriz's sister Begoña, mother, and Beatriz herself, I find this surprising. Instead, I wonder if Beatriz's silence was not that of a spectator but rather of a person feeling left out of her sister's new relationship and robbed of the parent-child and sibling bonds she had believed in.

Dr. Jorge De Vega, who was seated across from me, interrupted at this point, asserting, "This is a judicial case with large amounts of money at stake. Feelings are tinged with that little significant detail [financial compensation]." I do not believe that possible financial gain determined what the twins told the psychiatrist or their lawyers. Their feelings were their feelings. Money would help the twins, of course, and it is a satisfying feeling when responsible parties are held accountable for their mistakes. But money, no amount of it, could ever amend the lives of the three women and their families.

Dr. Casimiro Cabrera mentioned his surprise at the media attention the case attracted. "It had an impact all over the place," he said. However, he could not comment publicly, being under judicial order not to do so. Cabrera had been appointed to assess Delia's parents, Débora and Juan, who had brought a formal complaint against the Canary Islands Health Service within that past year, in 2009. Cabrera did assess them toward the end of September 2009. The psychiatrists had turned down requests for interviews from the media to protect their clients.

Before leaving, I asked the psychiatrists if general intelligence (IQ) tests had been completed by the twins and Beatriz, and they said no. De Vega agreed to test one of the twins after I left Las Palmas, although I made it clear that we would have to work through the attorneys to arrange this. I wanted the twins and Beatriz assessed by three separate testers at the same time to avoid any discussion among them of the test items; using separate testers is a common practice in twin studies. All three women were IQ tested as I had hoped, but not until early 2010. Knowing that Trujillo had conducted the psychiatric examinations on all three women, I wondered to what extent his impressions of one had been colored by his impressions of another. He had seen Beatriz two months prior to seeing Begoña and Delia, but he had seen Begoña and Delia only eight days apart.

Jessica and I had left Wednesday afternoon free after our interview with Trujillo so that we could go to the Las Arenas shopping mall. I wanted to visit the store where Clarisa had mistaken Begoña for Delia as well as the restaurant where the twins had first been reunited so as to better imagine what these meetings had been like. I also had another, more important purpose in mind—I wanted to find Clarisa.

Las Arenas

Jessica and I made our way by taxi to Las Arenas, which is about fifteen minutes from the University Hospital. The mall's modern concrete structure seemed at odds with the island's gorgeous beaches and parks. The three crystal pyramids on the roof gave the building a distinctive look, and there were great views from the top floor. Adding to its interest were the surrounding statues of stately lions, clusters of palm trees, and a replica of the Great Sphinx of Egypt. We headed first to Stradivarius, where Begoña had encountered the shop assistant Clarisa

Fig. 5.1. A replica of the Great Sphinx of Giza in Egypt, symbolizing strength and wisdom, is next to the Las Arenas (The Sands) shopping mall where the twins first met. Courtesy of Nancy L. Segal.

who had been certain that Begoña was Delia; Jessica knew the location of the store. However, that incident had happened eight years earlier, and Stradivarius had moved to a different place in the mall. In its prior location was Rip Curl, another popular clothing chain.

We found Stradivarius's new location and looked absently at the clothing racks and displays. Sales assistants come and go, and so it was unlikely that Clarisa would still be working there, but it was possible that someone, such as a manager, remembered her. Clarisa's first description of Begoña and Delia looking "as alike as two drops of water" had become a sound bite throughout the story's press coverage. In my mind Clarisa was a central figure in the story, the person singly responsible for the twins' meeting. Neither attorney had met Clarisa or knew her whereabouts, and neither seemed curious to do so, probably because her actions had no bearing on the case. Begoña did not know Clarisa's last name, nor did she know where to find her. But that was not surprising because Clarisa was

Delia's friend, not Begoña's. However, at that time it was still uncertain if Socorro could arrange for me to meet Delia, so going to Stradivarius was my best plan. I wanted to know how Clarisa felt about having brought the twins together and if her feelings about that decision had changed over the years. It turned out that one of the shop assistants we spoke with remembered the twins' incident—not surprising, considering the amount of press coverage the story had garnered—and knew someone who knew Clarisa. The assistant called her contact for us, but her contact was unable to provide identifying information.

We left Stradivarius and had a late lunch at the coffee shop on the mall's upper level where the twins had met for the first time (Beatriz had called it the "terrace"). It was the sort of nondescript eating establishment found in shopping malls anywhere in the world, with predictable menus and uninteresting furniture. But something extraordinary had happened exactly in this space eight years earlier. I looked around and wondered where they sat and if people had stared at them. After an hour or so, we took a cab back to Peregrina's office on Calle Luis Doreste Silva for my interview with the Spanish press. It was about five o'clock, and we were due back in his office at 6:00 PM.

Canarias 7

According to Peregrina and Socorro's initial instructions, I was to avoid speaking to the press. Therefore, I was surprised when Peregrina arranged for me to be interviewed by Antonio Fernández de la Gándara, a journalist from a local newspaper, *Canarias 7*. The paper had also sent a photographer. Gándara had covered the twins' story in ten previous articles but had never actually met the twins. I was concerned about this change to the media plan. But Peregrina seemed enthusiastic, and because he had been very helpful to me, I didn't want to disappoint him if he now felt that my input with the media would help the case. Gándara interviewed me for about an hour, with Jessica translating his ques-

tions to me and my answers back to him. I was careful to keep my comments in a scientific context and to not reveal that I had been meeting with the twins and their families, as Peregrina had instructed. Figure 5.2 shows an excerpt of the article that appeared the next day, both in print and online.

Fig. 5.2. Excerpt from the article describing my research visit to Las Palmas in the newspaper *Canarias 7*. Courtesy of Antonio Fernández de la Gándara and *Canarias 7*.

THURSDAY, SEPTEMBER 17

Canarias 7

Stacks of the September 17 issue of *Canarias 7* were at the front desk of my hotel lobby the next morning. A small picture of me was on the front page next to the teaser, "SEGAL: El Hospital Del Caso de Las Gemelas Debe Pagar Por el Error" ("SEGAL: The Hospital Should Pay for the Error"), directing readers to the full story on page 43. I couldn't read what Gándara had written in Spanish, but when Jessica arrived, she read the story quickly. Gándara said favorable things about me, but he also said that I was in Las Palmas for a week to study the twins' case, raising the possibility that the press would use me to try to find them. Fortunately, Gándara also said that I had not confirmed whether or not I had met the twins or if they had agreed to meet with me. Still, Jessica and I were worried that this news story would jeopardize our Saturday meeting with Begoña, our Monday meeting with her mother and sister, and the interview I was hoping to schedule with Delia. Then I had a real scare.

Jessica and I were still in the hotel lobby, trying to decide what to do next, when her cell phone rang. The call was from a *La Provincia* journalist whose newspaper headquarters was around the corner from my hotel. This journalist and I had arranged to meet, but it was so *I* could interview *her* about the case. (I had seen her article about the twins' case in *La Provincia* before I left California, so I knew she had been researching it.) Now the journalist had seen the story in *Canarias 7* and was canceling her evening appointment with us because she wanted an exclusive interview with me. The journalist's first name was also Delia, so when Jessica said "Delia" had cancelled, my heart nearly stopped. Jessica quickly explained that the journalist, not the twin, had called—this was a disappointment, but it was one I could accept. Later that day another *La Provincia* journalist, Miguel Ayala, who had written the only

story about the switched identical male twins in Las Palmas, cancelled a meeting with me for the same reason.

Jessica and I spent part of that morning assessing the effects of the newspaper story on my plans. We contacted Socorro to assess his reaction to the *Canarias 7* article and to see if he had arranged our meeting with Delia. Socorro was not pleased with the story, but he didn't think it would hurt the case in any way. I suspect his displeasure mostly reflected his not having been consulted first, given the lawyers' prior agreement about my not speaking to the press. Fortunately, Socorro still believed we could meet with Delia, but not at his office because someone might see us there; by then, interested journalists knew what I looked like, having seen my photograph in *Canarias 7*. Socorro suggested we meet Delia at his home or at a location other than his office, and he promised to tell us the time and place. Both attorneys had talked about the potential difficulties from press coverage of the case, and I was learning of them firsthand.

The Judge

I still hadn't seen the judge in this case, María Olimpia del Rosario Palenzuela, and I wanted to understand her role in the case's progression through the Spanish courts. Jessica and I decided to look for her at the address Peregrina had given us several days earlier. I believed Judge Palenzuela could speak only generally about the nature of the case because of the pending appeal, but I hoped she would provide insight into the inner workings of the Spanish legal system.

We found the right government building, which was set in the middle of a city block, and rode the elevator up several floors to the judge's office. The doors opened to a security officer seated at a table opposite the elevator. Jessica explained to her that we did not have an appointment but wanted to see Judge Palenzuela to discuss a specific case. My being a professor from the United States apparently gave considerable weight to our request. About twenty minutes passed, and then the judge appeared. We spoke with her in the hallway for approximately half an hour, but she did not wish her views about the case to be included in this book.

Change of Plans

I can't remember at what time we heard about the suicide, but it was sometime that day. Delia's twenty-year-old male cousin (nonbiological) had jumped to his death from Las Palmas's Puente de Silva, the highest bridge of the Islas Canarias. It is known, paradoxically, for its spectacular views and for suicide attempts. He was thirty years old and was dying from leukemia. The city had constructed barriers at the top of the 410-feet- (125-meter-) high structure to discourage such acts, but people still managed to take their lives at this site. This tragic and unexpected event meant that Delia's nonbiological family would gather that night at a morgue in Las Palmas. The family graciously suggested that Jessica and I meet Gara (Delia's nonbiological sister; also Beatriz's biological sister) at the morgue and conduct our interviews there, instead of meeting Gara at her home in the north part of the island as we had planned. Gara would be coming to Las Palmas with her daughter, sister Julia, and parents Débora and Juan. Jessica and I agreed to meet the sisters together, but I had another appointment first.

University of Las Palmas

Thursday afternoon, before the visit to the morgue, I was introduced to colleagues from the department of psychology at the University of Las Palmas: Drs. José Martín-Albo, Fernando Grijalvo, and Juan Luis Núñez Alonso, as well as their students David and Evelia. I visited their laboratory, and we later had lunch at Restaurante Embarcadero, a scenic seaside café not far from Las Canteras Beach. My hosts had seen the article and my photo in *Canarias 7*, and our meeting was a little awkward at first since I avoided their questions about the purpose of my trip to Las Palmas. I did so by focusing our conversation on my broader research interest in twins and on my colleagues' studies of self-esteem.

Gara

Located about thirty minutes from my hotel was an extremely large modern structure called the Tanatorio San Miguel (San Miguel Morgue). Jessica and I arrived at about 6:00 PM. It seemed as though hundreds of people were there that night congregating in small family groups inside and outside the building. Delia's family did not arrive for some time, but when they did, Débora and Juan greeted us warmly. We recognized Julia and knew that the woman standing next to her, holding the hand of her two-and--year-old daughter, Elena, was Gara. Julia and Gara were willing to complete the interviews at the morgue, but there was no private place. When they were ready, Gara, her daughter, Julia, Jessica, and I took a taxi back to my hotel. We spoke with Gara in the lobby from 10:30 to 11:30 PM.[4]

Gara's dark hair and skin matched her mother's, but her facial features were more like her father's and Beatriz's. She did not show a striking physical resemblance to her sister Julia, but their general appearance was enough alike to place them in the same family. Gara wore a pink V-neck T-shirt patterned with black crescents and stars, blue jeans, and white studded sandals. Julia also came back to the hotel and sat with us during Gara's interview, commenting occasionally. Gara's daughter, Elena, stayed close by her aunt Julia, calling Julia her "second mama," no doubt because Julia took care of her every day while Gara worked.

Gara told us she had left school when she was sixteen and had begun cleaning houses. "Delia was the smartest one," Gara said. "Delia completed [school], and I didn't want to go to school by myself so I quit." Her mother agreed to Gara's decision to leave school as long as she was employed. Gara eventually married and became a cook in a local Canarian restaurant after her daughter was born. Like the rest of her family, Gara learned about the baby switch from the television news and had been unaware of the Las Arenas reunion until one year prior to our meeting. She spoke informatively and sensitively about her reactions. "I was at home alone. I didn't think that case was related to us, but there were some similarities in the dates and they showed the front of my mother's house. [My family] talked the following day. I didn't believe it—I told my mum it was just a coincidence and that we shouldn't give it too much importance." But when Gara realized that the television news story did affect her family, she felt terribly sad and hurt.

Gara spoke about the time Delia had left home under the premise of moving into her boss's home, where she was a housecleaner, to help her boss with her son. Gara said she thought Delia's behavior was strange at that time. She saw her sister sometime afterward shopping with her then boyfriend, Rafael. Gara said, "[Delia] confessed that they had rented a house and were living together." At the time of our interview, Gara had not seen Delia in two months.

Gara compared the three sisters who had grown up together in Débora and Juan's home. "Julia and I have the same character, we're both quiet people. We're sisters and good friends—we were the two best friends among the three of us. We go out together and agree on many things. It has always been like that. We behave differently than Delia. We think twice before doing things. . . . Even though Delia was the cleverest one, she never finished things she started. But I never thought she wasn't my sister." Gara also talked about how the baby switch affected her parents. "My parents feel terrible, especially my mother. My father shuts up and hides his feelings. He's stronger—he keeps the suffering to himself. My mother doesn't stop crying." The residents of their close neighborhood had also been following the story, siding with Débora and Juan.

"Knowing the truth in this case has no advantages because we have lost a loved family member," Gara said with emphasis. She wished the entire inci-

dent hadn't happened, but she did not fault Clarisa for arranging the twins' first meeting. "That girl had no axe to grind," she said. Gara told me she does hold Delia responsible for her family's suffering because her parents sacrificed for Delia's cancer treatment and she believes Delia turned against them. But Gara thinks of Delia with sentimentality as her sister.

Gara had seen Beatriz only once for about an hour when Beatriz visited at her home. "During the first moments, I saw Beatriz as a stranger because I didn't know her. But after a while, I realized she had some similarities with us. I never saw Beatriz again." I believe Beatriz could not become close to Gara and Julia because she was closely bonded to Laura, Begoña, and her other siblings. But it was not just her family ties that stood in the way of close relations with her biological family. As noted earlier, I believe that Beatriz also felt torn between the lifestyle she had and the one she might have had. The twins' situation was different from Beatriz's. Despite their family pressures, Delia and Begoña could embrace their similarities and their understanding of one another, probably because they were not moving between two separate and very different worlds. Delia had feelings for her rearing family, but severing her connection to them must have seemed her only option; Begoña had grown up in the place where she belonged, but Beatriz was struggling.

When our interview ended, Jessica and I stood outside the hotel with the two sisters and Gara's daughter until a taxi arrived to take them home. Gara had been slightly on edge at first but had eventually relaxed, largely owing to Jessica's friendly manner, which she maintained while skillfully translating my questions into Spanish and Gara's answers into English. Gara worked long hours at the restaurant, and I appreciated the time she had taken to speak with me, especially on the occasion of a death in the family. While we waited, I noticed that Gara and Julia were closely matched in height and weight and wore the same studded sandals in different colors. Julia smoked a cigarette. I remembered that Beatriz smoked, too, and had done so more frequently since the discovery of the switch—Begoña, who did not smoke, called her sister a "regular smoker." As we waited, I looked at Gara's daughter, Elena, who was lively, playful, and pretty, with a round face and fair hair.

With no interviews scheduled for Friday, September 18, or Sunday, September 20, I used those days to sightsee in the city of Las Palmas and in the beach area of Maspalomas, located on the southern part of the island. This quiet time gave me the opportunity to reflect on the days I'd spent speaking with the twins and families involved in the switch. Jessica and I met Begoña again on Saturday, September 19.

SATURDAY, SEPTEMBER 19

Begoña

Begoña met us at my hotel on Saturday, September 19, driving a medium-blue French Renault Clio that can cost as much as 39,000 euros (US$50,000). The car's interior was immaculate, with blue-and-white-patterned cushions and seat belt covers. She drove us to her apartment located in a comfortable suburb about fifteen minutes away. It was spacious, with three bedrooms, a medium-sized living room, and an ample kitchen. The rooms were immaculate, too, and Begoña admitted she never fully relaxes because she thinks constantly about cleaning.[5] The only item I noticed that was out of place was a box of Special K cereal that had been placed upside down in the pantry.

Begoña's apartment was furnished in a range of coordinated earth tones, suggesting a motif that in the United States could be recognized as "southwestern," and was decorated with artwork she had collected on trips to North Africa and northern Spain. Some ceramic statues reflected her interests in Buddhism and Indian culture. Family photos were also displayed on tables and shelves throughout the living room and hallway. Begoña liked nice clothes and furnishings—the day we met at her home, she wore a loose, flowered top over white shorts,

Dolce and Gabbana sunglasses, several silver bangles, and the stylish DKNY watch she had worn during our first meeting. I spotted a shopping bag from Desigual, a high-end boutique I had seen in the Triana district of Gran Canaria.[6]

Begoña had been living by herself in this apartment for eleven years, but said she dislikes eating alone and had many friends whom she saw regularly. We met two of them that morning and four or five at the beach later that afternoon. But first Begoña completed several psychological questionnaires I had brought and then spoke more about how the hospital's mistake had affected her family.

Begoña's first concern had always been the effects of the switch on her sister Beatriz. "Beatriz suffers because of her biological family's indifference." She told us that by chance Beatriz had run into Débora, Julia, Gara, and Gara's daughter two days earlier at Las Torres (The Towers) shopping mall. "Gara was the only one who said hello to her, and the rest just left. They don't show their feelings. Beatriz has always felt rejected by her family and came home crying." Hearing this, I wondered if Beatriz shared a genetically based tendency toward introversion that characterized the members of her biological family. Failure to express their feelings may have been misinterpreted by both sides as rejection when, in fact, they really wanted to know each other.

"I have accepted [what happened]," Begoña said, adding that she sees herself as a very positive person trying to find the good side of a bad situation. After five years she had come to terms with the switch and did not feel traumatized by talking about it with us. However, she said her mother, Laura, had never accepted "what they did to her," suggesting how victimized her mother must feel. Begoña's next comment reflected her positive perspective on things and her attempt to give purpose to what had happened. "I believe we were switched because having a brother with Down syndrome and a twin sister with leukemia [would have been] too much suffering for a single family. God wanted to share the suffering." Begoña believes in destiny, she said, explaining that Delia suffered from leukemia partly because she had to learn that the parents she grew up with were not her biological ones.

Delia's parents and sisters were incompatible as bone marrow donors for her, but that fact was determined years before the switch was discovered. Therefore, Delia's illness was not the factor that brought the mistake to light, as Begoña's comments implied. However, Socorro revealed a fascinating observation by one of Delia's physicians who knew she could not find a donor among her parents and sisters: once DNA tests established that Delia was Laura's biological daughter and Begoña's identical twin, the doctor told her he had always questioned her relatedness to Débora and Juan but didn't want to share his earlier suspicions. He was probably being prudent because many children do not resemble their parents and to suggest otherwise would have enraged and alienated Delia's family. It is also unlikely that Delia's parents would have considered a DNA test based on one doctor's impressions.

Begoña talked more about her complex relationship with Delia, and I encouraged her to do so, because most accounts of the other switched-at-birth twins had not fully explored this side of the situation with the twins themselves.[7] "I would like to have a closer relationship with Delia, but that is really complicated, bearing in mind all the people involved. I felt a really special bond with Delia since the very first time we met; it's a natural bond only twins can understand." But Begoña admitted to feeling conflicted. "The first time I saw Delia, I was frightened. Imagine that you see a person who looks exactly like you.... How would you feel? I felt overwhelmed by the situation.... At that moment, I realized Beatriz didn't belong to my family." A series of disconnected and seemingly contradictory statements followed. "Delia and I cannot be friends due to our family environment.... I feel Delia has a need to be with me.... Delia would be my friend if we could have a normal relationship.... All this is difficult to explain because I don't have that much contact with Delia, but I do have contact with my friends." She explained that you take personal matters to your friends, not to your sisters. Had Begoña grown up with Delia, she might not have said this because identical twins share their concerns with one another more than with anyone else. Based on my conversations with Begoña, I believe Delia and Begoña had the potential to be as close as any identical twins I have known.

The twins' relationship has not had a chance to flourish because their family circumstances have prevented that from happening. However, Begoña and Delia may eventually realize that the number of hours identical twins spend together is unrelated to the social closeness and intimacy they can feel for one another. This is not the case for fraternal twins, whose closeness is associated with their degree of contact.[8] Begoña said, "For sure I would help Delia if she needed me. If I had to donate an egg [for her to have children], I'd do it. Delia hasn't told me she is infertile, but we've talked about donation before. I imagine Delia is interested in donation because she may have problems having children." Begoña understood that because she and Delia have identical genes, a child conceived with Begoña's egg would be equally related to both of them. Mothers (and fathers) transmit exactly 50 percent of their genes to each of their children, and an egg from Begoña could just as easily have come from Delia. In fact, DNA tests cannot distinguish between the mother and the aunt of a child born to one identical twin. Identical twins' identical genes turn them into unusual aunts and uncles because their nieces and nephews are their genetic children.[9] Another way to think of this is that identical twins who are aunts and uncles are genetically equivalent to the parents of their nieces and nephews, i.e., their twin's children.

Begoña would have been an ideal bone marrow donor for her twin sister when she developed leukemia at age sixteen, but her existence was unknown. In an ironic twist, Tairí, the switched-at-birth twin from Puerto Rico, was available to donate blood to her twin sister Mari when Mari was diagnosed with a brain tumor at age three and relapsed at age eight. But Tairí's mother said Tairí was too young at the time; seventeen is the lower age limit for blood donation.[10]

Begoña talked about her difficulty relaxing, a trait she said she shared with Delia. "I neither smoke nor drink alcohol. Beatriz some-times drinks a beer or a cup of wine. I used to exercise, but I don't have energy left with my current job [as supervisor of hotel maids]." I was relieved that Begoña was "relaxed" about the *Canarias 7* story that had appeared two days earlier. She hadn't read it carefully, but a friend told her it contained nothing to worry about.

Shortly before we left for the beach, we discussed Begoña's willing-ness to take an IQ test, and she said she was interested; I promised I would make the arrangements after I left Las Palmas. I wasn't surprised that Begoña agreed to the testing because she had told us she was returning to school and was thinking about a new career. Begoña also told me she had spoken with Delia and Begoña described my interview with her as "all great." I was happy to hear this but even happier to know that Delia was back from her honeymoon, increasing the likelihood of our meeting her the following week. This information also told me that these twins stayed in touch despite the difficulties imposed by their par-ents. It was also apparent that the twins had been together recently because Begoña didn't care for Delia's new hairstyle, commenting, "I will kill her hairdresser." Begoña had, in fact, attended Delia's hen party on September 5 with her mother, Laura. Begoña also told us that Delia is dressing more like her now.

Begoña's comment about Delia's new clothing choices reminded me of two-year-old Tairí, the switched-at-birth twin from Puerto Rico. Her father had told me that Tairí adopted her twin sister Mari's habits, such as finger sucking, once they were brought together again. I also remem-bered that Canadian twin Brent really enjoyed the grunge music his twin brother George listened to. Imitation isn't easy unless one has the interest, preference, and capacity to do so. What some people call imita-tion between identical twins may be more a matter of doing what comes naturally when given the option to explore something new. Delia's small village probably did not offer the range of fashion choices that Begoña enjoyed while living in Las Palmas, yet it makes sense that Delia would like and look good in the kinds of clothes her identical twin sister selected. I left with the sense that the twin sisters were closer than they let on or possibly realized.

Once the interview at her apartment ended, Begoña gave me a present, a small leather box that held a silver ring with a dark green stone. I was delighted.

We left Begoña's home at 12:30 in the afternoon and drove with Begoña to a quiet beach in a residential area. Several of Begoña's friends were waiting for us at a café, and we stayed to talk with them until nearly 3:00. Begoña meets them every Saturday when the weather is nice, and she returned to the café after dropping us off close to my hotel. Her friends talked about the differences between Begoña and Beatriz and their surprise at the turn Begoña's life had taken. One of her friends commented that many Spanish women in the 1970s decided to have children because conditions in the country started to improve once Franco's dictatorship ended. He said this baby boom explained why hospitals were crowded, raising the chances of switching babies and making other mistakes. However, the change in Spain's government would not have applied to Begoña, Beatriz, and Delia—they were born in 1973, two years before Franco died and five years before democracy in Spain was official. Moreover, the hospital where they were born was crowded because maternity hospitals were unavailable in some towns and villages on the island.

Begoña was charming that day, very gracious to us and to her guests, and it was easy to see why she had so many friends. We posed for pictures before leaving with the understanding that they were for our personal enjoyment, not for publication. She thought she could arrange lunch for us and her twin sister the following Monday in her neighborhood, but that never happened, and I never found out why.

MONDAY, SEPTEMBER 21

I also never found out why our Monday morning meeting with Laura
and Beatriz at their home was cancelled. It is possible that Laura and her
daughter had tired of talking about the case or didn't understand that I
was not writing a sensational article but rather a serious book. The good
news was that Socorro had arranged for us to interview Delia in the early
evening.[11] Delia had caught a bad cold during an outdoor luncheon
after her wedding, so Jessica and I took the one-hour bus ride and taxi
from Las Palmas to her home. She and her husband of ten days, Rafael,
were living approximately twenty-five miles southwest of Las Palmas in
a remote area that even our local taxi driver had trouble finding. We
stopped twice to ask directions while the driver negotiated the long,
winding roads away from the central bus station. One person told us the
street name had changed, but Delia said the street had been reconfig-
ured, making it difficult to find.

Rafael was in the yard when Jessica and I arrived, and he gave us each
two kisses on the cheek. He was a very friendly man with a big grin; a
coarse beard; long, dark hair; and several gold loops in his ears. His arm
was in a sling from a recent injury. We didn't see Rafael again until we
left—he seemed to understand that we had important interviews to conduct and gave us the time and space we needed.

Delia and Rafael had lived in this house for three years, but they had
originally met in Las Palmas. Delia explained that the number of men in
the small town in which she was raised was "limited," making it necessary for her to move in order to find a husband. Delia's home was small,
rustic, and completely private with wonderful views of the surrounding
hills. She and Rafael loved animals and had three dogs, two small birds,
and a parrot. Having been raised in the country, Delia has always had
animals around her.

Delia, Jessica, and I sat at a long table in Delia's kitchen, a large room
that blended into a smaller living room area. Delia had chosen furnish-

ings that seemed traditional in style, mostly dark wood tables and a hardwood floor. There were no family photographs.

Delia had the flu when we met and wore a light-colored wraparound sweater with no jewelry or makeup. She appeared to be several pounds heavier than Begoña, but their facial contours were the same. My colleague Professor Thomas J. Bouchard Jr. would have described them as different versions of the same song. Delia served us two desserts, marzapán and rosco de vino, local delicacies made with almonds, which were both delicious. That dessert was dinner for Jessica and me.

Delia's house was extremely neat, just like Begoña's. One of the first things Delia said was, "I like having my house tidy. I was worried today because I didn't have time to tidy up." It was like an echo—Begoña had also begun by telling us about her urge to clean. Like Begoña, Delia had also cleaned houses in the past, but unlike her twin sister, cleaning was not the first job Delia had taken after receiving her diploma at fourteen. Delia's occupational itinerary was longer and more varied than her sister's.

Delia had first studied accounting for three years as part of a vocational training program, but she didn't complete the five-year course. "I got bored and decided to work." She began cleaning houses, then started working for Circulo de Lectores, a company that sells books and audiovisual materials door-to-door. After that, Delia worked for marketing companies and eventually returned to cleaning houses in a town fifteen minutes from her home; she was still cleaning houses at the time of our interview. But Delia has had other interests—she worked for four years as a volunteer for a nongovernmental organization (NGO) project that sought to help children overcome their drug problems. She had to end this service because of both personal and media problems associated with the switch, but she had enjoyed it and said she might do it again in the future. Delia also told me she was considering going back to school to study interior design. Then we discussed the topic of her family.

"I never thought I wasn't part of the family. I thought I was different from [Gara and Julia] because we hadn't been raised together."

I asked Delia to please repeat this remark because it was the first time I had heard about Delia growing up separately from her sisters. (I did not understand Spanish, but Jessica immediately translated significant information so I could follow up on it.) It seemed that Delia had been raised by her grandparents, who lived quite close to her parents. Her mother Débora was only seventeen when Delia was born, and when Gara arrived fifteen months later, Débora was overwhelmed. But the family members were together every day, and after Delia's grandmother died, when Delia was sixteen, her entire family moved into her grandfather's house. This was also when Delia developed leukemia, putting emotional and financial strains on her family. Her parents eventually sold their house and moved permanently to the grandparents' home, where they were living at the time of the interviews.

Delia told us that she had always felt different from her sisters. "My sisters were angry with me all the time. They always thought they were right; I couldn't disagree with them. I was the oldest, but they treated me like the youngest." It may have been easy for Gara and Julia to believe they were right because they shared opinions that Delia did not. Delia was aware of this. "Gara and Julia are quite similar to each other. Beatriz, too. I haven't seen Beatriz often, maybe seven or eight times over all these years. We talk when something [significant] happens."

Delia felt she was the smartest of three sisters in her rearing family and was interested in taking an IQ test when I could arrange it. "I didn't need to study. I just read. I was good in all my subjects and I always had A grades. Subjects that were difficult for most students were easy for me."

I was surprised, after all I'd heard from others, to hear from Delia that she had been a happy child. "I had a good time with my grandparents. My grandparents were really nice. I thank them for who I am nowadays. I had the normal life of a teenager with the sort of problems everyone had." I shouldn't have been surprised to hear this because happiness comes from many sources, not just one's home. Growing up, Delia had grandparents who loved her and friends she enjoyed. She also did well in school. Most teenagers have conflicts with their parents and siblings, and Delia had been no exception. Having been raised primarily by grandparents, who are generally lenient and forgiving, may have provided just the buffer she needed against feeling too different from her family.

It is natural to believe that the people who raise us are related to us biologically because human families are generally organized this way. It is, therefore, not surprising that Delia never wondered whether or not she was part of her family. Even having been mistaken three times for someone else, twice for someone named Begoña, did not raise her suspicions. The first time it happened, Delia was at a discotheque about fifteen years prior to our interview when a boy she didn't know planted two big kisses on her cheeks. "I thought he was crazy," she said, but added that she now understood why he thought he knew her. "He thought he was kissing Begoña."

The second time Delia was mistaken for Begoña occurred about five years later when she was twenty-five. She had stopped at a café in Triana, the lovely area filled with shops and restaurants near Las Palmas's old section of Vegueta. Delia selected her food items from the counter and went to pay, but the cashier looked at her oddly. She asked Delia if she was from a certain part of town—the same neighborhood where Begoña was living. Delia said no, and the cashier replied, "You look exactly like my neighbor, Begoña." Begoña had told us this same story. Also, about this time, Delia was at a market in the old section of Las Palmas when she noticed a young woman staring at her. The woman asked her if she was Begoña. "I always thought those [incidents] were coincidences," Delia told me. "This is a little island." She added, "Nobody thinks a thing like [a baby switch] can happen." People in Las Palmas now know that these things do happen. And their little island actually increases the chance of meeting someone who might be related.

As Delia took us through the events leading to her meeting with Begoña, she provided one new detail. The shop assistant, Clarisa, who had mistaken Begoña for Delia, was not a close friend of Delia but an acquain-

tance. Delia said she was closer to Clarisa's mother, Mónica, who had actually arranged the Las Arenas get-together. It turned out that Delia's mother, Débora, had sold a house to Mónica. Unfortunately, Delia was not in touch with Clarisa or her family at the time of our interview.

Delia told us that her first response to seeing Begoña was simply to stare. "We were astonished because we didn't expect to be so alike. At the time, Begoña was heavier [than she is now], so we looked even more alike [than we do now]. Delia also described how the twins compared their hands, eyes, gait, gestures, and facial expressions and were amazed that everything matched; an exception was their birthdays because Delia had been given Beatriz's date of birth, which was three days earlier. "The waiter came and began joking. He said, 'Who are the twin sisters here? These two or those two?' We couldn't believe it." The waiter's casual comment must have hurt Beatriz deeply.

Delia continued, expressing the same shock and disbelief as Begoña and Beatriz had, but she also expressed fear. "I wasn't sure of anything, but I knew something strange was happening. I was so shocked I couldn't think. I didn't say anything when I got home because I was afraid. I was scared of my family.... I was afraid of their reaction." In fact, Delia never said a word.

Specifically, Delia feared having the DNA test that Begoña, Beatriz, and their mother Laura had taken at the Hospital Insular (Insular Hospital). This test showed that Delia and Begoña matched on all the measured DNA markers, identifying them as identical twins. Delia delayed taking the test out of fear of what she might find. When Delia was ready, Laura paid for the analysis that ultimately identified the true twins.

"[Once the switch was suspected], I didn't want to do the DNA test because I was afraid of my family's reaction. [Eventually] I decided to do it [a few years later] because I didn't have anything.[12] When I asked Delia what she meant by this statement, she explained that she had felt alone and as though she had no place to turn. She also had to have the DNA test results to file a lawsuit against the Canary Islands Health Service. Once the DNA analysis was completed, Delia hesitated to learn what it revealed. She said, "It took me a week to go [to the lab] to collect the results. [I was told] there was a 99.99 percent chance that Begoña and I were identical twins. . . . [Eventually] I had to move from my parents' house—it was the only exit."

Earlier, I had asked Begoña how she had felt about Delia's delay in taking the DNA test. Most people would have been eager to know the truth once the truth was so strongly suspected, but Begoña understood. "I don't mind the fact that Delia waited three years before having the DNA test done. Each person needs a different amount of time to face their problems." Of course, the DNA results probably seemed like a foregone conclusion by the time Delia had decided to take the test.

Delia continued, "I think [my parents] didn't know how to accept and deal with the new situation. I've always felt rejected by my family, but I associated the rejection with the fact that I was raised by my grandparents. That rejection became much worse when they found out they weren't my biological family." After knowing the DNA test results, Delia lived at home for about one year. "But at that point it was really difficult to live with my parents. . . . So after a year, I moved out. When I left, things seemed to be better, and I tried to go back to my parents' [house]. But as time went by, it became more and more impossible for me to do that."

Delia told us she had visited a psychiatrist for two years at Socorro's suggestion, beginning in 2004 or 2005. "[The psychiatrist] said I was insisting on going to a place where they didn't want me. I felt bad because I didn't want to stop talking to my parents." Delia's depressed state at that time may have made her especially sensitive to her psychiatrist's advice, making his words sound unusually harsh.

In 2004, Delia contacted Socorro with the intention of filing a lawsuit to receive compensation for pain and suffering, something her parents did not know about until they heard it on the news. "[This] changed my life. You have a family you live with, and suddenly you have nothing. Maybe this case would have been different if my parents had reacted in a different way. There is no money that can pay for what I've lived through.... I felt I had been living a fake life for almost thirty years. It wasn't me anymore. My life made a U-turn." Delia believes that of the three women, she suffered the most. "At least Begoña and Beatriz are supported by their family. [But] I think Beatriz suffered more than Begoña because she doesn't belong [biologically] in that family and Begoña does."

Delia spoke more specifically about what she had missed by being raised as she had been. "I feel more related to twins now, and I realized I had lost that special experience. It's something I cannot recover easily. I cannot change the fact of not getting to know my biological father." Despite everything that happened, Delia sees Débora, not Laura, as her real mother. "I can understand that Laura as a mother sees me as a daughter, but I as a daughter couldn't feel the same way.... Laura invited me to live with her, but at that moment I didn't have anything in common with them.... The feeling toward Begoña was different because I saw in her someone who was exactly like me. When I talk to her, I feel we have always known each other."

As mentioned earlier, about halfway through our interview, the telephone rang, and it was Begoña. The twins spoke only briefly, and while I was curious, I never learned the content of their conversation. The phone rang again, and this time it was a television reporter interested in speaking with me. I managed to put him off, but that call encouraged Delia to talk about her horrific experiences with the press. "I'm usually an easygoing person, but this entire situation has affected my nerves. I don't want the media to talk about my private life because they distort the truth. They create sensationalism where it doesn't exist." Delia said she didn't mind if I appeared on TV, but she didn't want journalists following her. She said the first time the case was on the news, it had been a "big scandal" that left her unable to leave her home for a week. Her cell phone had rung constantly. She also said that journalists had approached her parents in their village and had begun filming their house and neighborhood, although later the journalists denied doing so. Delia called her lawyer and asked Socorro to try to stop it, but Delia said the media coverage continued.

Like her twin sister, Delia seemed to have accepted her situation. She didn't know what Clarisa thought when Begoña walked into her shop, whether they were twins or rare look-alikes. But she said she believes that if Clarisa had not pursued the situation, she and Begoña would have met one another eventually. She was probably right.

Despite all that happened, Delia still thinks of Débora and Juan as her real parents. She would have liked to have her mother and sisters at her hen party, but those relationships were difficult. When our interview ended, Delia called a taxi to drive us back to the city, and this driver found her house within five minutes. The next day was my last full day in Las Palmas, and I planned to visit both attorneys. I had no idea what a stressful time awaited me.

TUESDAY, SEPTEMBER 22

On Tuesday morning, Jessica and I returned to Socorro's conference area one more time. It seemed Socorro had been contacted by *Television Española,* a Spanish government channel, and he encouraged me to be interviewed. "I have always told [the station] it was not the right moment. They even told me they agreed to do an interview and keep it aside until we found it appropriate. I am interested in helping the sisters if Nancy agrees that the moral damage is considerable." By moral damage, Socorro meant Delia's loss of a twin sister during her childhood and adolescence, her loss of an opportunity to meet her biological father, and her loss of finding an ideal bone marrow donor when she was sick.

I hesitated because I did not want to do anything to disturb the twins' trust in me. By then I was thankful enough that the *Canarias 7* story had not damaged our relationships, and I had assured the twins afterward that I would not accept media invitations. But because both twins were

guided by their attorneys, whom they believed acted in their best interests, I told Socorro I would do the interview *only if the twins agreed.* He
mentioned that the journalist who would conduct the interview was the
daughter of a woman Delia worked for, so refusing could be socially awkward. Another consideration was that Socorro had been helpful to me,
arranging the interview with Delia, and I wanted to reciprocate. Socorro
would also be part of the televised interview tentatively scheduled to take
place early the next morning before my flight back to Barcelona.

While we were still in Socorro's office, he called Delia, who agreed
to my doing the interview as long as I spoke from a scientific perspective
and did not discuss the twins' personal details. That was not a problem
in my mind, but before deciding, I insisted that Delia contact Begoña
and call us back. Begoña said she would do whatever her attorney, Peregrina, considered to be appropriate. However, I knew Begoña would not
be happy about the interview, and I was regretting the fact that I had not
declined the television opportunity as soon as Socorro had offered it.
But even if I had declined, Socorro might have persisted because he
really believed my interview would help his case. I was also concerned
that the two lawyers who were working on the same case were not
working together with the media, and I felt uncomfortably positioned
between them.

Jessica and I left Socorro's office promising to let him know what I
decided about the interview. We spent several minutes with Peregrina in
his office, mostly reviewing legal procedures relevant to the case. Peregrina told us he was unable to reach Begoña to discuss my interview;
later, when Jessica talked with Begoña by telephone, we confirmed that
Begoña and Peregrina had not spoken. Apparently, Begoña had turned
off her cell phone for much of that day. I believed that the prudent decision was to decline, and Jessica called Socorro to let him know.

Jessica and I stayed in touch by telephone the rest of the evening,
and when she finally reached Begoña, we learned that the possibility of
my interview had greatly upset her and her family. There was no ques-

tion that doing the interview would have been a catastrophic mistake. I never regretted my decision to turn it down, but I didn't know until the next morning that Jessica had finally reached Begoña to tell her my decision and that she was relieved. It was an uncomfortable end to a nearly perfect research week.

WEDNESDAY, SEPTEMBER 23

Jessica and I met for breakfast early in the morning on Wednesday, September 23, the day I was to leave Gran Canaria. I waited for her outside her apartment building, a four- or five-story structure located a block away from the Las Canteras beach. Now that we were not working, Jessica was casually dressed in a lightweight white sweater and blue jeans. Jessica knew the events of the past ten days better than anyone and, most importantly, had been able to relate to the twins and their families in a personal way that I could not since I could not converse with them directly. Jessica reassured me that morning by placing the turmoil of the past twenty-four hours in the context of the twins' respect for my being what Jessica called a "serious scientist." We walked along the beach, confident that I had made the right decision to not appear on TV.

When I returned to California, I resumed contact with both attorneys, who graciously facilitated my efforts to have the twins and Beatriz complete IQ tests. I was also in touch with Socorro and Peregrina when I signed the contract for this book, and both immediately sent me professional photographs of themselves for the first chapter, as requested. I have also enjoyed a Facebook correspondence with Delia, who regularly sends me pictures of her beautiful island and has been helpful in other ways. Delia put me in touch with Marcos, her twin friend who was also switched at birth, and helped arrange two Skype interviews that allowed Socorro, Peregrina, Delia, Begoña, an interpreter, my colleague Dr. Iris Blandón-Gitlin, and me to discuss my book plans.

In November 2010 I contacted Miguel Ayala, the *La Provincia* journalist who described the switched-at-birth twins Marcos and Matías. Ayala was unable to provide additional details about the case, explaining that the family was saddened by the loss of their son and did not wish to speak about it. In January 2011 an attorney representing the Canarian Health Service volunteered to talk to me about the lawsuit, but then declined after receiving my list of questions.

I have also visited each attorney's website for updates about the twins' case. Peregrina has a notice stating, "The American psychologist Nancy Segal . . . is in Las Palmas to study the case of two identical sisters separated in 1973 and reunited 28 years later."[13] The entry was dated September 17, 2009, the same day the *Canarias 7* article appeared. But his website did not say I had met the twins. Socorro also posted information and pictures from my visit on his website.

Reading the twins' news stories before conducting my personal interviews was like watching a movie and then reading the book from which it was written. I love films, but those based on existing sources often eliminate scenes, change lines, and rewrite endings. Reading the original story afterward is usually more satisfying because the full complement of events, dialogue, and best moments lets readers make greater sense of characters' hopes, fears, and dilemmas. It was like that for me when I went to Las Palmas. The twins' and their families' comments and conclusions gave substance and meaning to their eight years of suffering, which the media had mostly condensed into sound bites. Seeing their gestures and expressions provided a more complete picture of who they were, analogous to the detailed character descriptions offered in books.

6

SOMEONE ELSE'S BABY

I n 1967 the late Amram Scheinfeld, esteemed author of *Twins and Supertwins*, commented that the "mix-up [of twins] occurring now is extremely remote in view of the greatly improved methods used in hospitals for 'tagging' babies at birth."[1] Methods for matching mothers and babies have become increasingly sophisticated during the four decades since Scheinfeld's time; they include, for example, the use of electronically encoded ankle and wrist bracelets for both mother and newborn. Nevertheless, a 2001 study found that nearly 10 percent of the new mothers surveyed worried that they were going home with the wrong baby.[2] Such concern is understandable because historically, some mothers—like the fourteen mothers of twins and non-twins I have discussed thus far—have discovered that they were nursing the wrong baby, or they have discovered hours, days, or years later that they left the hospital with someone else's child.

Reports of switched-at-birth babies are newsworthy because such occurrences seem unimaginable and improbable. However, the frequency of such events is uncertain because some cases are not reported and others go undetected. An independent security management consultant, working for Talon Medical Ltd. in San Antonio, Texas, estimated that 20,000 accidental baby switches occur each year nationwide.[3] This figure, using an error rate of 1 in 1,000, was based on the number of transfers that occur (e.g., transporting the baby within the hospital for medical testing before the baby is safely home). The DNA Diagnostics Center's estimate of 23,000 infant-mother mix-ups each year corroborated that figure.[4] Nicholas Webb, Talon's head of technology, was quoted in a 2001 article saying that 20,000 baby switches probably do occur each year, but they are most likely corrected in the hospital before the infants go home.[5]

Webb is most likely correct, as evidenced by several documented hospital errors that were successfully averted. In 1998, an Oregon mother was handed the wrong baby to breast-feed after her nurse failed to confirm that the mother's identification bracelet matched that of her baby. The error was detected when a second nurse delivering a baby to another mother noticed that their identification numbers differed; the nurse immediately brought the right infants to the right mothers. That same year, a Massachusetts woman who delivered a female infant discovered that the infant she had been breast-feeding was a male and notified her nurse, who then corrected the situation. Unfortunately, not all mistakes are detected or even suspected, as the twins' stories have shown. These mix-ups cannot be tolerated because once discovered, the lives of those involved will never be the same.

How do mothers know their own children? No one would have asked this question in the year 1900 when fewer than 5 percent of women delivered their babies in hospitals.[6] At that time, delivering babies was a task performed by midwives who managed the births of new mothers in the privacy of their homes, where there was never any question as to the identification of the infant or its mother. However, that changed as the percentage of women delivering in hospitals increased to 97 percent by 1960.[7] Many women preferred hospital deliveries, believing that giving birth in the hospital assured them of better physical care than delivering at home with a midwife. Childbirth in a hospital is particularly safer for high-risk deliveries, such as of twins and other multiples. However, the percentage of home deliveries doubled from 0.6 percent in 1970 to 1.5 percent in 1977 because more and more women wanted to control the circumstances of the birth, involve their families, and lower their costs.[8] Interestingly, the protection a home delivery would provide against baby switching in particular was not mentioned. By 2006, only 1 in 200 women in the United States (0.5 percent) delivered their babies at home.[9] The American Congress of Obstetricians and Gynecologists does not favor home deliveries because of the increased physical risks to the infants.

An unanticipated and unfortunate by-product of this shift toward hospital deliveries is that newborns are not only housed with other newborns, they are also managed by unrelated and overworked caretakers who might inadvertently mistake one baby for another. In addition, the movement toward patient empowerment—the active role of patients in disease management and decision making—did not begin until the 1970s.[10] Even then, it is unlikely that in its early years patient empowerment extended to newborn identification because no one had really heard of baby switching. Then a 1998 report of a baby exchange that had happened in 1995 at the University of Virginia's Medical Center in Charlottesville brought this problem into the national consciousness.[11]

However, the Virginia baby-switching incident was not the first such case to come to light. In December 1978, two female infants, Arlena Beatrice Twiggs and Kimberly Michelle Mays, born in Florida, were given to the wrong families and raised by them. The mistake was discovered when the girls were nearly nine. Unfortunately, Arlena died from congenital heart failure shortly after the switch was confirmed by blood tests. The court determined that Kimberly's family would retain custody of the daughter they had reared.[12] This case received considerable press coverage, leading to a book and television miniseries,[13] but the Virginia case seems to have attracted even more. The many unexpected events associated with the Virginia case kept it in the public eye for more than a decade.

The mother of three-year-old Callie Marie was Paula Johnson. Callie's presumed father was Carlton Conley. Conley requested a DNA

test to determine Callie's paternity. However, the test showed that neither Johnson nor Conley was Callie's biological parent. A reporter, using
birth announcements and ingenuity, identified the family raising
Rebecca Grace Chittum, the daughter Johnson had delivered. Rebecca's
family lived eighty miles away.

The disturbing news did not stop there. Just one day after Johnson
learned that Callie was not her biological daughter, Rebecca's rearing
parents (Callie's biological parents) were killed in a car accident. They
never knew that the daughter they had been raising belonged to a different family and that their biological daughter was being raised by
someone else. Rebecca's parents also had a daughter named Lindsay two
years younger than Rebecca.

The cause of the switch was never determined, but a videotape and
photos of the newborn girls showed loosely fitting identification
bracelets that might have slipped off.[14] The hospital suggested that the
mix-up was deliberate, but that was never confirmed. Perhaps the hospital was trying to place the blame for the mistake on an outside party to
avoid financial responsibility.

Decisions regarding custody and visitation strained relations
between the two families, both of which filed lawsuits against the hospital. In a curious twist, Rebecca's biological father, while estranged from
Callie, began to visit his birth daughter periodically, and during these
visits he met Rebecca's Aunt Pam whom he married in 2001. Rebecca
and her sister Lindsey moved in with the couple.

In the wake of discovering that Callie was not her biological
daughter, Paula Johnson remembered that Callie had lost two and a half
pounds by the time Paula took her home. Paula had sensed that something wasn't right and contacted the hospital. In fact, a review of medical records showed that both families had raised concerns over their
babies' weight and appetite changes, but they were ignored by hospital
staff. We cannot know if these parents were simply asking questions or
seriously doubting the identity of their infants. But it is easy to under-

stand why a mother suspecting a baby isn't hers might be reluctant to voice her concerns. Some new mothers lack confidence in their ability to recall their infant's features or to distinguish physical changes that are possible (e.g., skin tone, due to water and weight loss) from those that are impossible (e.g., sudden appearance of a deformity). Recall that Dulce, the mother of switched-at-birth twins Tairí and Mari, whom I discussed in chapter 2, did challenge her nurse about one twin's appearance, but she was condescendingly told not to worry because infants change all the time.

Some new mothers may feel embarrassed to question their baby's identity, worrying that their fears will appear irrational.[15] As recently as March 2008, two Illinois mothers, Kassie Hopkins and Mary Jo Bathen, were given each other's baby boys.[16] The switch occurred when the infants were taken at the same time to get circumcisions. Both babies were wearing ID tags, but they were removed and incorrectly replaced. Both mothers said they experienced "eerie feelings" when they received their babies, but only one spoke up in the hospital while the other took the baby home.

A more extreme instance of a mother keeping silent occurred in 1951 when a Wisconsin woman "knew"—for forty years—that the infant she had been given was not hers. She didn't pursue the matter because she was afraid of hurting her marriage and causing a stir in her small town.[17]

There is the different, but also extreme, example of a Dutch mother named Wilma Stuart who seriously questioned the biological origins of one of her fraternal twin sons based on his appearance.[18] In 1993 Wilma delivered artificially conceived fraternal twins, Teun and Koen. She was immediately aware of Koen's extremely dark skin tone, which made him look quite different from her, her husband Willem, and his twin brother. Desperate to make sense of the situation, Wilma wondered if intermarriage somewhere in the family line might have been responsible. She also raised her worries many times with doctors and nurses. However, they were unconcerned or invoked the usual explanation that *babies change*. Sometimes it doesn't matter if mothers raise their concerns delicately or push hard; hospital staff can react to both in the same uninterested way.

Wilma lived with her concerns until the twins were nearly one year old, when a new pediatrician asked her if she realized that the boys looked very different.[19] She burst into tears. DNA testing subsequently determined that Koen was Wilma's child but not Willem's—the fertility clinic had accidentally fertilized one of Wilma's eggs with the sperm from a Black man who was there on the same day. Wilma remembered him. Wilma arranged for the man to meet Koen when he was still a toddler—she was hoping he would eventually show Koen what it was like to be a minority living in the Netherlands—but the man was not interested in pursuing a relationship with the child. Koen and Teun grew up as Wilma and Willem's twin sons and are now seventeen.

Most people hold doctors and nurses in high esteem, deferring to their knowledge and experience and never imagining that such mistakes in infant identity or embryo implantation are possible. Infant identification is too important to allow for errors, and when they are suspected most parents initially deny them, as did Mme. Joye, the mother of Philippe and Paul, and Andrzej, the father of Kasia and Nina. However, mothers now have the tools to resolve maternity uncertainty as quickly as possible, partly because patient empowerment came of age independently of, but conveniently for, suspected baby switching. Following the Virginia case, efforts were made nationwide to acquaint new mothers with procedures and protocols for protecting infant identification. Mothers delivering babies still respect their doctors and nurses but now understand that these professionals can make mistakes.

I will now take a closer look at why maternity uncertainty, a current societal concern, was not a problem throughout the course of human history. And I will consider why the parallel problem of paternity uncertainty (i.e., how fathers cannot be fully certain of who their children are) has been the focus of considerable research attention. I will also review findings and implications from scientific studies that show the ways in which a mother can distinguish her own baby from others. Lastly, I will share my extraordinary experience with Dr. Antonio Garrido-Lestache, a Spanish pediatrician who has made mother-infant identification his life's work.

Maternity versus Paternity Uncertainty

A woman can be certain that she is related to her offspring by an average coefficient of relatedness of at least .5, and her offspring can have the same degree of confidence in their relatedness to her. This contrasts sharply with the situation of the male, who can never be certain that his mate's children are related to him at all.[20]

The human birth process assures a mother that the child she bears belongs to her biologically, but such is not true for a father. Hidden ovulation, internal fertilization, and continuous female receptivity mean that a male can never know with complete assurance that he is the biological father of a child delivered by his partner.[21] Even a DNA test cannot prove paternity, but it can disprove it. This phenomenon, known as *paternity uncertainty*, has been of interest to evolutionary psychologists attempting to identify physical and behavioral characteristics associated with individual survival and reproduction.[22] For example, research shows that males are especially sensitive to signs of sexual disloyalty by their partners, behaviors that might signal that a given child is not truly theirs. Females also experience jealousy following assumed or actual sexual transgressions by their partners, but their suspicions of emotional disloyalty are generally more upsetting to them than possible sexual infidelity. That is because emotional distance on the part of unfaithful males may make them less likely to support the care and well-being of their family.

Some studies have shown that most babies visually resemble their fathers more than their mothers; this may be a mechanism to assure men that they are truly the fathers of a given child.[23] I found it remarkable that my twin sister's son Adam mirrored his father's facial features for about one year, before transforming into a near replica of my sister. The interpretation of this finding is that a male is more likely to believe that he fathered a child who resembles him and, consequently, is more likely to invest in that child than a child who does not resemble him. Of course, the theory isn't perfect because children and parents can vary considerably in appearance for both genetic and nongenetic reasons. For example, some blue-eyed infants are born to two brown-eyed parents who each carry one copy of the recessive gene coding for blue eyes. Dark-haired children may have what appear to be light-haired mothers who prefer to dye their naturally dark hair blonde.

Attempts to replicate studies of father-infant similarity have produced mixed results. Some researchers have found that ratings of infant-parent resemblance by independent judges, based on photographs, do not favor either mothers or fathers,[24] while others have reported greater resemblance between infants and mothers than between infants and fathers.[25] I believe that because fathers' own perceptions would matter most with respect to their investment in their children, researchers should gather father-infant similarity ratings from fathers themselves and study them with reference to the fathers' parenting behaviors.[26] Such a study would also be valuable for determining whether mothers favor children who look like them over those who do not. A twin study would be well suited to this goal—when Dulce took her twins Mari and Tairí (really Samantha) home, she did not feel an immediate bond with Samantha, so she made a special effort to love that baby. Of course, given the nature of direct involvement in childbirth, mothers have not been expected to question their relatedness to their children. However, in a non-twin baby switch in Wyoming, a newborn's darker complexion caused her father to "openly and frequently" claim she was not his child. The child was ridiculed and mistreated by her father and her other siblings.[27]

"Maternity uncertainty"—a mother's insecurity over whether or not the baby she is given to take home is really hers—is a term that is virtually absent from textbooks and other parenting research. This makes sense because a mother's concern as to the identity of her newborn is a relatively recent phenomenon in childbirth, a consequence of the 1960s spike in the delivery of babies in hospitals. As mentioned earlier, maternal doubt over the identity of a baby was simply not a factor in early human history—not part of the female behavioral repertoire—when mothers delivered babies in small groups surrounded by female relatives or when births took place at home with the assistance of midwives. This may explain why most modern women still do not question their baby's identity even if their babies do not look like them. Most of the twins' mothers I have written about in this book were curious about their baby's physical changes between their birth and the time they came home from the hospital or their baby's physical difference from the rest of the family. But most of these women never thought about whether or not the baby was hers. Even Begoña and Beatriz's mother, who was told that she had delivered identical twins, reconciled Beatriz's unusual skin tone and hair color by deciding that genes from her husband's distant relatives were somehow responsible.

But things have changed since the mid-1900s. The Canary Islands twins, the other six known switched-at-birth twin cases, and the known and suspected incidents of non-twin baby mix-ups have given maternity uncertainty significant scientific status. It is no longer the case that "no woman has ever faced the adaptive problem of 'maternity uncertainty.'"[28] The cases that are known, coupled with those that are unknown but possible, pose a threat to any new mother. I predict that maternity uncertainty will continue to evolve into an important topic in its own right as further infant mix-ups are exposed. Knowing that hospital procedures are in place to minimize such occurrences may allay parents' fears, but they could have the opposite effect by highlighting the potential for error.

HOW DO MOTHERS KNOW
WHO THEIR CHILDREN ARE?

Physical recognition is an important aspect of the bond that develops between mothers and babies, and it may explain why mothers' feelings of attachment to their infants decline as their periods of separation increase.[29] Doctors are divided as to whether newborn twins should be released separately from the hospital if just one twin is physically able to go home; they cite the advantages of reduced medical expense and routine setting for the healthier twin and the disadvantages of possibly impaired bonding and breast-feeding difficulty for the less healthy twin.[30] Delia, Begoña, and Beatriz were discharged from the hospital on different dates (twenty-five days, five days, and three months after birth, respectively), and it was Delia, the later-released twin, who was switched. Extended hospitalization of newborns understandably increases the risk of a mistake. Most "twins" in the other switched-at-birth pairs went home on the same day, although they did so after being in hospital or foster care for between two days and two months.

There is a rich body of literature showing that new mothers are exquisitely sensitive to the smell, sound, touch, and sight of their newborn infants. In fact, mothers are often able to use these sensory modalities to distinguish their own infant from others after only several hours of contact. A 2009 review referenced new mothers' heightened hormonal arousal as facilitating their responsivity to their newborns.[31]

Smell is a powerful, but unappreciated, clue to infant identity, largely because humans rely mostly on visual cues for recognition. In 1983 Michael J. Russell and his colleagues at the University of California, San Francisco showed that mothers could identify their infants by smell after being with them for only six hours. Russell recruited twenty-six mothers from a well-baby nursery, half of whom were tested at six hours postpartum and half of whom were tested at forty-eight hours postpartum. Mothers in the first group had had only one-half

hour of contact with their infants, whereas mothers in the second group
had had approximately forty hours of contact. Each mother was blind-
folded and asked to sniff three different infants who had been similarly
washed and covered, one of whom was her own. The process was
repeated three times with the ordering of the babies shifted for each
trial. It turned out that nearly two-thirds of the mothers in the first
group (61 percent) and in the second group (58 percent) identified their
infants correctly, results that were significantly greater than chance (33
percent). Even one-half hour of infant exposure, followed by six hours of
separation, was enough for mothers to know which child was theirs.[32]

When this experiment was repeated with ten fathers who had experienced variable amounts of infant contact, the results were quite different. Fathers made fewer correct identifications than mothers (37 percent), a percentage that did not differ from chance. These results suggested that new mothers are biologically primed to recognize features of
their own infants that distinguish them from unrelated infants. The possibility that the infants' odors were recognized because they matched
those of their mothers seemed unlikely; because mothers and fathers
both transmit 50 percent of their genes to their children, they should
have been equally successful if genetic factors were primarily responsible.

Of course, approximately one-third of the mothers' responses were
incorrect, showing that odor is not a perfect means for knowing one's
infant. Infants' different odor intensities and mothers' different smell
sensitivities may explain why the percentage of correct answers was not
higher. Nevertheless, all these mothers had had early opportunities to
know their infants, in contrast with most of the mothers of the switched
twins, who had only observed their premature newborns through glass
panes and incubators. There was no opportunity for the twins' mothers
to know their babies. These mothers also couldn't hear their babies cry
so as to identify their sound.

It has been known for some time that mothers can distinguish their
own baby's cry from the cries of other babies. An early study used a

simple but elegant method for testing this observation.[33] Tape recordings were made of the cries of thirty-one newborns when they were between 14 hours (about 0.5 day) and 144 hours old (6 days). Infant crying was elicited by the examiner, who scratched the sole of the baby's foot with his or her finger. Each mother listened to five recordings played separately in a random order, one of which was the sound of her own baby crying. Of the twenty-three mothers tested less than forty-eight hours after delivery, slightly over half (52 percent) correctly identified their infant's cry. However, all eight of the mothers tested after forty-eight hours were correct in their identifications. It appeared that some degree of learning is required by mothers in order for them to identify their infant's cry, but such learning occurs quickly. Consistent with these findings is more recent work showing greater responsivity to infant cries by experienced than by inexperienced new mothers after the period of postpartum changes.[34] It is likely that, as with smell, new mothers have a heightened receptivity to their infants' sounds, further demonstrated in a second part of the same study.

A different group of ten new mothers in three- and four-bedded maternity wards were asked to record the number of times they were awakened by the cries of their own infant versus someone else's infant over the course of three successive nights. The first time the clock struck midnight after birth was counted as the first night, so in some cases, the third night was less than forty-eight hours after delivery. It turned out that out of twenty-six waking-up episodes, fifteen (58 percent) were mothers' waking for their own infants; however, from the fourth night onward, twenty-two out of twenty-three waking-up episodes (96 percent) were for mothers' own infants. Again, as with smell, mothers seemed to learn the sounds of their infants after relatively brief periods of exposure.

A 2009 study by Kathleen Wermke of the University of Wurzburg in Germany produced a startling finding, namely that two- to five-day-old infants' cries display the melodic patterns of their mothers' native tongue.[35] The investigators recorded 2,500 cries emitted by 60 newborns, 30 from French-speaking families and 30 from German-speaking families. The French infants' cries showed a low-to-high pitch transition, while the German infants' cries showed the reverse. Comparable intonation patterns are found in the speech of French and German adult speakers, respectively. It has been known since 1980 that babies can hear voices during the later months of their prenatal life and prefer their mothers' voices to the voices of others once they are born.[36] Now it appears that, prior to birth, babies are processing the language patterns of the people around them.

This research reminded me of Ernstli and Paul, the switched-at-birth twin and non-twin from Fribourg, Switzerland. Ernstli heard only French during prenatal life, while Paul had heard only German, yet these exchanged babies were placed with families that spoke different languages. I wonder if the twins' mother Mme. Joye sensed that her true twin son Philippe's cries were more familiar to her than Paul's. I also wonder if Mme. Vatter, the woman who raised Ernstli, thought that his cries differed from those of other babies she knew.

Touch is another fascinating sensory modality for infant recognition. Research has shown that premature infants consume more milk, gain more weight, and show greater mental and motor development if massaged daily for three 15-minute sessions relative to premature infants who are not massaged.[37] The benefits of infant touch have, in fact, been underestimated for many years. Touch is also a way that new mothers can recognize their infants.

Maternal stroking of an infant with the fingers during the course of early care is a frequently observed behavior. However, mothers may be unaware that tactile interactions are opportunities to learn the distinctive qualities of their infant's skin. A 1992 study conducted by psychologist Marsha Kaitz and her colleagues at the Hebrew University of Jerusalem, Israel, tested mothers' accuracy in distinguishing their own infants from two other infants by means of tactile cues.[38] Eighty-two mothers categorized as having spent between five and fifty-five minutes, between one and ten hours, and more than ten hours with their babies were asked to stroke the hand of three infants and to then identify their own. Mothers were first guided to the right side of a bassinet in which a baby was facedown with arms extended and right hand lying flat on the mattress. The examiner brought the mother's fingertips in contact with the dorsal surface (back side) of the infant's hand so she could stroke the hand with her index and middle fingers in the direction away from the baby's fingers.

Only five of the fourteen women (36 percent) who had spent less than one hour with their babies could recognize them, a finding that did not significantly exceed chance (33 percent). However, forty-seven of the sixty-eight women (69 percent) who had spent an hour or more with their infants could identify them correctly, a result that significantly exceeded chance expectations. Interestingly, mothers who had spent more than ten hours with their babies were not more successful than mothers who had spent one to ten hours. It appears that once mother-infant interaction exceeds one hour, maternal proficiency at infant tactile recognition does not increase with greater contact.

An interesting question raised by this study was the nature of the tactile cues enabling mothers to know who their babies were. Most mothers explained that their decisions were based on the texture or temperature of the infant's hand, but several mothers who could not be specific said their choice was based on the hand that "felt most familiar." Their comments were consistent with the view that some degree of interaction is required for mothers to recognize their babies by touch. The investigators also believed that the hormonal state of these mothers when they were parturient (in labor about to give birth) increased their responsiveness to their newborn infant's characteristics, including skin quality.

This study had several important methodological features. First, the women could not prepare in advance for the required task since the goals of the study were not revealed to them before the test. Second, in the few cases in which an infant vocalized during the test session, the test was discontinued and resumed ten to fifteen minutes later because the mothers might have become attuned to their babies' sounds during that time. Third, a cloth was draped over the mothers' noses and eyes during testing to prevent any odor or visual cues from biasing their choices. It is, therefore, likely that mothers' knowledge of their infant's skin was acquired during the course of ordinary early mother-infant interaction.

Visual cues are central to human recognition and are the most common means we use to identify family and friends, provided we have normal vision. This raises the question of whether or not new mothers can recognize their infants' faces following brief periods of contact (up to five hours). A visual-recognition study showed that they can, but with some qualifications. Clearly, facial recognition of infants requires mothers and babies to be together for at least some period of time, moments denied to most mothers of the switched-at-birth twins.

In another study, Kaitz and her colleagues assembled two groups from a total of 124 new mothers to see if the mothers could correctly select their infants' facial photographs from a series of seven infant photos.[39] Forty-nine mothers were primiparous (i.e., had just delivered their first baby), while seventy-five were multiparous (i.e., had delivered babies previously). The two groups were further organized into those who had been with their babies for between thirty minutes and five hours, between five hours and ten hours, and between ten hours and fifteen hours for a total of six groups. Color photographs of the infants' faces were taken while they slept. (Newborns sleep between sixteen and eighteen hours each day, albeit in two- to four-hour intervals, so it was likely that most mothers had seen their babies in a resting state.)[40] Babies with facial rashes or other distinctive markings were excluded from the study, and pretesting by assistants showed that the baby's face in each photograph closely matched each baby's face in real life.

Mothers separately examined each of the seven photographs in their given album for two to four seconds, going through the seven pages twice. They were then asked to leaf through the album one more time to identify their own child. Mothers who were uncertain as to which baby was hers were encouraged to guess. Only eight of the twenty-seven primiparous mothers with the least amount of infant exposure (30 percent) chose the photograph of their own baby. However, thirty-four of the forty-three multiparous women with little infant exposure (70 percent) were successful at this task. The other four groups of primiparous and multiparous women with greater hours of infant exposure made correct choices between 78 percent and 86 percent of the time. The researchers proposed that the poor performance of the first-time mothers with the lowest levels of infant contact might be due to their elevated anxiety, discomfort, or fatigue. Such factors have been shown to adversely affect cognitive and perceptual skills. In fact, more primiparous mothers in the study rated their labor experience as "difficult" (55 percent) than did the multiparous mothers (13 percent). Not surprisingly, far more multiparous mothers described their labor as "easy" (25.3 percent) than did the primiparous mothers (4 percent).

Fathers' early interactions with their infants were not as lengthy or as intensive as the infants' contact with their mothers. In a related study, fifteen out of twenty-three new fathers (65 percent) recognized their infant's photograph after seeing the infant just once in the delivery room.[41] In fact, fathers were more successful than mothers in this respect; only one out of six new mothers (16.7 percent) recognized her baby's photograph following the same brief period of exposure. It was possible that mothers' judgments were adversely affected by medication and/or fatigue; males generally excel on mental rotation and spatial perception problems, while females generally outperform males on facial recognition tasks.[42] Interestingly, studies have shown that female newborns prefer to look at faces, whereas male babies prefer to look at mobiles.[43] These sex differences in facial recognition and preference may be associated with females' greater early care of newborns, specifically their need to understand the infant's needs and condition from facial cues.

In contrast, mothers and fathers with between ten and forty-five minutes of infant exposure showed the same levels of success: nine out of thirteen (69.2 percent) and fourteen out of eighteen (78 percent), respectively, made correct choices. Thus, new fathers, like new mothers, are
closely attuned to their infant's facial characteristics—this process may
function, albeit unconsciously, to confirm their paternity of the child.

These simple but clever visual-recognition experiments reveal a
great deal about how mothers know their own babies. However, I would
like to see studies in which mothers visually identify their own baby
from a set of seven live infants. Infants' vocalizations and odor cues
could be eliminated by covering the mothers' ears and noses. Photos may
not completely capture the full range of features, some known (e.g., skin
tone, hair color) but possibly others unknown, that tell a mother that a
baby is hers. Perhaps the question is empirical, but comparing baby identification success rates based on images versus live infants would be
worth doing.

There is an important distinction to be made between recognition
and discrimination in this study and in all the studies involving infant
identification by sensory modalities. That is, it may be easier to discrim-
inate, or differentiate, one's own infant from several others shown in succession than to simply recognize a given infant as one's own with no
others nearby to compare. In the former case there is a basis for comparison, whereas in the second case there is not. The difference is similar to
that between a multiple-choice test and a short-answer test—perhaps
the answer is obvious when it is seen but not when it must be produced.
The real question is whether or not mothers can identify their infants
from a single smell, sound, touch, or image when there are no other
infant smells, sounds, touches, or images around.

To the extent that it is harder to identify a single infant through the
different sensory modalities, mothers given the wrong non-twin infant
to take home may be especially disadvantaged relative to mothers given
the wrong identical twin. Most of the mothers of the switched-at-birth

twins did not suspect a mistake, but not all of them were told whether or not their twins were identical. One exception was Tairí and Mari's mother, Dulce, who had spent time with her twins and knew that her identical "twin" babies did not look alike when she took them home.

There is another infant identification study worthy of description because it was conducted specifically in response to baby-switching reports that appeared in the press. A 2001 investigation by Joan DiPasquale Davis at the University of Steubenville in Ohio focused on whether or not maternal anxieties linked to the possibility of infant misidentification would prevent mothers from recognizing the odors and cries of their babies.[44] Forty-four mothers who had delivered their babies between twenty-four and ninety-six hours prior to the study were recruited for participation while in the maternity ward. The mothers first underwent interviews concerning their health, medication, and delivery and completed a pregnancy anxiety scale. They were also asked: "Have you ever felt anxious that the baby delivered to you might not be yours?" Project staff gathered three nightshirts worn by each infant and recorded each infant's crying while changing the infant's nightshirt. Each mother listened to the individual tapes of each of three infants once, or twice if requested, and indicated which cry was made by her own infant. Mothers also sniffed three separate nightshirts and selected the one they believed had been worn by their own babies.

Most mothers (90.5 percent) reported anxiety over childbirth and delivery, while far fewer reported anxiety over possible baby switching (9.1 percent). Only one of the four women who had baby-switching concerns had also reported anxiety in all three areas assessed by the anxiety scale: childbirth and delivery, pregnancy, and hospitalization. This suggests that worry over baby switching reflects a specific concern rather than a generalized anxiety. Interestingly, concerns over baby switching did not impair mothers' ability to recognize their infants' sounds and smells. Each of these four mothers with baby-switching concerns correctly identified her baby's cries, and two (50 percent) correctly identified their babies' odors, a percentage similar to that of the mothers who were not anxious about baby switching.

The group of mothers anxious about baby switching was small (four), so the results from this study require replication. However, as indicated in the article, if a nurse manages twenty new mothers at a time, then two of those new mothers can be expected to show anxiety over receiving the wrong infant. This means that nurses and other hospital staff need to find ways to calm these mothers' fears and, most importantly, to prevent such mistakes from happening.

I expect that mothers participating in infant recognition studies try hard to correctly identify their baby's smell, sound, skin, and face. However, some babies' features are probably more identifiable and therefore easier to remember than others. There is also evidence that maternal interaction is easier with bigger babies than it is with smaller ones and that babies' health status plays a role in how mothers respond to their infants.[45] A study of preterm infant twins found that by eight months of age, mothers interacted more frequently with the healthier twin than the less healthy twin, a difference displayed by some mothers at four months.[46] If these preferences are present even earlier in the mother-infant relationship, they could conceivably affect maternal recognition of the twins' characteristics. That is, mothers might show preferential treatment, albeit not consciously, toward the twin whose features were clearer in her mind.

While not discussed in the various studies I have described, it is likely that the mothers making correct choices felt confident and happy, while the mothers making incorrect choices felt inadequate and distressed.[47] None of the mothers knew the goals of the studies in advance, so they could not prepare by focusing on their infant's skin or by memorizing their infants' faces. However, during the experimental sessions it is possible that they thought about their babies' qualities to a greater degree than they would have during the course of ordinary interactions. Perhaps mothers' abilities to recognize infants are heightened in situations that challenge their abilities to do so—not just during research participation but when they are worried about possible baby switching or abduction. This would explain why the four anxious mothers in Davis's study were as accurate in identifying their babies as the mothers who were not anxious. In fact, I would predict that mothers worried about baby switching might be extremely good at knowing and recalling their infants' physical features, possibly outperforming mothers who do not express these concerns.

Javier Urra, a Spanish psychologist and current president of the Ethics Committee of the College of Psychologists in Madrid,[48] said "[Baby switching] is something that has always been in parents' imagination, but no one wants to think about it."[49] I do not believe all new mothers have seriously considered possible baby switching—the Canary Islands mothers had never heard of it, although news reports of their situation would make it a concern for others. Still, even a slight possibility of going home with the wrong baby might make mothers especially attuned to their infant's unique characteristics, as Davis's study suggested. In fact, following the 1998 baby-switching case in Virginia and five 1998 and 1999 baby-switching cases in Orange County, California, hospital staff across the United States began encouraging women to familiarize themselves with their babies' characteristics as a precautionary measure. Since then many hospitals have instituted programs using standard procedures and advanced technologies to protect mothers and babies. One such program makes use of a simple, inexpensive, and highly reliable technique, further developed for infant identification by a caring and forward-thinking physician from Madrid, Dr. Antonio Garrido-Lestache. Here's what I learned from him.

DR. ANTONIO GARRIDO-LESTACHE

Dr. Antonio Garrido-Lestache was quoted in a July 2008 article in the Spanish newspaper *El Pais* as saying that the switching of the Canary

Islands twins violated children's fundamental right to their personal identity and family circumstances.[50] Garrido-Lestache is a renowned pediatrician, famous for his 1999 implementation of Spain's standard fingerprinting system for identifying newborns.[51] He had become concerned about child welfare soon after he received his medical degree in 1954 from the Universidad Complutense de Madrid at age twenty-three. He recognized the importance of infant identification soon after that, even before baby switches were reported in the press, because he claimed they occurred with some frequency. He has lectured widely on the topic, most notably at the 1989 United Nations Convention on the Rights of the Child, and has been recognized for his efforts by Queen Sophia of Spain. I requested a meeting with him in late September 2009 when I returned to Barcelona from Las Palmas. I visited him at his office at the Hospital del Nino Jesus in Madrid.[52]

Dr. Julia Moreno y Vázquez, Garrido-Lestache's family friend, met me at Madrid's Atocha train station. She served as my interpreter for the day since Garrido-Lestached spoke only Spanish. Moreno, a professor of economics and diplomacy in Madrid, was a warm, intelligent, and stylishly dressed woman who appeared to be in her fifties. She found me at the station by holding a large sign that read "Dr. Nancy" in bold letters. The reverse side of her sign, an illustrated poster depicting the important needs of young children, is displayed in my Twin Studies Center library in Fullerton, California. Moments after I met Moreno, she introduced me to Cristina, a third-year psychology student who was also Garrido-Lestache's granddaughter. Cristina looked like many college students in the year 2009 with long dark hair, blue jeans, and short black jacket. Cristina seemed to love child psychology almost as much as she loved her dog, Bob, and we discussed the possibility of her pursuing graduate study in the United States.

I finally met Garrido-Lestache, a distinguished seventy-eight-year-old gentleman who wore a dark gray jacket, gray pants, light blue striped shirt, and complementary tie. Garrido-Lestache was enthusiastic about

Fig. 6.1. Dr. Antonio Garrido-Lestache; Dr. Julia Moreno y Vázquez; and
Garrido-Lestache's granddaughter, Cristina; in Madrid. Courtesy of Nancy L. Segal

and proud of his work in infant identification and more than happy to
discuss his efforts at length. He had prepared a packet of materials for me,
including articles on baby switching, brochures on his fingerprint identification system, and his 2001 book, *La Identificación de Recien Nacidos en
la Casa Real Española* (*The Identification of Newborns in the Royal
Spanish Household*).[53] The book's cover shows Queen Dona Victoria
Eugenia (1887–1969), wife of King Juan Carlos I of Spain (1886–1941),
holding her infant son Principe de Asturias, Don Alfonso de Borbon
(1907–1938). Don Alfonso died of hemophilia at age thirty-one.

Garrido-Lestache became interested in infant identification due to
his concern over the lack of a system for protecting children from hospital exchanges or related mishaps. He believes that every prospective
mother harbors three fears: the presentation of the baby (vertex or
breech), the infant's physical condition (healthy or unhealthy), and the
infant's identity (mother's own child or someone else's). Garrido-

Lestache was not the first person to show interest in legally mandated infant identification practices, but he was the first to implement them as a routine procedure. His system, first presented to delegates at the 1989 United Nations Convention, is based on the biological uniqueness and stability of mothers' and babies' fingerprints.

The scientific study of fingerprints is known as dermatoglyphics, a term coined from the Greek words *derma* (skin) and *glyph* (carving). Fingerprints are stable and enduring characteristics that are present at or about the eighteenth week of gestation.[54] Fingerprints can be analyzed for the number of lines or ridges on each fingertip, called the ridgecount, as well as for the configurations formed by the ridges, known as pattern types. The three basic dermatoglyphic patterns are the arch, loop, and whorl, but each has particular variations (e.g., tented arch, double loop, double whorl), increasing each person's dermatoglyphic complexity and individuality. Greater fingerprint resemblance between identical than fraternal twins shows that fingerprints are influenced by genetic factors, but identical twins can show varying degrees of fingerprint discordance due to ordinary prenatal influences, such as twins' differences in fetal position, or adverse effects, such as differences in brain trauma.[55] Because identical twins' fingerprints are rarely the same, a switched-at-birth twin case could not be resolved by trying to match the prints of the separated infants.

Mistaken exchanges of individuals are not limited to newborn nurseries. In April 2006, two Taylor University students, Laura Van Ryn and Whitney Cerak, were involved in a fatal car crash on an Indiana highway in which Laura died and Whitney survived.[56] Possibly because Whitney was found next to Laura's personal effects, authorities believed Laura and not Whitney was the survivor. Over the course of several weeks of intensive treatment, it became clear that this was a tragic case of mistaken identity—the woman initially identified as Laura Van Ryn was really Whitney Cerak. Had fingerprints been filed in a national database, this unfortunate situation, so painful for the families, could have been avoided. And had anyone worried about the identity of Spanish children in the 1970s, Delia and Beatriz would have grown up knowing their biological parents and siblings.

Garrido-Lestache's system requires taking prints from two of the baby's fingers on the right hand (index and middle fingers) and two of the mother's fingers on the right hand (index finger and thumb). He has designed a special document that requires the entry of these prints at the time of birth to ensure correspondence between the legal and biological identity of the child. A public information pamphlet states, "This system, which has been implemented in other countries, solves the problems that arise with identification in hospitals and guarantees the right of parents to know who their children are, since this document is recorded in the register of births and in the national identity card of the child."[57]

Garrido-Lestache stressed the importance of using a biological marker for identity because it is stable and reliable, noting that identification bracelets can easily slip off. He also argued that legal documents in the absence of biological data could conceivably apply to more than one infant because they are not tied to something unique and unchangeable.[58] Simply put, a birth certificate is not physically attached to any one child the way a fingerprint is, and it could be mistaken, or intentionally used, as a document belonging to another child. In contrast, a fingerprint is unique, it only belongs to the person from whom it was taken, and its origin can be verified. Furthermore, the essential features of fingerprints remain unchanged throughout life, despite the development of lines and creases associated with aging. An exception is advanced leprosy, which can destroy fingerprints, but if the fingerprint ridges (lines) remain, they can be associated with the person's fingerprints if available prior to the disease onset.[59]

Spain's royal families' births were witnessed to make certain that the correct heir eventually assumed the throne. However, this process relied on visual identification only, meaning that legal documents could conceivably be applied to any baby of the same age and sex. Attempts to circumvent this problem included dentition, photography, and tattoos, but each had specific associated problems. For example, photographs were impractical because of young children's rapid physical development. For Garrido-Lestache, fingerprints are the ideal method for establishing personal identity easily, economically, and accurately. Even footprints had been used for infant identity in Spain, but they were omitted from Garrido-Lestache's procedures because babies' growth makes it difficult to compare later images with the original print.

I have recorded the fingerprints of hundreds of twin children and adults, a process that requires several minutes per pair. The tip of each finger is pressed against an inkpad and then rolled from one side to another onto a special card with spaces labeled for each of the ten fingers. According to Garrido-Lestache, infants' fingerprints can be recorded just as easily using a different approach.[60] The best time for doing this is twenty minutes after birth when the infant's condition has stabilized. The baby's right hand is washed, and the baby is placed lying on its stomach on a table. An identification official lifts the baby's hand about 3 to 4 centimeters (1.18 to 1.57 inches) and gently separates the fingers, and an assistant places the ink plate under each finger, lowers it to the plate, then lifts it onto the identity card. This procedure is repeated until the required number of prints has been recorded. The baby is not harmed in any way by this technique. If a newborn is premature, or needs immediate medical attention that precludes fingerprinting, then DNA analysis can be performed using a hair sample.

Garrido-Lestache believes that society as a whole needs to participate in the process of infant identification. One of his articles on the subject outlines several requirements necessary for implementation. They include the provision of training courses for hospital staff; the appointment of identification officers in maternity units; and the hiring of additional forensic specialists in intelligence, documentation, and fingerprinting. "Bulls are worth millions, horses are guarded, and dogs have identity cards," he told me. "Kids should have them too." When he mentioned this to Spain's Queen Sophia, she encouraged him to develop a process for identifying babies.

It is not just the careful registration of animals but not humans that disturbs Garrido-Lestache. In a written statement in 2000 he said, "Tree registration is so important that in Madrid, each tree has its own individual document. Children, however, are given so little consideration that this comparison is outrageous. I feel our activities are now better targeted than in the past."[61] His words were another reminder of Mme. Joye's distress that chickens, but not babies, were meticulously labeled.

I could not end my interview without asking Garrido-Lestache to describe his reaction to the Canary Islands twins case. "I see [baby exchanges] all the time," he said. "Years ago the nurses said that [baby switches] were impossible, but now they know I am right. It was a very unpleasant situation." He added that the sum of three million euros initially requested in damages by the Canary Islands twins' attorneys was too modest, based on a case he had worked on twenty years earlier. "All people have the right to identity. . . . Adults should have the same rights as children. The damage [from baby switching] is less serious when you are young than when you are seventeen and discover you are in the wrong family."

I thought about Garrido-Lestache's point and wondered if perhaps children's greater flexibility and benefit of time lend them an adaptive advantage over adults in a switched-at-birth situation. Again, I believe children and adults both suffer, albeit differently, and the nature and intensity of their responses depend on their personal situation at the time of discovery and during the years that preceded it. Interestingly, most discussions of personal identity focus on infant protection with little mention of adults' rights. Delia's sense that her life took a U-turn and Beatriz's knowledge of her physical differences extend these issues beyond the nursery.

Garrido-Lestache said he is certain that all five of his adult children were the babies his wife once delivered. He also said he was present at all five births. Fathers are increasingly encouraged to take active roles in the birth of their children, not just to support their partners but to foster their caretaking involvement. Being certain of going home with the right child is an important by-product of witnessing the birth. However, witnessing the birth does not guarantee paternity.

On my train ride back to Barcelona, I examined materials included in the packet I had received from Garrido-Lestache. Information about ICN—Identificación y Custodia Neonal (Newborn Identification and Custody)—a company headquartered in La Coruña, Spain, stood out because it was exactly what Garrido-Lestache had envisioned for his country. The company's website states, "The *sistema* (system) of ICN guarantees the newborn's right to be able to be identified at the moment of birth."[62] ICN uses state-of-the-art equipment: a handheld device includes a biometric camera to scan and record the baby's fingerprint and a biometric sensor to record information from the mother. The system offers a wireless Internet connection, a fingerprint recognition system, a code reader, and a data encryption system so that fingerprints taken on later occasions can be compared with those taken at birth. Its technology has been implemented in hospitals throughout Spain.

ICN was formed in response to Spain's 1999 decree mandating the systematic identification of newborns. That decree resulted from the 1989 United Nations Convention on the Rights of the Child. Only 2 countries—the United States and Somalia—out of 194 did not ratify the declaration resulting from that convention. In November 2009, Somalia's cabinet ministers announced plans for ratification, and at the time of this writing President Obama requires Senate approval of the declaration before he can sign it.[63] In reference to the declaration, Obama stated that the United States must "return to its position as a respected global leader and supporter of Human Rights."[64]

One of the most significant remarks Garrido-Lestache made during my visit was to emphasize the importance of involving all of society in the process of infant identification and protection. One way Spain has

Fig. 6.2. Spanish Stamp Commemorating Infant Identification and Interpol. Courtesy of Dr. Antonio Garrido-Lestache.

fulfilled this goal was its July 2005 issuance of four million copies of a commemorative postage stamp with a face value of 0.28 euros (US$0.36 in 2005). This unlimited edition stamp recognized the seventy-sixth anniversary of Interpol (International Criminal Police Organization) in Spain, a group that has supported Spain's efforts in infant identification. The stamp combines images of a newborn baby, a fingerprint, the flag of Spain, and the symbol of Interpol, reflecting the importance of the problem and the efforts and resources behind it.

STEPS TOWARD INFANT IDENTIFICATION

Hospital Procedure

Garrido-Lestache claimed that only Argentina and Venezuela and possibly Chile have achieved a national level of sophistication regarding children's fingerprint identification commensurate with Spain's. In contrast, national discussion of a universal fingerprinting system in the United States has not occurred. There has also been a lack of national discussion in the United States over the use of DNA as a biological marker of infant identity, although a workable system has been patented. However, the Infant Protection and Baby Switching Prevention Act was introduced into the House of Representatives (H.R. 4680) in 1998.[65] The legislation was sponsored by Representative Sheila Jackson-Lee of Texas.

H.R. 4680 would have required all US hospitals, reimbursed under the Medicare system, to "establish and implement security procedures to reduce the likelihood of infant patient abduction and baby switching." Failure to comply with the regulations would have resulted in civil sanctions between $25,000 and $50,000, depending on the size of the hospital. Individuals or organizations altering or destroying an identification record, defined as the newborns' footprint, fingerprint, photograph, written description, or identification tag, would have been subject to criminal penalties. Unfortunately, this bill was never enacted into law. Related legislation proposed in the 106th to 111th congressional sessions was likewise never approved. The latest version of the bill (H.R. 222) was introduced in January 2011 to the 112th Congress .

Third-year law student Tara R. Crane, while enrolled at the Southern Illinois University School of Law, cited several problematic features of this legislation.[66] First, if a hospital were fined for violating a regulation, the money would be paid to the regulatory agency, not to the parents of the switched-at-birth newborns who would be the real victims. Second, a criminal violation would require that intentionality be demonstrated on the part of the responsible individual, and most mix-ups are due to carelessness. Crane concluded that the bill would have failed to fulfill its goal of promoting infant identification safeguards.

Discussion of infant identification procedures in the United States has generally taken the form of guidelines issued by bodies such as the Joint Commission (formerly the Joint Commission on Accreditation of Healthcare Organizations), the American Academy of Pediatrics (AAP), the American College of Obstetricians and Gynecologists (ACOG), and the Federal Bureau of Investigation (FBI). However, while efforts toward implementing infant identification procedures have been encouraged, they have occurred at the local hospital level rather than nationally. Preferred methods have mostly included more secure identity bracelets for mothers and babies and more effective alarm systems should bracelets be removed or babies be taken from the nursery. Stricter protocols, guidelines, and education for staff and patients have also been implemented, although the nature and extent of these programs have varied across facilities. It is possible that the patient empowerment movement I alluded to earlier has inadvertently shifted some responsibility for infant identification from hospitals onto parents, but ideally both should be involved as both stand to suffer in the event of a mistake. Interestingly, the mothers' role in protecting infants' identity was not addressed in the literature I received from Garrido-Lestache. The implication was that in Spain, this responsibility belongs to the hospital and the state, an approach that is very different from that in the United States.

In April 1998, the Chicago-based Joint Commission took two steps toward the prevention of baby switching. It asked the 5,100 hospitals under its jurisdiction to report all baby mix-ups and started tracking such occurrences by means other than hospital communications, such as the press.[67] The Joint Commission is bound by confidentiality agreements not to disclose the identity of hospitals reporting such incidents, a practice that protects medical institutions in a number of ways. Announcements of baby switching damage a hospital's reputation, potentially leading to loss of patients, accreditation, and staff.[68] This probably explains why St. Joseph's Hospital in Orange County, California, initially failed to report the five baby-switching incidents that had occurred there between 1998 and 1999. One such incident, the "Valentine's Day mix-up," in which a mother left the hospital with someone else's baby, was later called "every parent's nightmare" by the hospital's president Larry Ainsworth. Another St. Joseph's Hospital mix-up involved two mothers who breast-fed the wrong baby, mandating hepatitis B and HIV testing of the infants. These mistakes were not reported at first because hospital officials claimed they did not meet criteria for "'reportable'" problems.[69] St. Joseph's silence on these switches is understandable because hospitals do not wish to lose prospective patients. However, infant identification errors must be reported so that problems with newborn management can be found and eliminated. It is difficult to imagine that a baby switch is not reportable.

Preventative steps taken by St. Joseph's are representative of those taken by hospitals elsewhere. In the wake of the intense media attention surrounding its five baby switches, the hospital allocated $500,000 toward electronically encoded wristbands for mothers and babies. The hospital also increased enforcement of its existing policy requiring nurses to compare mothers' and infants' wristbands whenever infants are transported between mothers' rooms and the baby nursery. The incident in which a mother took the wrong baby home was detected only when she, and not the nurse, checked the baby's wristband against her own. St. Joseph's also emphasized the importance of its infant transport procedure, stipulating that nurses deliver only one baby to mothers at a time—a nurse carrying two infants had inadvertently given the wrong babies to mothers sharing a room.

The tightening of nursing policies and procedures seems to be a cosmetic cure, at best. Such changes may be immediate constructive responses to mistakes, but following the resolution of such cases, staff are likely to become less vigilant, especially when media attention starts to ebb. The sophisticated system offered by ICN in Spain would seem to offer greater protection against switches than reinforcing or modifying existing hospital policies.

Various factors other than those mentioned above may contribute to infant mix-ups. Among them are nurses' misreading of numbers on bracelets and identification tags (especially if numbers are not clearly shown), insecurely attached bracelets that may slip off due to shrinkage of newborns' limbs after water loss (a common occurrence in newborns),[70] confusion of newborns with similar names (as happened in Puerto Rico to the two Hernández mothers of twins), miscommunication between nurses and mothers (particularly when their native languages differ), and poorly recorded footprints and fingerprints (due to inadequate staff training).[71]

Parent education has also been encouraged by hospitals following the 1998 Virginia baby-switching incident.[72] Consequently, nurses have been advised to have parents acquaint themselves with their infant's physical features as a safeguard against switching and possible abduction.[73] Pat Staten, associate director of the Joint Commission, claims that parents should be "doing more than counting fingers and toes."[74] Parents are encouraged to check their baby's identification bracelet against their own at all times.

A more formal program provided by Prince George's Hospital in Cheverly, Maryland, called "Tea and Tour," is more proactive. This program allows prospective parents to visit the hospital's maternity unit to better understand the procedures used to protect infant identity.[75] The hospital's reasoning is that parents will feel more comfortable knowing such procedures are in place. However, parents taking the tour might become complacent, assuming no personal responsibility for their baby's identification. They should always exercise awareness. Prince George's Hospital tags newborns with an identity sensor clamped to the infant's umbilical cord. When the clamp is released, staff confirm that the serial number on the sensor matches the serial number on the mother's bracelet.

Some maternity arrangements in some hospitals protect infant identity even if they were not intentionally designed to do so. Couplet care, also known as mother-baby care, is an alternative approach to the post-partum hospital management of mothers and babies.[76] Traditionally, mothers and newborns have remained separated from one another and have been assigned to nurses with specific specializations in mother and infant care. In the 1940s, the practice of rooming-in, in which mothers and babies share their room but not their nurses, was instituted in some facilities. By 1992, 27 percent of Florida hospitals had instituted couplet care in which the same nurse was responsible for mother and baby; today, both couplet care arrangements are offered more frequently to new mothers in Florida and nationwide. By 1998, 60 percent of maternity units in US hospitals had implemented various forms of couplet care, and 30 percent were in the process of doing so.[77]

Couplet care that assigns mother and infant management to a single staff member regards mothers and babies as both physically and psychologically interdependent. "The emphasis is on the provision of maternal-newborn care that fosters family unity while maintaining physical safety."[78] The specific physical safety aspects of couplet care were not detailed in the report I reviewed. However, infants' physical safety may be increased due to fewer transports and greater nurse familiarity with both mother and baby. A study comparing mothers' levels of satisfaction with one-nurse versus two-nurse couplet care showed similar results; however, these two situations did not compare the mothers' concerns over whether or not babies were theirs with those of mothers who were not in couplet care.

I would like to see a study comparing baby-switching concerns between mothers in couplet care arrangements and mothers in traditional postpartum care. It is likely that mothers receiving couplet care, in conjunction with the collection of fingerprints or other biological data, would feel most at ease regarding the identity of their infants. However, once hospitals adopt more technical methods of infant identification, couplet care as a protection against infant switching may become irrelevant.

Several highly sophisticated procedures for the biological identification of babies have been developed, some prompted by the reports of baby-switching incidents. The surprise finding is that these procedures have not as yet been widely implemented.

Dermatoglyphics, DNA, and Digitization

In 1988, the American Academy of Pediatrics (AAP) and the American College of Obstetricians and Gynecologists (ACOG) stated, "Individual hospitals may want to continue the practice of footprinting or fingerprinting, but universal use of this practice is no longer recommended."[79] This view was based on studies showing that infants' footprints taken by hospital personnel were often recorded improperly, rendering them useless for identification. These findings were confirmed by a 1993 study showing that 89 percent of newborns' footprints (provided by twenty infants from five centers) were unreadable by a police expert.[80] Both the AAP and ACOG advocated analyses of DNA or human leukocyte antigen (HLA), genes relating to the immune system, for reliable identification of newborns.

Garrido-Lestache was an advocate of fingerprints, not footprints, given that infant growth compromises comparison of earlier and later images of the foot. But Garrido-Lestache also emphasized the importance of excellent training in fingerprinting techniques, a policy that would apply to any scientific procedure. I find it puzzling that two professional organizations, AAP and ACOG, while recognizing the difficulties posed by footprints, did not suggest that they be discontinued *and* did not recommend them—conflicting conclusions expressed in the same sentence. Perhaps these organizations hesitated to advocate discontinuing footprinting lest they be held accountable in the event of switches. Subsequent to their policy statement, several highly sophisticated infant identification techniques have been developed and applied on a limited scale.

The DNA Diagnostics Center (DDC) in Fairfield, Ohio, performs DNA testing on mothers and babies when their biological relatedness is in question.[81] The company's website section on child identification services states, "DNA is the ultimate identifier. Our child ID services are meant to give parents peace of mind in many circumstances, including suspected baby switching and child identification services." DDC additionally advocates DNA testing to assure relatedness when called for in specific situations, such as meetings between adoptees and birth relatives, reunions of relatives through immigration, and transplantation of embryos into mothers' wombs, services it has provided for the last ten years. DDC does not discuss DNA analysis with respect to making it a mandatory national procedure, but some geneticists have.

In 2001, Rick Staub and Caroline Caskey of Texas were issued a patent for their development of the first systematic DNA-based method for newborn identification and tracking.[82] Staub is the senior manager and laboratory director of Orchid Cellmark, a DNA-testing laboratory in Dallas, Texas. The invention is intended to ensure identification of newborns at birth and maintain correct mother-infant pairing until hospital discharge. Staub and Caskey's procedure involves performing DNA analysis on infants and/or mothers on one or more occasions while they are in the hospital. In support of their method, Staub and Caskey noted in their patent document the aforementioned difficulties associated with footprints, as well as the inability to guarantee an association between an infant's footprint and a particular mother other than that a particular print appears on the mother's hospital record. They dislike external devices, such as wristbands or other tags, because of possible alteration or replacement. In further support of their invention, Staub and Caskey cited a survey of two hundred expectant mothers, of whom 85 percent indicated their willingness to pay for a methodology that would guarantee their newborn's identity.

In its simplest form, Staub and Caskey's method would extract the infant's DNA at birth, placing the sample on a tamper-proof card with the names of the mother and infant in the presence of a witness. A second DNA sample would be obtained at the time of hospital discharge and compared with the first sample. Variations on this process would include multiple samplings of both mothers' and infants' DNA, as well as the collection of mixed samples (samples containing both maternal and infant DNA) obtained from umbilical cord blood or amniotic fluid (before birth) or from manually mixing samples containing both maternal and infant DNA. At the time of Staub and Caskey's 2001 patent, analyses of both mothers' and infants' DNA were technically feasible, but some felt they were not cost-effective on a routine basis, as would be necessary in a maternity ward.

I believe the most attractive feature of Staub and Caskey's method is that DNA analyses would be performed either before or immediately after birth *and* upon hospital discharge. This practice would confirm that the initially identified mother-infant pairing was present when the mother took the baby home.

Obtaining fetal cells from amniotic fluid or chorionic villi (microscopic projections on the outer membrane surrounding the fetus) prior to birth is done to screen fetuses for serious genetic conditions, such as hemophilia, Tay-Sach's disease, and Down syndrome. The most common procedures, amniocentesis and chorionic villus sampling (CVS), are invasive, posing a slight chance of miscarriage; fetal cells would be gathered by amniocentesis according to Staub and Caskey's method. In December 2010 researchers at the Chinese University of Hong Kong discovered a way to fully analyze a fetus's genome from cells carried in the mother's blood.[83] This technique, while not yet cost-effective, has been applauded for eliminating the risk associated with current screening methods. But this technique could also be used to type maternal and fetal DNA prenatally for the purpose of newborn infant identification. In cases of multiple pregnancy, comparing twins' DNA profiles would reveal if they were identical or fraternal, information that might potentially avert an accidental switch.[84]

A different kind of infant identification process evolved out of the trend toward electronic medical records (EMRs). Wonju Hospital in South Korea had received many patient requests for a system that would allow fast access to medical information about their infant as well as information sharing with relatives. Intel developed a device that can accomplish these tasks with the added benefit of protecting infants against baby-switching incidents.[85] A successful pilot program led to the adoption of a radio frequency identification (RFID) device at Wonju.

Following the birth of a newborn, the RFID device generates two identical tags based on the mother's identification number. One tag is inserted into the baby's ankle bracelet, and the other tag is inserted into the mother's wrist bracelet; the baby's bracelet is in place before the tag is created. Nurses use a personal digital assistant (PDA) to record the baby's vital details. Every time the baby is involved in a new activity, such as a bath or feeding, the RFID tag is scanned, and the action is recorded as a new event. The PDAs communicate wirelessly on a local network that transmits the information to the hospital's Ethernet system, making it available to family members through specially designed kiosks in the hospital. Infant identification is protected by a PDA RFID reader that verifies all mother-baby transactions. At the time of discharge from the hospital, the reader is used to make a final check that the mothers' and babies' tags match. However, proponents of fingerprinting and DNA analysis would argue that bracelets can be removed and reattached, even when they are part of sophisticated systems.

The dermatoglyphic, DNA, and digital systems seem simple and error-free, but all new technologies require adequate staff training to be effective. I believe the above methods will increase the confidence of hospitals and patients in the correct identification of infants, but human error is always a concern. Whether or not these newer procedures will be significantly more effective in preventing baby mix-ups than skillfully performed fingerprinting is unknown. A key to infant protection is not only public awareness that baby switching can and does happen but also an examination of how and why it happens. Had Débora and Laura been aware that such mistakes are possible, they may have taken their infants' physical differences more seriously.

Parties responsible for infant identity mistakes must be held accountable, and families and children who are unnecessarily hurt by such events must be compensated. Cases coming to light are relatively rare, and precedents that can guide legal decisions are often nonexistent. Determining compensation for damages is not easy.

7

DETERMINING THE DAMAGES

One hundred and thirty-seven reared-apart twin pairs participated in the Minnesota Study of Twins Raised Apart
(MISTRA) between 1979 and 1999, but of the entire group, only one
lawsuit was filed against a single party responsible for a twin pair's separation.[1] The Ottawa Children's Aid Society was sued by the families of
switched identical twins, Brent and George, whose story I described in
chapter 2. For the Minnesota Study's remaining twins, separated mostly
due to illegitimate birth, maternal death, parental incapacity, or financial
hardship, meeting their co-twin was a joy. These twins, most of whom
were adoptees, were delighted to meet a biological family member, especially someone who looked like them. The decisions that divided these
twins were unfortunate but generally reflected each family's circumstances at the time. In contrast, the switched-at-birth twins were never
intended to be apart—nor were the switched non-twin children meant
to be separated from their families.

CASE DETAILS FROM THE TWINS' ATTORNEYS

The discovery of nearly every documented switched-at-birth twin case
described in this book was followed by a lawsuit, filed either jointly or
separately by the families involved. The Canary Islands case is note-

worthy because it was the only case on record filed by the twins themselves. Moreover, Delia and Begoña chose different attorneys—Delia worked with Socorro, while Begoña, Beatriz, and Laura worked with Peregrina—although their lawyers sometimes worked together on court-related matters. Peregrina said that before the claim was taken to court, Delia came to his office with Begoña, then decided to work with Socorro.[2] "I don't know why [Delia] made that decision. She came to my office to comment on how surprised she was to find she had a twin, but we didn't talk about the legal process," he told me. Perhaps Delia believed that a different attorney would give closer consideration to her specific interests and complaints since her situation—as a lone twin reared in an unrelated family and a leukemia patient denied access to her identical twin's bone marrow—was unique.

Socorro provided his own opinion of the twins' legal arrangements when I saw him in his office in 2009.[3] "The fact that this case was taken by two different lawyers is symptomatic—it's the proof that the families do not have a good relationship. . . . Peregrina and I call each other, we comment on things, we exchange information, but we work independently. . . . The natural relationship that exists between sisters or mother and daughter does not exist in this case. This is a crossroad between two people who belong to different family environments, and with two different families [there are] two different kinds of problems." Peregrina also acknowledged that he and Socorro were partners on this case, but Peregrina disagreed that the twins' choice of two lawyers reflected negative feelings.

Both attorneys were aware of Delia and Begoña's difficulties in developing their relationship as twins. The twins had also talked to me about this problem, alluding to Delia's fear of her parents' reaction and Begoña's concern for Beatriz's feelings.

In another odd twist, Delia's parents, Débora and Juan, filed a separate lawsuit against the Canarian Public Health Service and hired Peregrina, the lawyer working for their daughter's twin, Begoña, to represent them. Perhaps their decision to use an attorney other than the one representing their daughter was intended to distance themselves from Delia. After all, Débora and Juan were grief stricken and angry that Delia had known the truth for eight years while, by the time of litigation, they had known it for only one. To complicate matters further, at the time of this writing, Peregrina had been working on Débora and Juan's case with yet another attorney; when Jessica and I met the family at the morgue, someone told us that the gentleman we saw talking to Débora and Juan was "the other lawyer."

In September 2009, Peregrina told me he was in the "early stage of [the parents'] case," and that the administrative file (materials provided to the court by the health service) was incomplete. He, therefore, filed a petition to the judge requesting that he be provided with any missing materials. These same bureaucratic failures had delayed the processing of the twins' and Beatriz and Laura's case as well, keeping the case in court for an additional year and a half. "We think [the health service] acted in bad faith," Peregrina asserted. Débora and Juan's case had also been delayed due to scheduling difficulties regarding their psychiatric assessment. Peregrina told me, "They were [scheduled] today [September 14, 2009], at 9:00 AM; we went there, and the Canarian Public Health Service didn't even know the appointment existed."

LEGAL PROCEEDINGS

Spain's jurisdictional system is composed of four courts: civil (claims for civil and commercial issues); criminal (claims for violation of the criminal code); social (claims for social security and employment issues); and administrative (claims based on acts of public administration).[4] The lawyers presented the twins' case against the Canary Islands Health Service in the administrative court. What constitutes administrative proceedings varies from country to country, but these courts deal with "judicial remedies" for individuals who feel wronged by "acts of governmental bureaucracy."[5] In the United States, such grievances are addressed in ordinary courts or in courts dealing with specific matters, such as federal taxes.[6]

The twins' claim went through a series of filings, judgments, and appeals between 2004 and 2009. Table 7.1 provides a timeline of the events that transpired. These events are described more fully later in this chapter. The table shows that the case moved slowly through the court, with gaps between events lasting up to four years.

Going to court was not the first legal step that the lawyers took. Initially, people in Spain must bring their case to the public administration directly and wait six months for a response. In the event that the administration (in this case the Canarian Health Service) does not rule within that time, then the parties involved can go to court; silence on the part of the administration can be considered a denial of the claim. The Health Service did not respond to Socorro and Peregrina's 2004 claim, so they

Table 7.1. Progress of the Twins' Case through the Spanish Court

March 16, 2004	Socorro and Peregrina filed a complaint against the Canary Islands Health Service (Ministry of Health). The Health Service did not respond, so the lawyers went to court in 2005.
March 10, 2005	The twins, mother, and sister took action against the alleged overruling of the legal claim filed on March 16, 2004. The Canary Islands Health Service offered them very modest compensation, while denying liability.
March 30, 2009	A decision from the judge was rendered.
April 2009	Socorro and Peregrina, as well as the Canary Islands Health Service, filed appeals in response to the decision.
December 11, 2009	The court of appeals (three-judge tribunal) upheld the terms of the March 30, 2009 decision.

Note: Most of the information in this table was provided by Socorro's secretary, Carolina.

filed a lawsuit. The Health Service's subsequent offer of only 700 euros to each client (US$904.00, based on 2005 exchange rates) was rejected by the lawyers on the grounds that it hardly came close to reflecting their clients' pain and suffering.[7] It is worth noting that the Health Service's denial of liability rested on the fact that it was organized differently in 1973 when the twins and Beatriz were born; in fact, the current health service (Servicio Canario de Salud) did not exist at that time. Nevertheless, the Health Service, in the form in which it functioned in the 1970s, was responsible for the delivery and care of the three newborns.[8] In its defense, the health service tried to assert that the babies were exchanged by the parents following their discharge from the hospital.[9] In 2005, Socorro and Peregrina argued their case before the judge, asking for three million euros in damages. There is no jury in the Spanish courts.

In May 2008, when I first contacted Socorro's office to learn more about the twins, he and his associates were eager for information about how similar cases had been resolved in the United States and elsewhere. As mentioned previously, there were no Spanish legal precedents to which he could refer because Spain's previous baby-switching cases had not led to lawsuits. Delia and Begoña's case was unique in this respect. Socorro explained, "In Spain, when we talk about charges, we refer to criminal proceedings, but in this case we were dealing with administrative proceedings. We couldn't file the case against the doctors and nurses in the criminal court because the [time] period had passed. . . . We filed a claim so that the court could consider the hospital's unacceptable practices and, as a consequence, [the health service] could be held responsible." In describing the case, Socorro used the Latin expressions *res ipso lucutor* (the thing speaks for itself) and *pretium doloris* (the price of the pain; a common expression in French law). He meant that the hospital's extreme negligence toward his client was clear and deserved compensation.[10]

Moral damage was the basis for the lawsuits filed by the two attorneys. In Spanish law, *personal moral damage* is defined as the "damageable assets that belong to the noneconomic sphere of the person." They include the personal rights of "life, mental and physical integrity, freedom, honor, privacy, self-image, identity, [and] creativity)."[11] Judges in Spain determine which damages are recoverable and how they are quantified with reference to compensation.

Peregrina explained that the twins' case was filed for "pain and suffering," the kind of moral damage that is not highly valued in Spain. Peregrina defined pain and suffering in his clients' case as the emotional distress caused by Begoña's loss of association with her twin sister and Beatriz's loss of association with her biological family. Socorro considered Delia's moral damages as having been deprived of growing up with her biological parents and twin sister and never knowing her biological father. He stressed that not having Begoña as an ideal bone marrow donor exacerbated her suffering when she developed leukemia, even though she was unaware of being a twin at the time; recall that Delia underwent a risky medical procedure because a suitable donor could not be found. "I consider the psychological damage part of the moral damage, but in this case the [psychological damage] is a less important part. It's more important to consider the other things we are talking about." By this, I understood Socorro to mean that Delia's loss of her twin as a suitable bone marrow donor and the loss of her biological family were serious personal injuries and would weigh more heavily in his argument to the court than the psychological consequences associated with them.

According to Socorro, it was difficult to find independent expert witnesses at that time. A newspaper article about the case had described the aforementioned Madrid pediatrician Garrido-Lestache, who was responsible for Spain's infant identification program, as an expert witness, but Garrido-Lestache told me this was not so. However, the twins, Beatriz and Laura, had been evaluated by an expert witness, the court-appointed psychiatrist, Dr. Trujillo.

THE COURT'S DECISION AND THE APPEALS

Knowing how slowly cases proceed through the courts, I did not expect the twins' case to settle before I came to Las Palmas in 2009. However, I received a somewhat surprising e-mail message from Socorro on March 4 that same year, six months before I arrived. Socorro wrote to say, "[Trujillo] reported that the psychiatric sequelae [were] not very important. . . . We are now waiting for the judge's decision. I think the media will publicize it." Four weeks later, the court's decision appeared in the local press.

The decision, determined by Judge Palenzuela, was given to the lawyers on March 30, 2009, and made public on March 31. The text, translated from the Spanish, began:

> Given the expert evidence offered, bearing in mind that the damage can only apply to the period from the knowledge of the exchange until the administrative claim, a court-appointed expert said that the effect on the appellants is mild, without the obvious impact such an extraordinary event would have on their personal, work and social lives.

The total amount to be offered in damages was only 900,000 euros (US$1,195,460 at the time of the decision).[12] Begoña, Beatriz, and Laura were to receive 180,000 euros each (US$239,092), and Delia would receive 360,000 euros (US$478,184). These amounts were considered commensurate with each person's relative degree of suffering. The criteria for deciding the total amount and distribution are unknown. However, Delia's higher award was justified on the basis that she "was caused major damage by not having any kind of relationship with her biological family and the difficulty exacerbated when the treatment of a serious illness was diagnosed which surely would have been alleviated, in part, if she was aware of the existence of a twin sister."[13] The lawyers and Canarian Health Service were given fifteen days to appeal the decision, which they did.

Socorro authored an eloquent and persuasive statement on behalf of his client, Delia. He took serious issue with the administration's view and judge's opinion that the effects of the hospital's mistake on Delia were "mild," further asserting that the psychiatric expert failed to actually demonstrate mild effects. Translated from the Spanish, Socorro wrote,

> At no time did the expert conclude that the damage caused was of a minor nature but on the contrary, said that the damage affected fundamental and essential aspects of life . . . with serious attacks on [such things as] identity, personal dignity and family. . . . That is why we do not understand the conclusion that the effect is "mild."

After citing the various losses that Delia had suffered, Socorro concluded, "With all due respect . . . [this] trial has not shown proportionality or balance between the moral damage . . . and the compensation awarded."

Meanwhile, the Canary Islands Health Service had filed an appeal against the court, rejecting the sentence that required the government to pay the twins 900,000 euros in compensation. Peregrina issued a scathing press release in June 2009 in response to this appeal.[14] He cited evidence that personal data, including the baby's name, the record number, and a mother's fingerprint had been missing from the medical charts. The twins were even referred to as boys in some sections.[15] Peregrina called these errors and omissions "far-reaching deficiencies that directly affected the identification of the newborn."

Peregrina noted other problems, such as poorly handled transfers of the three babies among their incubators, cribs, and treatment areas as well as corrections, erasures, and missing signatures from the medical charts. Peregrina was astounded that in 1973, when the twins and Beatriz were born, scientific procedures were not in place for the accurate identification of newborns. An expert witness, then chief of pediatrics at the Hospital del Pino, confirmed that documentation displayed in the hospital's administrative record was "incomplete and faulty."[16] The witness said he was surprised because similar documents completed for other infants were in good order. He confirmed that the babies had been handled exclusively by hospital personnel, who delivered them to their mothers. It cannot be known at what point the mix-up occurred, but hospital staff appeared to be responsible.

Socorro reflected on the court's decision when I met him in Las Palmas in September 2009. "During the proceedings, [Trujillo] answered all my questions in ways that were consistent with my opinion. But later he came to the conclusion that the damage was mild. You don't need to be a psychologist to realize Trujillo wasn't right." Socorro also said he was surprised by the judge's opinion. "Considering the damage to be 'mild' means that the judge did not understand the nature of the damage. . . . I think the court interpreted the psychiatrist's analysis as saying [our clients] were psychologically affected, but not *that* affected, and decided that 'mild damage' was enough. . . . If you read the statement, you have the impression that the judge overlooked many things in the case. Keeping in mind that this was a unique case in Spain and, consequently, the one that was going to set court precedent, I expected a more well-reasoned judgment. I think even the Health Service thought something was amiss. The judgment doesn't clarify why [the judge] specified the precise amount that she did." Neither Peregrina nor Socorro spoke with the judge subsequent to the ruling.

In December 2009, the appeals filed by the lawyers and health service against the March 30, 2009, decision were rejected. A tribunal composed of three judges determined that the government would pay the twins and their families the 900,000 euros that the court had decided upon previously. A blog entry by Marisol Ayala, a former Canary Islands newspaper writer, applauded, in a candid and sarcastic vein, the rejection of the government's appeal.[17] Ayala asked if the Canary Islands Health Service, which tried to claim that the babies had not been switched at the hospital, believed that the newborns looked at each other from their cribs, put on their shoes and bathrobes, and jumped into the hallway. Then, after roaming around, did they return to the wrong cradle accidentally?

During my last visit to Peregrina's office, I asked him to review the judicial process associated with the lawsuit and the appeal. He said, "Before going to court, I raised a complaint with the Canarian Health Service [which provides nationally sponsored medical care to the citizens of Las Palmas]. They didn't respond, so I felt obliged to take legal action. . . . [Socorro and I] presented proofs and conclusions orally, and the judge [Palenzuela] gives the final opinion. . . . The judge is an impartial figure . . . there to consider the proofs presented, analyze them, and give judgment."

Reflecting on the time of the appeal in April 2009, Peregrina said he did not think the chance for higher compensation on appeal was high. "I think the quantity they offered in the first instance [900,000 euros] is quite a lot for what we are used to here." He said that Begoña and Laura were satisfied with the distribution of the award, but Beatriz felt dejected. "Delia received a higher compensation although both cases were similar." Beatriz was correct in that both she and Delia had been raised by unrelated families. In fact, Peregrina had wondered if Beatriz hadn't suffered the most because she was not as strong emotionally as Begoña. Socorro did not comment on Delia's response as to how the compensation was distributed, but Delia didn't complain.

I believe that Delia's higher compensation can be explained by various factors, several of which were noted by Socorro during the court proceedings. First and most importantly, Delia's lack of access to Begoña as her ideal bone marrow donor had put her life at risk. Second, the death of Delia's biological father when she was a child meant that she would never have the opportunity to meet him. Third, Delia's relations with her rearing family were poor, and they worsened further still when her parents learned of the switch. Of course, Beatriz's lifelong feelings of being different from her rearing family were problematic and cannot be discounted. Her discovery that she was not a biological member of that family traumatized her further, leading to serious emotional and physical complaints. But Beatriz was loved and supported by Laura, Begoña, and her other three siblings, a situation that may have tipped the legal administration somewhat against Beatriz and in favor of Delia.

Each person's experience of the discovery was subjective, shaped by his or her individual personality, social understanding, and life history. My interviews showed me that everyone in both families suffered enormously, though some implied that they suffered more than the others. In contrast, juries, judges, and other disinterested parties aim to assess damages objectively, attaching weights to each person's loss based on legal criteria and their own professional experience. However, even the decisions of supposedly impartial parties are inevitably affected by their personal belief systems, accumulated life experiences, and public opinion pressures. These factors, in conjunction with the attorneys' variable legal skills, produce decisions that strike some people as fair and others as unfair. Beatriz was not assertive, but Delia was, and that might have made all the difference in how their respective lawyers and psychiatrist assessed and presented their case.

Beatriz's disappointment at her reduced award reminded me of another disappointed twin in a similar case. Canadian twin Brent Tremblay received lower compensation than Marcus Holmes, who had been raised as George Holmes's accidental (virtual) twin. Brent had been raised apart from his twin in an adoptive family, most likely intended for Marcus. Brent's mother, upset by her son's financial outcome, wrote in her diary, "Everyone focused more on Marcus, but which is more traumatic? To find out you were not adopted and should have been (Marcus)—or to find out you were adopted and weren't supposed to be (Brent)?" Like the Canary Islands case, the overall complaint (the baby switch between Brent and Marcus) and the responsible party (the Ottawa Children's Aid Society) were not in dispute. But both cases also demonstrate the tension between clients' subjectivity and judges' objectivity in assessing relative damages. Although both cases have been concluded, the question of who suffered the most in each can still be argued.

THE CASE FOR IDENTICAL TWINSHIP

As mentioned, Socorro had difficulty finding expert witnesses who could testify to Delia's difficulties as he was preparing to go to trial. Neither he nor Peregrina was able to obtain testimony from individuals qualified to address the significance of twin loss for both Delia and Begoña. In fact, Socorro appeared to give more importance to Delia's other losses, such as having lost her biological father and the opportunity for a bone marrow transplant from Begoña. Having personally testified many times in legal cases involving wrongful death, injury, and custody of twins, I believe Delia and Begoña's loss of their twin relationship should have been given greater weight. My reasoning is based on research showing an exceedingly close bond between most identical twins, as well as reared-apart twins' greater affinity for their co-twin than for their adoptive siblings.[18] Even young twin children meeting for the first time can show unusual attraction to one another.[19] Research also shows that adult twins generally grieve more intensely for the loss of their co-twin than for the loss of other relatives.[20] And twins whose twin brothers and sisters are stillborn or perish shortly after birth nonetheless mourn their loss without ever having known them.[21]

Twinship remains significant and meaningful in twins' lives despite physical separation or loss. Twins' reared apart who meet as adults can never recover the lost years between them, and twins who lose a twin at birth grieve for a relationship unfulfilled. That is why I object to the court's judgment that the twins' and Beatriz's suffering began at the time the mix-up was discovered. Suddenly finding a twin in adulthood revises everything about one's personal identity—who one is and who one should have been. Some discoveries are small, such as Delia's discovery that she and Begoña had the same odd gait; others are monumental, such as the twins' immediate social connection and rapport, denied to them for twenty-eight years. Life events that happened previously take on new meaning after a twin is found. Begoña and Beatriz had never felt like twins and had difficulty reconciling the physical and behavioral differences between them. With news of the switch, they suddenly understood why. Still, I believe a case could have been made for Beatriz having lost her twin, an extremely devastating loss from which the nearly seven hundred twinless twins I have studied never fully recovered. Begoña stayed loyal to her sister, but Beatriz lost whatever sense she had of herself as a twin, an identity that true surviving twins can still claim but that she could not.

Trying to explain the reasons behind the close connections between identical twins has challenged psychologists for years. Some of the other aforementioned switched-at-birth twins provide keen insight into this question. Edyta, who grew up apart from her twin sister Kasia, recalled, "We were meeting each other for the first time, but I felt as if I knew everything about her."[22] George said of Brent, "My brother Marcus was doing his thing, and we couldn't wait to do ours."[23] And ten-year-old Ernstli, finally somewhat accustomed to his new home, said to his twin, "I have found the other half of me."[24] I believe twins' perceptions of their shared intellectual skills, personality traits, and physical features may trigger identical twins' unusual attraction to one another. Their rapport may be analogous to, on a much grander scale, the affinity travelers feel when meeting someone from their hometown.

The fact that twins were part of the Canary Islands case added a unique layer of complexity to the situation. But whether twins or non-twins are switched at birth, the damage does not begin when the mistake is detected. Instead, it has been constantly occurring, accumulating continually over the lifetimes of the individuals in question, although they don't know it. Once the switch is discovered, nothing in life is the way it once appeared, the greatest damage being the destruction of beliefs about one's place in the family and to whom one actually belongs. Andrzej, father of the Polish switched-at-birth twins, told me that Nina, raised as Kasia's "twin" for seventeen years and now married with a child, recently asked her aunt, "What is to become of me?" I have tried to think of other more commonly occurring examples or analogies that convey this sense of radical change and disorientation. Perhaps it is like discovering that your favorite author has been plagiarizing published texts. Or learning that someone whom you truly respected has been living a lie. Or finding out that your life's work was never really appreciated by your boss, who hired you as a favor. But it is probably closest to discovering that the person with whom you shared a significant relationship for thirty years never really loved you and that you, in fact, were living the lie.

THE OTHER CASES

Of all the switched twins, Delia, Begoña, and Beatriz were the only adults to file lawsuits on their own—the twins' mother, Laura, filed with Begoña and Beatriz, but Begoña took the lead. Brent, George, and Marcus's families filed on their sons' behalf. But as adults, the twins and non-twins who were younger at the time of the discovery can look back on the appropriateness of the legal decisions that affected their lives.

In June 1948, the justice of the peace of Fribourg, Switzerland, determined that the switched seven-year-old boys, Ernstli (Charles) and Paul, were to be returned to their biological families. As noted earlier, the nonswitched identical twin Philippe Joye is the only surviving member of the threesome. In a March 2008 newspaper interview, sixty-six-year-old Philippe recalled, "It was terrible for Charles. In our house we didn't speak a word of German. [Charles's] adjustment was difficult. He wondered when he would return home, not understanding what was happening. . . . Paul is not happier—his mother cannot stand this 'new' child who is nothing like Ernstli."[25]

Charles, who passed away in 2008, wrote candidly about the return of the two children in a book about his life.[26] In a section titled "They were not my mothers but still . . . ," he wrote,

After the exchange I was reunited with my real mother, Madelaine, who I had to share with a husband and a brother. In comparison to my monopolistic position with my first mother I was frustrated and I have never had the same relationship with her that my brother Philippe had. . . . After the exchange, my relationship with my first mother was very limited since if I recall correctly I met her only three times when I would run away from the house of Joye. . . . It was only when I reached 10 that I finally had to admit that I had only one mother. . . . [Mme. Vatter] half-opened the door without letting me in and said, "Go back home, you are not my son." Today I understand [Mme Vatter's] decision to keep her door shut. . . . In my opinion she could not come to terms with the consequences of this exchange.

Charles also reflected on the decision to return the two boys to their families. He disagreed with his brother Philippe, who felt the return severely damaged many people and seriously affected the twins' childhood and adolescent years. But Charles understood his brother's views—his mother, Mme. Joye, had a loving relationship with Paul but "instead of him she found a little boy whom she could not recognize as her own." The twins' father, Philippe Joye Sr., most likely considered the situation from a long-term perspective. Charles wrote, "For my father the exchange had to be done because what would have happened if ten years later whilst meeting me in the town of Fribourg I would have asked, 'Mr. Joye, why did you not do the exchange as I was your real son?'"

Charles concluded, "I do not think there was another solution. In an ideal world it might have been possible to make arrangements to facilitate the transition, but my first mother [Mme. Vatter] did not have the psychological strength to accept the situation." I believe that the children should have stayed with the families who loved them and to whom they were so closely attached. Informal birthday celebrations, school events, and family vacations could have been arranged easily because the families lived in the same town. Mme. Vatter may have had the strength to take part in these get-togethers.

I wonder if the final outcome for the Fribourg twin switch was determined by considering the short-term versus long-term consequences of the exchange. In the short term, the exchange was excruciating for the two small boys, who could not comprehend why they were being taken from their families. The exchange was also painful for Philippe, who missed his brother Paul, had to become familiar with a new twin brother, and lost the parental attention that was needed to help Charles adjust. In the long term, the exchange let Charles and Philippe enjoy their identical twinship and let their parents and Paul's mother raise their own sons. But the two mothers never recovered from the trauma of relinquishing the children they loved, so this long-term result does not seem completely advantageous.

I believe the basis for the decision is captured in a very significant point raised by Charles in his book. Recall that Charles imagined a hypothetical meeting between his father and himself ten years later (when Charles would have been seventeen) at which teenage Charles might have challenged the wisdom of not making the exchange; by then, Charles would have been aware of being denied relationships with his biological father, mother, and twin brother. It is likely that this long-term consideration swayed the magistrate in reaching the decision.

I have always been a strong advocate for keeping twins together, but there are exceptional cases. I believe that if the two children had stayed with the families that raised them and had been given frequent visitation opportunities, everyone in both families would have been spared lifelong pain and suffering. Such an arrangement would not have been difficult because the families lived in close proximity to one another. When the twins and Paul were older, they could have made their own decisions about how to live their lives. There are models in place for such arrangements.

Of those families who have participated in my research since 2006, most parents of separately adopted Chinese twin children bring the twins together as much as possible, especially on their birthdays and holidays. They hope their children will come to know each other well so they can decide on their own how much time they want to spend together in the future. My research is not limited to separated twins from China. The parents who each adopted a one-year-old identical male twin from Vietnam met several times each year despite a thousand-mile distance between them. The twins, Ben and Henry, enjoyed each other's company so much that departures were very painful for them and for their families. When the twins were almost four, Ben's family relocated across the United States to Henry's hometown to allow the boys to grow up together as friends, neighbors—and twins.

An inescapable difficulty faced by all of the families I've detailed was that their legal cases were presented publicly. The story of Philippe, Paul, and Charles was covered in newspapers worldwide, and the decision as to whether or not to switch Charles and Paul again was debated among the twenty-five thousand citizens of their town. The Joyes were accused by some of trying to benefit socially and financially from the case. These accusations were made because some people covet the money and attention that others seem to acquire easily. However, these charges were unfair: I believe that Mme. Joye's memoir, *He Was Not My Son*, shows that she only wanted to do what was right. The Joyes did not seek media attention; the case was popular with the press because of its scientific quality and human interest. Mme. Joye's book also strikes me as an outlet for her overwhelming emotional unrest.

The press also chronicled the lawsuit filed by the Ofmańskis and Wierzbickis in Poland, exacerbating their pain by making it widely known. People learned that "yellowing hospital notes" were key pieces of evidence in the accidental exchange of Nina and Edyta.[27] They also learned that the seven family members—the two sets of parents, twins, and non-twin sister—were awarded a total of 1.9 million zlotys, equivalent to 425,000 euros or US$566,000 in 2006. Andrzej Ofmański, the twins' father, said, "I'm not looking for the guilty party or parties. That would be impossible all these years later. But we want compensation. In the United States, we'd get millions of dollars. In Poland, we're asking for very little, just enough to buy [an apartment] for our girls."

Andrzej explained that in Poland, lawyers are not allowed to receive a percentage of the compensation as they are in the United States.[28] In Poland, lawyers' fees are set in advance, and the huge sums discourage many people from seeking justice. However, in conjunction with his work at the television station, Andrzej had met an attorney who agreed to accept the case. The families paid the requested trial fees out of their own funds. Nine years after the discovery and seven years after the legal proceedings began, the two families were the first in Poland to receive compensation in a trial against a healthcare institution in this type of case. They agreed to the price of three small apartments, based on housing costs in 2009 when the case settled.

The story of the Polish twins has not really concluded because everyone is still dealing with the aftermath. Nina worries that Kasia will stop loving her, but Kasia believes their shared time together outweighs their lack of biological connection. Edyta has severed the relationship with her rearing family and with Kasia, her real twin—no one has heard from her for months. The two mothers remain seriously depressed at the time of this writing. The Ofmanksi family has pictures of all three girls displayed in their home. Andrzej said, "Now I'm the father of three. I love all three, I treat them equally."[29] But he also said he wishes the truth had never been known.

Legal proceedings surrounding the 1985 double twin switch in Puerto Rico involving Tairí and Mari and Samantha and Jennifer also played out in a public way. The case also ran an unusual course in court. As noted earlier, Tairí and Mari's grandfather, Pablo De León López, filed the lawsuit because as a Saint Croix resident he could sue in federal court. As residents of Puerto Rico, the twins' parents, Juan and Dulce, could have filed only at the local level. De León contended that he had visited the twins twice a month and had grown especially attached to Samantha (then called Tairí), whom he had nicknamed "La Canita" (straw) because of her blonde hair.[30] He charged the Corporacion Insular de Seguros (CIS), the hospital's malpractice insurer, for his own pain and suffering and that of his son and daughter-in-law. The jury decided on an award of

US$800,000, leading to a new motion by CIS claiming it could not be sued in federal court. That motion was dismissed.

There was no question that the hospital was negligent in caring for the twins or that the families suffered from the switch. However, Judge Hector M. Laffitte reduced the $800,000 jury award to $110,000. A court document cites his reasons for reducing the amount: "No medical or other expert testimony was presented in connection with the damage claim; that De León contracted no lasting physical or mental impairment; that he saw his granddaughters no more than twice a month before the mix-up was discovered; and that afterwards, he maintained his relationship with La Canita to the degree possible."[31] The family preferred not to comment to me on the nature of the settlement.

When I spoke with Laffitte in January 2010, he remembered being struck by the different backgrounds of the two families—Tairí and Mari's parents were comfortable financially, whereas Jennifer and Samatha's mother lived in the housing projects.[32] He also recalled Dulce's upset over the discovery. "She was not really allowed to present evidence [because] she was not a plaintiff. The lawyer talked me into accepting her testimony, and her emotions swayed the jury."

The mother of twins Jennifer and Samantha, Rosaura Hernández, also hired attorneys. In July 2010, I corresponded with José A. León Landrau, who represented Hernández, but only after the judgment had been entered by the court. (Rosaura's original lawyer, Angel Derkes, is no longer practicing law in Puerto Rico and could not be reached.) Landrau told me that once the judgment was final, Rosaura and her twin daughters put the past behind them.

DETERMINING THE DAMAGES

Lawsuits cannot replace what these parents and children lost. Parents lost that most cherished of experiences, namely raising a child that is theirs. Switched twins and non-twins raised by people from whom they may differ greatly may feel like outsiders in their own family. Other brothers and sisters also miss out on true sibling relationships that should have been theirs. Relationships between husbands and wives can also unravel. The answer to the question of whether or not individuals can be adequately compensated for a mistake that so drastically altered their lives is no. The best that families can hope for is to identify the responsible parties and, by calling attention to their grievance, attempt to prevent future incidents from happening. Tairí and Mari's mother Dulce was advised by her attorney to file a claim, partly for these reasons. Dulce said the hospital where she delivered her twins has replaced wristbands with electronic sensors.[33]

Newspaper articles about the Canary Islands case drew responses from readers, most of whom were supportive but some of whom were dismissive. The latter may have been driven, in part, by the fact that the twins' financial compensation would be drawn from their taxes. But I expect that virtually everyone, when pressed, would agree that some form of compensation was necessary. The switched-at-birth twins cases raise questions about assessing both the emotional cost and monetary value of potential lives not lived relative to those that were.

One might argue that if the actual life (the one that was not intended but was created due to the switch) was judged to be less favorable than the potential of the one intended, then a financial award is justified. But if the unintended life appeared to be better than the likelihood of the one that was supposed to be, would financial compensation be justified? The answer to this question is also yes. The *circumstance* under which the change occurred is the crucial point—and in all the documented switched-at-birth twins cases, the circumstances were not intended, and the cause was negligence.

The difficulty in determining the damages in cases like these is well expressed in a court document, written in English, associated with the claim made by De León, Tairí and Mari's grandfather: "In cases like this, juries and judges face an unenviable task. It is agonizingly hard to place a monetary value on a grandparent's misplaced affection, or on loss of contact with a descendant during her formative years, or on the emotional turmoil attendant to disruption of one's nuclear family. To pretend that this translation of distress into dollars does not involve a certain amount of guesswork would be to ignore the obvious."[34]

There have been attempts by the twins and their families to answer a different question: Would the twins and their families have been better off not knowing what had happened in the delivery room years ago? Kasia and Edyta's father says yes: "I'd have preferred to continue living as we did before." Brent's father despaired because he perceived that knowledge of the switch destroyed his happy family unit. And Mme. Joye, now deceased, may have ultimately regretted the school she chose for her two boys—the same school that Ernstli attended—where the switch was apprehended. She mourned Paul's loss more than she celebrated Ernstli's (Charles's) presence.

Some of those who have unknowingly experienced a switch will remain happy twins or contented parents, never realizing that they or their children are biologically connected to other families. Among them must be some fraternal twins and non-twins who are less likely than identicals to discover a switch: since they look different, no one confuses them. But if they should somehow meet as adults, establishing their relationship could be difficult, especially if parental DNA is unavailable due to death or inaccessibility. In the event that other siblings are available, analysis of mitochondrial DNA (extracellular DNA transmitted intact by mothers to all their children) would confirm or disprove shared maternal ancestry. If the switched-at-birth child is male, and there are brothers in the presumed biological family, then Y chromosome analysis could assess sibling relationships and shared paternal ancestry. That is because Y chromosome transmission occurs only from fathers to sons and the Y chromosome is passed on intact except for possible mutations. Identical twins share the same DNA, so confirming their relationship is straightforward, unaffected by parental or sibling DNA analyses.

228 Someone Else's Twin

Switched-at-birth twin cases do not go away quietly, if at all. Both Socorro's and Peregrina's websites include legal documents, press reports, televised segments, and other materials relevant to the twins' case.[35] The quantity of material is impressive, reflecting the social significance of, the legal importance of, and the human interest in the twins' unusual life stories. Socorro maintained that their case was not an absurd claim and acknowledged its important place in Spanish legal history. "[It] was quite a complex demand—it was the first one in Spain, and we made use of the United Nations Convention on the Rights of the Child."[36]

The 1989 United Nations Convention on the Rights of the Child remains the first legally binding mechanism for acknowledging human rights relevant to individuals younger than eighteen years of age.[37] Relevant to any of the switched twins' cases is that the parent-child relationship enjoys unique social and legal status, as stated within the convention's fifty-four articles and two optional protocols. The family is regarded as a fundamental societal entity and a natural environment for the growth, protection, and well-being of children. The preamble states that the child "should grow up in a family environment, in an atmosphere of happiness, love and understanding." Article 3 states that children's best interests be given "primary consideration."[38] Of course, parents unable to raise their children due to unfavorable circumstances may seek alternative rearing situations, such as adoptive homes or placement with relatives. This is assumed to be done with children's best interests in mind.

The twins' and Beatriz's parents wanted to raise their daughters, yet they did not raise them due to hospital oversight. In accordance with the 1989 Convention's statement, and as stated by Socorro, "the fundamental right to non-interference in personal identity and the family, the fundamental right to personal dignity . . . and the fundamental right to physical and moral integrity" were violated in Delia's case.[39] The same claim extends to Begoña, Beatriz, their parents, and every family member involved in the switched-at-birth cases described in this book. But Delia, Begoña and Beatriz were adults, over the age of eighteen years, so Socorro actually applied the convention's principles to them retrospectively. I believe his approach was appropriate and legitimate. Even if the three women and their families were unaware of the switch when the twins and Beatriz were growing up, their family circumstances and personal identities were jeopardized during that time. The court's claim that their damage began when the mistake was discovered, and affected only the years that followed, is further challenged in view of these considerations.

Questions as to whether or not and to what extent children's best interests (i.e., association and protection by their parents) are violated or upheld are important and timely in view of the many diverse approaches to child conception and child rearing now available. These new approaches, such as donating sperm and eggs to infertile couples and the more frequent participation of surrogate mothers in bearing children they do not raise, direct attention to the circumstances of thousands of adopted and abandoned children seeking to establish contact with their biological families. Adult children who seek to identify their biological parents or siblings may or may not desire social or financial relationships with these individuals. Parents who seek the children they gave up for adoption may or may not be interested in connecting permanently with them. The obligations of these individuals to one another are not straightforward, although adults are better positioned than children to understand these situations and to resolve them, albeit sometimes with legal assistance. Adopted adult children may respect the rights of their biological parents, who may not wish to pursue a future relationship with them due to familial responsibilities, privacy issues, or other concerns. Adult children conceived by sperm or egg donation may also understand that the donor responsible for their conception may prefer to remain uninvolved in their life for similar reasons. The same can be said for biological parents and donors seeking the identity of the children they conceived but did not raise.

The relationships and responsibilities that come with unusual conception and adoption arrangements are more complex when the children involved are still minors. The attachment of adopted children to their rearing parents may conflict with the desires of biological parents who wish to claim them at a later date but legally cannot. In any case, adopted children who are minors lack the authority to make custodial decisions for themselves. Adopted children and children conceived through egg or sperm donation may experience confusion as to who their parents are if parenting is shared by the people with whom the child is related only either legally or biologically but not both. These issues, as they apply to baby switches, have been the focus of several legal analyses. Unfortunately, none of these analyses addresses the question of switches discovered in adulthood, but I will consider extensions of these ideas to the Canary Islands case and others.

> What makes an impression on children are the
> day-to-day interactions with the adults who care
> for them. It is through this activity that an adult
> becomes a parent figure to the child.
> —CHRISTI BAUNACH[40]

Attorney Christi Baunach's essay explained the *doctrine of equitable adoption*, a principle granting the same status to rearing parents as to biological parents when there has been no statutory adoption. (In statutory adoption a law or laws set forth the conditions of the adoption and the responsibilities of the parties involved). The assumption is that the children who have lived with rearing parents for "a significant number of years," even in the absence of formal adoption proceedings, are considered the children of these parents and are entitled to all benefits that would be available to their biological children. Note, however, that the precise number of years that would define such a relationship is unspecified. The burden of proof becomes the love of the parent for the child and the reliance of the child on the parent.

In past cases, the doctrine of equitable adoption allowed a son to contest the will of a father who had never adopted him legally but who had acted as his father in every respect during the son's childhood. The doctrine also allowed a daughter to obtain her father's Social Security benefits although she was not formally adopted by him until she turned nineteen. The principle is analogous to that of common-law marriage in which couples "enter into a marriage relationship, cohabitation sufficient to warrant a fulfillment of necessary relationship of husband and wife, and an assumption of marital duties and obligations."[41]

In her essay, Baunach further applied the doctrine to the previously mentioned Florida baby-switching case involving two girls, Arlena Twiggs and Kimberly Mays, discovered in 1989 when the children were almost nine. Each had been raised by the other child's parents. When Arlena became ill, blood tests were taken, and shortly before she died, the tests revealed that she was not the child of her rearing parents. The infants' identification tags had been switched, causing each to go home with the wrong parents. A 1993 book by author and journalist Loretta Schwartz-Nobel, *The Baby Swap Conspiracy*, suggested that the mix-up was deliberate.[42] In 1978, Barbara Mays delivered a terminally ill child after many years of trying to conceive, while Regina Mays delivered her seventh healthy child three days later in the same hospital. According to Schwartz-Nobel, Kimberly Mays's parents and doctors arranged the switch and altered the hospital records so Mays would have a healthy child. Mays died of cancer in 1998.

Following the discovery, Kimberly's custody was in question; at the time she insisted on remaining with her rearing father, Robert Mays. Baunach reasoned that acknowledgment of a psychological parent-child relationship, by granting custody to the rearing parent and allowing visitation by the biological parent, would be in the best interest of the child (Kimberly). Six months after the judge allowed fourteen-year-old Kimberly to remain with Mays, the father who raised her, she moved in with the Twiggs, a move that the state's lawyer attributed to the personal problems of a teenager.[43]

The doctrine of equitable adoption was exactly what I had in mind when I proposed leaving custody by the rearing parents intact and allowing visitation for the Swiss twins Philippe and Charles (Ernstli) and the non-twin Paul. The two-year-old twin children in Puerto Rico, Tairí and Mari and Samantha and Jennifer, were young enough to be returned to their biological families, and the parents and children did maintain contact for a number of years. However, at one point Dulce was advised to terminate visits with Samantha, the twin she had raised, a decision that may not have been in Samantha's or Dulce's best interests. Samantha protested strongly, and Dulce worried about the child she had come to love. In these two cases, the decisions seem to have been based on legal considerations at the expense of family ties.

Baunach also stated, "In a mistaken baby switch situation, the legal system confronts the child with the fact that his or her 'parents' are not really related to the child at all, thus crumbling the world as it stood for the child."[44] I would add the words "or adult" after "child" in this sentence. The circumstances may differ, but the world still falls apart.

Law student Tara R. Crane's 2000 essay, "Mistaken Baby Switches," addressed several relevant issues, most notably the statutes of limitations that refer to the time at which the discovery of the switch occurred.[45] The statute of limitations could begin when the mistake is first discovered, but that moment is not always clear. For example, Crane noted that the statute of limitations "arguably could commence sometime during the child's development, that is when no physical characteristics resembling the parents emerge or when the child develops a genetic disease that is not common to either parent's family. These are events that could arguably place the parents on notice that the child is not their biological offspring, thereby beginning the statute of limitations."[46] This might move many twins' discovery dates back in time. For example, it could be the day that Philippe and Paul first met Ernstli at school or the day that Dulce wondered why her newborn twins did not look identical. It could also be the day that Brent and George first met as look-alike friends or the day that Laura and Débora took their babies home, each surprised at how little their babies resembled them or their husbands. It could also be the day that Begoña and Delia met for the first time at the Las Arenas Mall.

I believe the problem with defining the statute of limitations as beginning at the time of first suspicion, rather than the time of biological proof, is that none of these mothers or twins ever considered, in those moments, that a baby switch had occurred. It's widely known and accepted that children do not always look like their parents due to the random process of genetic transmission. Legal proceedings cannot go forward in the absence of biological proof, and to suggest otherwise could diminish the family's case by claims of insufficient evidence of a switch.

Crane also underlined the greater difficulty in assessing emotional damages associated with baby switching compared to physical damages, which are unlikely in such cases. Proof of intentionality on the part of hospital staff may sometimes be required to establish blame and to obtain compensation; the only instance of possible intentional baby switching that has been alleged was the Twigg-Mays case in Florida. Furthermore, damages meant to punish responsible parties for human error do not necessarily prevent errors from recurring. Most importantly, Crane made the crucial distinction between contested adoptions and baby switches: that parents of adopted children give them up willingly, whereas parents of switched-at-birth twins do not. Like Baunach, Crane noted that strong parent-child bonds develop over time. "This relationship is considered just as significant as any right biological parents would have."[47] I agree with her conclusion that children's best emotional, social, and physical interests must be considered in court proceedings. But as I noted with respect to Paul and Charles, short-term and long-term interests do not always mesh.

Custodial decisions were not at issue for Delia and Beatriz because of their age at the time of discovery. However, their relationships with their newly discovered biological relatives were not always easy, and their relationships with their rearing relatives were challenged from time to time, in Delia's case more so than Beatriz's. Though Beatriz was assured of her family's love, she harbored doubts. The dearth of articles addressing adult children's rights in baby-switching cases is unfortunate, but it probably reflects the rarity with which such cases are reported. I am aware of only four involving twins: two in the Canary Islands, one in Poland, and one in Canada. But the lack of attention paid to these adult children may also reflect the assumption that adults can cope more easily than children when such mistakes are discovered. As I indicated in chapter 6, this may not be so since children have their lives ahead of them, whereas adults have fewer years during which to adapt. The current availability of DNA testing for assessing biological relatedness may uncover additional switched-at-birth twins in the future. If so, I hope these cases are given the attention they deserve so we can learn from them.

Modern methods of collaborative reproduction, the situation in which sperm and eggs are donated by individuals outside the rearing family, have implications for custodial decisions.[48] A baby created in this way may have four "parents"—the egg and sperm donors and the adoptive parents. These situations draw distinctions between biological and psychological parenthood. If a third woman is involved and gestates the fetus for the potential rearing mother, the relationships and responsibilities among the parties may become even more complex, but the best interests of the child should prevail. When the child in such an arrangement reaches adulthood, the best interests of that adult child are still in question. We can begin by asking if Delia's friend Clarisa, who confused Begoña for Delia and brought about their reunion, acted in the twins' and families' best interests by bringing the look-alikes together.

Clarisa acted quickly—after all, the twins were reunited several hours after she had seen Begoña for the second time. Perhaps Clarisa did not realize the enormity of the responsibility she had assumed. I remember a conversation I had with New Jersey firehouse captain Jimmy Tedesco in the late 1980s after he had reunited identical twins Mark Newman and Jerry Levey.[49] Tedesco had encountered Jerry at a firefighter's convention and was struck by Jerry's resemblance to his friend Mark. Tedesco worried that his plan to bring the twins together might backfire, but he believed it was a chance worth taking. He was right. Mark and Jerry had been given up for adoption, not switched at birth. Jerry's parents had known he was a twin, information they had kept concealed thinking he would never meet Mark. Jerry's parents were noticeably uncomfortable telling me about their decision, which they ultimately regretted.[50]

Had Clarisa stayed silent, or if she had never met Begoña, everyone's lives would have proceeded without the turmoil. The family members are divided on this issue—the twins spoke of the inevitability of their meeting, probably because they had each been confused for the other on several occasions, but Beatriz wished it had never happened. Delia's parents, Débora and Juan, also looked back on their former life as peaceful and uncomplicated. Most parents of older switched twins, such as Andrzej Ofmański in Poland and Jim Carroll in Canada, agreed. Juan and Dulce, parents of Tairí and Mari, reversed the switch when the twins were two, but Juan's thoughts on the issue were mixed: "I would have preferred not to know the truth. . . . Maybe if we hadn't learned of the truth, it could have been better. But I have to thank God for what happened because I found my daughter, my biological daughter, and I also met another child who loved me as a father. It would have been more painful if this had happened even later on." Consistent with that view, Andrzej Ofmański said he wished that the switch had been detected when the girls were young.

There may be an age threshold at which switched-at-birth children can be returned psychologically unharmed to their rightful families. Attachment to a caregiver generally develops between the ages of six to eight months and eighteen to twenty-four months. During these years, children show varying degrees of upset following separation from a familiar person to whom they have become securely bonded. However, a child's temperament, the separation context, and the adult's behavior significantly affect their separation outcomes.[51] Some studies have shown that even children adopted as late as eight years of age, but who had received good care during their first year of life, can form successful social relationships with sensitive and caring adults.[52] These research findings can serve as guidelines only because, ultimately, decisions to return switched children to their biological homes should be made on a case-by-case basis.

Tairí, the only known twin to have been returned to her biological family at age two (aside from Samantha, who was unavailable for an interview), has little recollection of living with Rosaura and her non-twin sister, Jennifer. The families arranged visits among the children before the final exchange took place in order to ease the transition. But based on Juan and Dulce's experience, I believe that for the parents, discovering a baby switch at any age is a painful experience from which they may never recover.

Most people would probably say that the truth is better known than unknown in that it allows for an accurate appraisal of events and better-informed decision making. It is likely that those I have written about in this book would have supported this view before discovering the switches that so disrupted their lives. Knowing the struggles the twins and their families still endure, and putting myself in their place, I wonder how many people might change their minds about knowing the truth in such circumstances. I might.

Interviewing a large sampling of switched-at-birth identical twins and their unrelated siblings would provide greater understanding of the relative genetic and environmental influences on our physical and behavioral characteristics. Greater resemblance between the separated twins than between the unrelated twins, or virtual twins, would demonstrate genetic effects on the traits under study. Only three switched-at-birth twin pairs and their unrelated siblings have been scientifically studied to assess their similarities and differences. In the next chapter I will review these findings and place them in the context of the larger twin literature. I will also consider the current and future situations of Delia, Begoña, Beatriz, and their families.

8

THREE LIVES

Delia's, Begoña's and Beatriz's lives are not just compelling human interest stories and legal landmarks—they are the stuff from which science is made. Scientific knowledge about the origins of behavioral and physical traits is broadened by studying such pairs because the knot of genetic and environmental factors is disentangled. As I explained earlier, the switching of the babies rearranged the three sisters into several genetically and environmentally informative sibling sets. Genetically identical twins (Delia and Begoña) were raised apart, genetically unrelated "twins" (Begoña and Beatriz) were raised together, two sets of biological siblings (Beatriz and Julia, and Beatriz and Gara) were raised apart, and three sets of unrelated siblings (Beatriz and Miguel, Beatriz and José, and Beatriz and María) were raised together. Here are the pairings:

- Delia and Begoña: Reared-apart identical twin pair (MZA)
- Begoña and Beatriz: Virtual twin pair (VT)
- Beatriz and Julia: Reared-apart sibling pair 1 (SIBA-1)
- Beatriz and Gara: Reared-apart sibling pair 2 (SIBA-2)
- Beatriz and Miguel: Reared-together unrelated pair 1 (UST-1)
- Beatriz and José: Reared-together unrelated pair 2 (UST-2)
- Beatriz and María: Reared-together unrelated pair 3 (UST-3)

Other interesting relationships were also generated by the switch, namely children separated from their biological parents (e.g., Delia and Laura, and Beatriz and Débora), as well as children reared by unrelated parents (e.g., Delia and Juan, and Beatriz and Laura). These different kinships have been studied extensively by behavioral geneticists concerned with factors affecting intelligence, personality, and interests.[1] Like twins and siblings, these family relationships are valuable because they help identify the genetic and environmental influences on human traits at the center of nature-nurture debates.

I will examine here the similarities and differences among Delia, Begoña, and Beatriz based on a series of behavioral tests and questionnaires I administered to them. I will do the same for the Swiss brothers (Philippe, Paul, and Charles) and for the Canadian brothers (Brent, George, and Marcus), using information available to me from scientific reports and other publications. Based on findings from previous twin and adoption studies, I have not been surprised by the greater resemblance between the results for identical twins Philippe and Charles and Brent and George, as compared to those for virtual twins Philippe and Paul and George and Marcus. I expected the same pattern of findings to emerge for Delia, Begoña, and Beatriz, but there I found several surprises. Some background material on studies of reared-apart twins and virtual twins will provide a context for the findings.

REARED-APART TWIN STUDIES

The rare pairs of identical or monozygotic (MZA) and fraternal or dizygotic (DZA) twins separated at birth and later reunited have been the focus of several psychological and medical investigations. The first study, conducted in Chicago in 1937, included nineteen MZA twin pairs.[2] This work was followed by a 1962 study in England that included forty-four MZA twin pairs[3] and a 1965 study in Denmark that included twelve.[4] The Minnesota Study of Twins Reared Apart (MISTRA), launched in 1979 and lasting for twenty years, recruited 137 reared-apart twin pairs, 81 MZA twins and 56 DZA twins.[5] Since the 1980s, reared-apart twin studies have also been conducted in Sweden, Finland, and Japan. Several case reports of reared-apart twins raised separately in the United States and Korea are also available.[6]

Most of the 137 twin pairs in the Minnesota Study of Twins Reared Apart were separated because of unusual family circumstances, but there was one notable exception. In the 1950s, the Louise Wise Adoption Agency in New York City separated twins on the advice of its consultant, Columbia University psychiatrist Viola Bernard. Bernard believed twins would benefit from separate placement because they would occupy a special niche in their adoptive families, unencumbered by competition from the co-twin.[7] Bernard probably acted on occasional impressions from her clinical practice because there was no available research to support her claim. Nevertheless, the adoption agency implemented her suggestion, separating five identical twin pairs and one identical triplet set. The triplets, reunited as a result of mistaken identity, participated in the Minnesota Study in 1980. They consulted with attorneys about filing a lawsuit over their separation but did not pursue it.

Reared-apart twin studies have shown genetic influences on virtually every measured physical and behavioral characteristic, but the degree of genetic influence varies somewhat from trait to trait.[8] Genetic effects based on data from the MISTRA are highest for anthropometric (human body measurement) and physiological measures such as fingerprints (.97), height (.86) and brain waves (.80), followed by general intelligence (.69–.75), information-processing speed (.56), personality (.50), social attitudes (.49), and job satisfaction (.30). These percentages do not mean that half of one's personality is shaped by genes or that 70 percent of one's job satisfaction is shaped by the environment. Rather, the percentages mean that some portion of the trait variation among the members of a population is associated with genetic differences among them, while the other portion is associated with experiential differences. The .86 value for height indicates that 86 percent of the height differences among people are explained by genetic differences and the remaining 14 percent are explained by environmental influences, as well as measurement error. As alluded to earlier, one of the most interesting and provocative psychological findings of the last thirty years is that most of the environmental factors that influence behavior are those that are not shared among family members but are experienced uniquely by each individual. Siblings' sharing the same home contributes only modestly to their behavioral resemblance and then only during childhood.[9] The relative importance of genetic influences is captured by the similarities between reared-apart twins.

That a closer social relationship exists between identical twins than fraternal twins has been established. This difference was mirrored in my 2003 assessment of relationships among the identical and fraternal reared-apart twins studied in Minnesota.[10] But the most intriguing finding was that twins meeting for the first time indicated feeling closer to and more familiar with the twin they had never known as compared to an unrelated sibling they had known their entire lives. This finding demonstrated that similarity, or perhaps perceptions of similar features, may be at the heart of close social relationships and that living together does not guarantee closeness among family members. Research has shown that friends are similar to each other before they are friends[11] and that spouses mate assortatively (match) on selected traits such as social values.[12] The immediate rapport described by many reared-apart twins is consistent with these findings.

VIRTUAL TWIN STUDIES

Virtual twins (VTs) are same-age, unrelated, twinlike sibling sets. Earlier, I explained that they come about mostly when families adopt two same-age children simultaneously or adopt one child who is the same age as their biological child. My criteria for defining VTs are (1) the siblings must be reared together before one year of age, (2) the siblings cannot differ in age by more than nine months, which is the maximum age difference between two children in most classrooms, and (3) the siblings, if still in school, must be enrolled in the same grade to preserve the twinlike nature of their relationship.[13] The average age difference for the 142 VT pairs in my study is only 3.22 months.

Since starting my virtual twin studies in 1991, I have discovered other, less common ways in which VTs can be created. I learned about the latest one in 2010 while writing this book. A mother informed me that she and her female partner had conceived their daughters with sperm from different men and delivered their babies only four months apart. This situation reminded me of the 2010 film *The Kids Are All Right* about a same-sex couple (played by Annette Bening and Julianne Moore) that has two children through sperm donation and assisted insemination, except that their son and daughter were several years apart and were related as half-siblings through a common sperm donor. However, it is likely that virtual twin pairs have and will be created in this way. Another way to create VTs is through accidental twin switches, which produce the special class of VTs who *believe* they are fraternal twins—like Begoña and Beatriz.

I have studied over 140 virtual twin pairs thus far and am finding new sets all the time. After discovering my first pair in 1989, I had hoped to identify several additional pairs and have been surprised to discover they are not so rare after all. I believe VTs may be increasing in frequency because many women are marrying later in life, thereby delaying the childbearing years and compromising their chances for conception. Adoption and artificial reproductive technologies (ART) are allowing many infertile couples to raise families they might not otherwise have—but adoption alone and adoption combined with ART can unwittingly produce VTs, usually to their parents' delight. Two families in my study have each provided three VT pairs, generated by an adoptee paired with members of a triplet set the parents conceived by in vitro fertilization. And as I recently discovered, same-sex couples may be the next wave of VT parents. However, VTs that were formerly "fraternal twins" due to a baby mix-up are not joyful additions to the family because of the emotional turbulence their discovery brings.

The average age of my sample of 142 VT pairs is slightly over seven and a half years, but they include individuals as young as four and as old as fifty-four. I have found that even though co-VTs have shared family environments, they show little similarity in general intelligence. They are less alike than identical or fraternal twins raised both together and apart. VTs are also less alike than full siblings who, while they share half their genes on average, have different life experiences due to their difference in age. Table 8.1 summarizes the average IQ correlation (measures of within-pair resemblance) for these sibling pairs, based on a large number of studies in the psychological literature.

Table 8.1. Average IQ Correlations for Twins, Virtual Twins, and Siblings[14]

Pair Type	Correlation	% Shared Genes[15]
Identical Twins—Together	.86	100
Identical Twins—Apart	.73	100
Fraternal Twins—Together	.60	50
Fraternal Twins—Apart	.47	50
Full Siblings—Together	.47	50
Full Siblings—Apart	.24	50
Virtual Twins	.28	0

Table 8.1 shows that (1) IQ similarity goes up with the percentage of shared genes and (2) IQ similarity increases, but only slightly, when the same types of relatives are reared together versus apart. An exception concerns full siblings reared apart, who would be expected to be more

alike in intelligence than virtual twins because full siblings share, on average, half their genes, while VTs share no genes at all, by descent. It is possible that the reared-apart full-sibling group includes a significant number of half-siblings; that is, children who share approximately 25 percent of their genes (either half their mother's genes, on average, or half their father's genes, on average, but not both). Siblings reared apart tend to come from homes in which parents may not be living together and may have had multiple partners. The somewhat higher correlations of IQ between twins reared together than between twins reared apart may reflect the fact that most reared-together twin studies include children for whom a shared environment would affect intelligence, whereas the reared-together studies include adults.

The VT correlation shows that approximately 25 percent of the individual differences in young children's intelligence are associated with shared environmental effects. Shared environments are the only factors these children have in common. However, the interesting finding is that this correlation drops over time as children get older and are less under the influence of their parents. Using a subsample of VTs, I found that their IQ correlation at age five was .30 and at age ten was .11.[16] A reduction in intellectual similarity was also found in a study of ordinary adoptive siblings, in which the correlation dropped to zero as the children approached adolescence.[17]

In 2002 Dr. Shirley McGuire, at the University of San Francisco, and I began a collaborative study called TAPS (Twins, Adoptees, Peers, and Siblings). In an analysis that combined young identical twins, fraternal twins, and virtual twins, we and our University of Alabama co-investigators found that body mass index or BMI ([weight in kilograms]/[height in meters]^2) was significantly influenced by the shared family environment (25.7 percent).[18] BMI is a better measure of body size than height or weight alone because it considers the relationship between height and weight that is associated with body fat and health risk.[19] Previous studies had not detected shared environmental effects on body mass index, possibly because they lacked the different kinships used in our analyses. We also found substantial genetic effects on BMI (63.6 percent) but little impact from unshared environments or the unique experiences children have apart from their families (10.7 percent).

The closer social relationships between identical twins than fraternal twins and their more similar mental skills have been well established, so it was reasonable to expect VTs to follow fraternal twins along these lines. In 2008, I conducted a twin–virtual twin study of tacit coordination, the situation being "two parties have identical interests and face the problem . . . of coordinating their actions for their mutual benefit when communication is impossible."[20] The study included fifty-three identical twin pairs, eighty-five fraternal twin pairs, and forty-two virtual twin pairs between seven and a half and thirteen years of age. The task I gave to the children was to answer a list of twenty questions (e.g., name a book; name a movie) such that they and their twin would produce the same answers, but independently and without collaboration.[21] As I expected, the identical twins were the most successful group on this task, followed by the fraternal twins and virtual twins in that order. These data suggested that the VTs were not as attuned to one another as were the members of the other pairs even though, like twins, they were the same age and had been raised together. This same relationship pattern was repeated in our TAPS studies of social closeness[22] and interpersonal trust, although the difference between the fraternal twins and virtual twins in the trust study was small.[23] Virtual twins appear to spend as much time together as fraternal twins at young ages, possibly explaining why these two groups did not differ greatly on the trust variable.

The twin and virtual twin studies provided an informative framework for assessing the similarities and differences among Delia, Begoña, and Beatriz in the traits I had measured. The published studies provide average findings for twins and non-twins, but there is variation among the pairs. Some reared-apart identical twins are less alike in some traits than twins in other pairs, and some virtual twins can be very much the same.

I always interviewed the Canary Islands twins and sister separately, speaking through my interpreter Jessica.[24] Likewise, they completed written questionnaires individually as well as under our supervision. Ideally, twins should be interviewed by different individuals to avoid biased administration and interpretation. For example, if an examiner knows one twin's answer to a question, this knowledge may affect the examiner's questioning of the co-twin; I raised this issue regarding Trujillo's psychiatric interviewing of all three sisters. However, because I don't speak Spanish, I could not alter my line of questioning with Delia, whom I met second, in accordance with the responses I'd heard from Begoña, whom I met first. But Begoña raised several issues on her own, such as her difficulty in relaxing, that I also raised with Delia.

SIMILAR, BUT NOT THE SAME

I collected self-reported height and weight data from the twins; Beatriz; and Beatriz's two biological sisters, Julia and Gara.[25] Self-reported body size measures show very high agreement with measures made by investigators.[26] The findings are interesting because there are striking similarities and noticeable differences in the women's body sizes. Beatriz's unrelated siblings (who were also Begoña's biogical siblings) were unavailable for study.

The BMIs of the MZA pair (Delia and Begoña) were much closer than the BMIs of the VT pair (Begoña and Beatriz). Interestingly, and as expected, Beatriz's BMI was much closer to the BMIs of her two biological sisters, Julia and Gara, than to Begoña's, a finding that is consistent with genetic influence on body size. The twins' height difference of 6.0 cm (2.36 in.) was above the average 1.47 cm (0.58 in.) height difference of a small number of identical female twins reared apart[27] and the 1.57 cm (0.62 in.) height difference of a sample of identical female twins reared together.[28] However, height differences of over two inches have been reported for identical twins and may be due to the prenatal stressors associated with multiple pregnancies.[29] The twins' weight difference was also somewhat larger than the average weight difference of 5.26 kg (11.6 lb.) for identical female twins reared apart[30] and 5.23 kg (11.53 lb.) for identical female twins reared together.[31]

Findings like these lend themselves well to analysis by a case history approach that tries to link differences between co-twins to differences in their life histories. Delia suffered from leukemia at age sixteen, leading to her series of medications and surgeries. She is currently in remission, but her recent weight gain appears to be tied to her health history. Interestingly, the twins were closer in weight when they met eight years prior to my study of them, explaining why Clarisa had equated their likeness upon meeting to "two drops of water." But marked body size differences do not necessarily overwhelm identical twins' matched faces and forms, even when they are raised apart. The firefighter twins, Mark and Jerry, varied in weight by over 100 pounds, but Mark's friend was still struck by how much Jerry looked like Mark. He did not confuse Jerry for Mark, however. Bob, a reared-apart triplet who was mistaken for his brother Eddy at Sullivan County Community College, was just seven pounds heavier and exactly the same height.

Delia and Begoña's different medical histories can offer possible insights into factors that trigger disease and prevent its expression. Identical twin resemblance for leukemia is highest in childhood and declines with age. The percentage of pairs in which both twins are affected ranges between 5 percent and 25 percent for children between the ages of one and fifteen years, but eliminating infants from the analysis reduces the figure to 10 percent.[32] Begoña and Beatriz were divided over whether or not their family had a history of leukemia. It is suspected that when one identical twin develops leukemia and the other twin does not, then some factor in their early environment, either before or after birth, triggered the condition in the affected twin. It is possible that Delia's leukemia was triggered by an unknown environmental exposure, such as to a toxic chemical or other substance. Delia's unrelated sisters and parents were disease-free, but Delia came into the world with different genetic predispositions.

The 1 cm (0.39 in.) height difference between Beatriz and Begoña was quite a bit less than the 7 cm (3.15 in.) and 9 cm (3.94 in.) height differences between Beatriz and each of her two biological sisters, Julia and Gara, respectively. Beatriz was only somewhat closer in weight to her two sisters than to Begoña, but her BMI was closer to theirs than to Begoña's. Interestingly, Julia and Gara were very close in height and identical in weight. As such, they were more similar in body size than any of the other twin and sibling pairs. Genes explain both similarities and differences among family members.

Height and weight data were also available for the Canadian twins Brent and George, the virtual twins George and Marcus, and an unrelated sibling pair, Brent and his adoptive brother Wade, with whom he differed in age by six years.[33] Their data, gathered a number of years ago and reported in my previous book,[34] are summarized in table 8.2.

Table 8.2. Height, Weight, and Body Mass Index (BMI) Data for Reared-Apart Twins, Virtual Twin Brothers, and Unrelated Male Siblings Reared Together

| Sibling | Height | | Weight | | BMI |
	(cm)	(in.)	(kg)	(lb.)	
Brent	176.50	69.49	76.50	168.65	24.44
George	173.50	68.30	80.00	176.37	26.40
Marcus	173.00	68.11	103.00	227.03	34.45
Wade	190.50	75.00	115.67	255.00	31.69

The identical twins, Brent and George, were very similar in height, weight, and BMI. Marcus's height hardly differed from that of George, the unrelated brother he was raised with, but Marcus was quite a bit heavier, an effect captured by the size of his BMI. Brent's younger adoptive brother, Wade, was considerably taller and heavier than Brent. These body size patterns are expected given the genetic influences indicated by reared-apart and reared-together twin studies.

Height and weight measures were unavailable for the other known switched-at-birth twin pairs mentioned in this book. But in her memoir, Mme. Joye expressed acute awareness of Paul's robustness and Philippe's delicacy. She wrote, "Monsieur Barbichon lifts a fat and well-combed Paul down from his chair. The barber cannot help saying, 'How heavy is he for his age, he is not yet seven, is he?' . . . Monsieur Barbichon lifts Philippe into the chair. He weighs him. 'It's incredible the difference there is between these two kids. This one is as light as a feather by comparison!'"[35] Mme. Joye replied that the weight difference between her "twins" was fifteen pounds. Fifteen pounds is a sizeable weight difference, given an average reported difference of about 4.50 pounds for male fraternal twins just under age six.[36] Perhaps Monsieur Barbichon did not make the important distinction between genetically identical and nonidentical twins, something many people fail to do. Equating twinness with likeness is not uncommon.

The physical features of the three boys were studied exhaustively by the physicians in Geneva whom the magistrate assigned to determine the biological relationships among them.[37] The doctors observed far greater resemblance between Philippe and Ernstli (Charles) than between Philippe and Paul in facial features, iris color, iris pattern, hair color, hair texture, ear shape, fingerprint characteristics, nail form, capillary structure of the fingernail manifolds, electrocardiographic readings, encephalographic wave patterns, and shape of the tympanic membranes (ear drums). In addition, x-ray analyses showed "striking resemblance" in the cranial configurations of Philippe and Ernstli and "similar skeletal structure" of their hands, in particular their lack of radial carpal bones. Philippe and Ernstli also displayed the same type of red-green color blindness and the rare absence of their two median inferior incisor teeth.

The Swiss physicians, while impressed by Philippe and Ernstli's striking similarities, considered the twins' successful reciprocal skin grafts to be the most decisive proof of their relatedness and as being consistent with their being identical twins. Aside from the skin grafts, a match between presumed identical twins on any one of the other features the physicians measured would not be proof of monozygosity or identical twinship, but in combination such matches would make a compelling case. For example, the rarity of the twins' similar dental anomaly made their being identical twins very likely, but a researcher would not determine relatedness—or assign twin type or zygosity (identical or fraternal)—on the basis of that similarity alone. Twin researchers can, however, legitimately decide twin type on the basis of standard physical similarity questionnaires that jointly consider co-twins' resemblance in highly heritable (genetically influenced) traits such as hair color, eye color, and height, as well as on the basis of confusion by parents, teachers, and close friends.[38] Twins who are frequently confused by the people who know them are usually identical. Physical resemblance forms were purposefully designed to show excellent agreement with the resemblance in biological markers, such as multiple blood groups. Currently, analysis of standard DNA regions is the best available method for determining relatedness and determining twin type. Even fingerprints would be questionable because of their sensitivity to unknown prenatal effects that can cause identical twins to differ.

The Swiss doctors stated, "In addition to the morphological features, the psychomotor factors as well as the mental ability and general behavior [of Philippe and Ernstli] showed a strong likeness."[39] But not all identical twins are as alike as Philippe and Ernstli (Charles), a finding that keeps twin research active and exciting. If researchers can discover why two genetically identical people differ in height or ability or personality, that information can be used to understand the development of those traits in the non-twin population. Delia and Begoña were very much alike, but they did not show perfect similarity. As such, I was intrigued by them.

SEPARATE MINDS

The identical Canadian twins, Brent and George, earned very similar IQ scores, while the unrelated pair, George and Marcus, scored quite differently. This is the pattern I had predicted for Delia and Begoña and for Begoña and Beatriz.

I expected Delia and Begoña to obtain fairly similar IQ scores, not just because they were identical twins but also because of their similar attitudes and aspirations that reflected their academic interests and ability. Delia had earned a diploma and had studied accounting for several years. She had mostly cleaned houses and held a string of other nonprofessional jobs, but she displayed intelligence and talent. Her parents and sisters acknowledged her superior intellectual skills, which, according to Delia, helped her excel in school without much preparation. Delia also had outside interests, shown by her enthusiasm for the animals she cared for, the problem children she had helped, and the carefully chosen furnishings she had placed in her home. But everyone mentioned Delia's inability to finish projects she began. Delia struck me as having a great deal of ability that needed productive channeling.

I saw similar traits in Begoña. Begoña hadn't finished school, but when we met she was working toward her high school diploma through an adult education program. She had mostly cleaned houses, but in 2009 she was supervising the maid service at a well-known Las Palmas hotel, a position requiring superior managerial and social skills. Begoña talked about her plan to become a lawyer, insisting this future goal was unrelated to the baby mix-up. According to Laura, her mother, "[Begoña] now wants to go to the university. She didn't want to study when she was a child, but as an adult, she has never had problems passing exams for work positions." When Jessica and I had visited Begoña at her home, we learned of her interests in travel, art, and religion. Like Delia, Begoña also appeared to have considerable talent waiting to be expressed.

The twins and Beatriz were administered the Spanish version of the

Wechsler Adult Intelligence Scale (WAIS) IQ Test. The WAIS is a widely administered standardized test of general intelligence developed by David Wechsler in 1955 for individuals age sixteen and older.[40] The WAIS includes six verbal subtests and five nonverbal (performance) subtests that yield a verbal IQ score, a performance IQ score, and a full-scale IQ score. The verbal subtests include Information (general knowledge), Digit Span (auditory recall), Vocabulary (word knowledge), Arithmetic (numerical reasoning), Comprehension (social awareness), and Similarities (concept formation). The performance subtests include Picture Completion (attention to detail), Picture Arrangement (logic and sequence), Block Design (pattern matching), Digit Symbol (coding pattern copying), and Object Assembly (recognition of familiar configurations).

The WAIS is administered to each person individually by a trained examiner and requires approximately one and a half hours to complete. The test has undergone several revisions, later released as the WAIS-R (1981), WAIS-III (2007), and WAIS-IV (2008). The Spanish WAIS was copyrighted in 1977 and 1995.

Begoña and Beatriz completed the WAIS on January 21, 2010, and Delia completed it on February 8, 2010, about four months after I'd left Las Palmas. I arranged to have the three women assessed by different examiners to avoid biased administration. Begoña and Beatriz were tested in separate rooms in Peregrina's law office by examiners from the Psicologia Infantil FORTEA (Child Psychology Center, established by the psychologist María del Sol Fortea), and Delia was tested in Socorro's office by Dr. Jorge De Vega, the psychologist I had met at the psychiatric hospital when I interviewed the psychiatrist Trujillo.

The results were remarkable for several reasons. Delia and Begoña scored considerably less alike, and Begoña and Beatriz scored considerably more alike, than I had expected. Reared-apart identical twins' different IQ scores can have a number of explanations. My colleague Dr. Michael Fuhrman from the University of Minnesota suggested looking first at prenatal factors that might be linked to IQ differences between the twins; if prenatal factors could be ruled out, then perhaps rapport with the tester and/or level of task engagement affected their performance.

Laura and Débora had provided me with information about the twins' births. Begoña, who weighed 2.5 kg (5.5 pounds) at birth, was released to Laura when Laura left the hospital, while Delia, who weighed less than 2.0 kg (4.4 pounds), stayed in the hospital for twenty-five days until Débora took her home. Even though Delia and Begoña had been premature infants, neither of their mothers had indicated any obvious behavioral problems in their daughters. Based on the available information, prenatal factors did not appear to be associated with the IQ findings.

Fortunately, most test administrators document their observations of a person's behavior during testing, and the comments I received were insightful. One twin admitted to feeling "nervous and anxious," but she insisted on completing the test anyway. In contrast, her twin sister was described as "motivated at all times, funny, very outgoing, and talkative. [She] recognized that the test required effort and tried at all times to do her best." The twins' different approaches to the testing situation could be partly associated with their performance.

Another way to think about the twins' IQ discrepancy is to consider the statistical phenomenon called regression to the mean. Regression to the mean occurs because people with relatively high scores on their first test administration tend to score lower on their second test administration.[41] Similarly, people with lower scores on their first test administration tend to score higher on their second test administration. In other words, the scores of both groups move closer toward the mean on the second testing. There are several reasons for this. People doing well the first time do so because of their ability and/or chance factors such as feeling well rested or just being lucky. These people will continue to do well on the second administration, but some of their scores will decline due to a poor night's rest, overconfidence, or bad luck. In contrast, many people doing poorly the first time will continue to do poorly the second time, but some of them will improve due to a good night's rest, better preparation, or less bad luck. It is possible that if the twins were tested again, their test scores would show some convergence—the higher-scoring twin might feel overconfident and make careless mistakes, while her sister might be less anxious and more task oriented.

The IQ findings for Delia and Begoña do not detract from twin studies showing substantial within-pair resemblance between identical twins, nor do they challenge genetic explanations of individual differences in mental ability. Findings based on individual pairs do not carry the research weight of data gathered on large twin samples from which generalizations to the overall population are made. But individual pairs, like Begoña and Delia, can suggest reasons why some identical twins are less alike in some ways than in others.

SELF-ESTEEM

Self-esteem refers to an individual's overall evaluation of his or her self-worth. The Rosenberg Self-Esteem Scale (RSES) is a widely used ten-item form developed in 1989 by Professor Morris Rosenberg at the University of Maryland.[42] In 2007, the scale was translated into Spanish and validated using a large sample of students from the University of Las Palmas.[43] Two of the investigators of that project, José Martín-Albo and Fernando Grijalvo, were psychology department faculty and my hosts during my free Thursday afternoon in the Canary Islands.

The ten items of the RSES include five positively worded statements and five negatively worded statements. Examples are "I feel that I have a number of good qualities," and "I certainly feel useless at times." Respondents indicate their agreement with each statement using a four-point (1 to 4) scale, ranging from "Strongly Disagree" to "Strongly Agree." Final scores range from 10 to 40, with scores below 20 indicating low self-esteem.

Delia and Begoña obtained identical scores on the RSES, indicating good levels of self-esteem. In fact, their scores closely matched the average score obtained by the 296 female participants in the Spanish validation study. Overall, self-esteem reflects many aspects of a person's feelings of self-worth as experienced across a variety of different situations. I believe that the relationship between Begoña and Delia added a meaningful dimension to both of their lives—a situation that could certainly enhance self-esteem.

CLOSER THAN SISTERS

> I know Delia and I can understand each other and reach agreements even if we have different opinions. Beatriz and I have different ways of thinking.
> —BEGOÑA, 2009

Delia and Begoña accomplished in seconds what many sisters never achieve after a lifetime together—a mutually deep understanding of how the other thinks and feels. This level of connection and compatibility may seem reasonable between twins reared together, but it also characterizes relationships between many pairs of identical twins reunited as adults. In 1982, when I became associated with the Minnesota Study of Twins Reared Apart, I started looking systematically at how well reared-apart identical twins got along. I first examined the biographical essays of seventy-six previously studied pairs and found twin relationship information available for fifty-four. The striking finding was that forty of these fifty-four pairs (nearly 75 percent) got along extremely well, as indicated by their contact frequency (e.g., "A strong mutual affection sprang up between them, and they have managed, in spite of limited funds, to spend a week or so together every year."[44]), the investigators' observations (e.g, "They have always been closely attached to one another, and now go out courting together."[45]), and other indica-

tors. However, no one had systematically compared relationship qualities between identical and fraternal reared-apart twins because no one
had studied separated fraternal pairs until they were recruited by the
Minnesota Study. Professor Bouchard and I developed a comprehensive
Twin Relationship Survey for this purpose.

The identical reared-apart twins expressed significantly greater closeness and familiarity than the fraternal reared-apart twins, although there
was some overlap. But as I indicated above, my most intriguing finding
was that the reared-apart twins as a whole gave higher closeness and
familiarity ratings to the twin they had just met than to the unrelated sibling they had always known. I expected Delia and Begoña to give each
other high ratings, but I was actually more interested in knowing how
these ratings compared with their ratings for their other sisters.

When Delia met Begoña for the first time, she expected they would
become "closer than best friends." Begoña also seemed "more familiar
than a best friend" to Delia, sentiments Begoña echoed almost perfectly.
Today, both twins agree that the other is still "as familiar as a best
friend"; however, they also agree that they are "less close than best
friends, but closer than casual friends." They say that the physical distance between their homes and their heavy workloads keep them apart,
but they stay in touch by telephone. I remembered that traveling
between Begoña's home in Las Palmas and Delia's home in her small
town was not easy.

Delia did not feel as close with or as familiar toward her two sisters as
she felt toward Begoña. Thus, Delia's ratings are more consistent with my
findings on the Minnesota twins. In contrast, Begoña indicated that
Beatriz is "as close as a best friend" and "more familiar" than most people
she has always known. Begoña's answers may partly reflect the fact that she
was raised believing that Beatriz was truly her twin sister. Clearly, differences between family members do not have to prevent the development of
close social ties. Begoña told me that while she and Beatriz do not always
understand each other, that does not mean she does not love her.

THREE LIVES

I see Delia and Begoña as another fascinating version of identical twin-ship, one that shows striking similarities and curious differences. My col-league, Professor Bouchard, who directed the Minnesota Study, debated personality findings with then Harvard University geneticist Paul Billings on ABC's *Nightline* program in October 1989. In the context of the debate, Bouchard told viewers he recognized two types of twin resemblance, one based on anecdotal evidence and the other based on measured traits. Anecdotal evidence consists of reunited twins' personal observations, such as Delia and Begoña's unusual gait, their matching hands and feet, and their instant rapport—similarities they noticed at their first reunion. Bouchard said such observations can "overwhelm the twins" who are unaccustomed to seeing someone who looks and acts like them. Measured traits are the mental ability, personality, and health his-tory data that investigators like those of the Minnesota Study gather on large numbers of separated sets. Identical co-twins (members of a twin pair) tend to be less alike on these measures than those reported anec-dotally, although biological traits like brain waves and fingerprints show greater co-twin resemblance than behavioral traits like extraversion and job satisfaction.

Even though identical co-twins rarely attain the exact same scores on psychological tests, their scores are usually closer to each other's than to those of the other identical twins in the group of twins being studied. This pattern of findings, in addition to the greater resemblance between identical than nonidentical co-twins, has demonstrated genetic influ-ence on virtually all traits that have been examined using twins both reared apart and together. That is, conclusions regarding the relative roles of genes and environments on behavior are based on large numbers of twins. Results from single case studies are informative but are not always representative.

The fact that baby switches occur means that sometimes investigators studying the origins of behavior or disease will unknowingly include unrelated parent-child and brother-sister pairs in their participant samples. These pairs would reduce the magnitude of the genetic effect on the behavior or condition under study, because biologically unrelated people are less likely to resemble one another on genetically influenced traits, such as general intelligence and bipolar depression, than related people. Researchers do not typically screen participants for genetic relatedness, assuming, as do the volunteer families, that families are biologically intact. Including a few unrelated relatives in a sample of several hundred families would probably not bias the results to a significant degree, but including them in a very small sample could spuriously lower the genetic effect.

Baby switches pose another research issue. My late Minnesota colleague, Dr. David T. Lykken, coined the concept *emergenesis* to describe the genetic transmission of traits that do not run in families.[46] This concept sounds paradoxical; however, Lykken explained that complex behavioral traits, such as unusual creativity or musical skill, may be influenced by unique gene combinations inherited by a single individual from his or her parents. When that person has children, the genes responsible for his or her creativity or musicality are "disassembled" because parents transmit only half their genes to each of their children. Emergenic traits are suggested when identical twins are very similar and fraternal twins and full siblings are very dissimilar. That is because identical twins share all their genes and, therefore, all their gene combinations, whereas fraternal twins and full siblings share only half their genes, on average, making it unlikely for them to inherit the same combinations of genes. Emergenic effects on behavior may be artificially enhanced by baby switches because unrelated children might show remarkable traits not displayed by their alleged parents, fraternal twins, and siblings. This is an important consideration in twin and family studies, especially since the frequency of baby switches is unknown.

Investigators cannot ethically assign twins to different homes or put unrelated children together in order to study their physical and behavioral development. However, extenuating circumstances such as maternal death or extraordinary events such as baby switches can intervene to create reared-apart twins, virtual twins, and other unusual kinships. Even the fairly common practice of divorce can separate siblings or cause children to be reared by an unrelated parent. These situations are scientifically significant because they highlight the genetic and environmental factors affecting traits of interest. Inviting these twins and siblings into psychological and medical laboratories helps them understand why they are extraverted or introverted, happy or sad, or healthy or unwell.

Research participation also gives reunited relatives opportunities to build meaningful relationships with newly discovered parents, siblings, aunts and uncles, and nieces and nephews. But no one wishes for circumstances that pull families apart.

AFTERWORD

THIS DAY FORWARD

I t has been nearly two years since I met the twins and their families in the Canary Islands. I think about them often, wondering how the discovery of the twin switch has been affecting their lives and how it will continue to do so in the future. Both Delia's and Begoña's attitude of inevitability, the belief they would have found out sooner or later about the switch, shows that they have generally accepted the changes in their lives. I believe Delia and Begoña will continue to develop their relationship despite the odds. Identical twinship exerts a powerful pull, keeping twins together even when outside influences work against them. I have seen this many times.

Jack Yufe and Oskar Stohr, separated at six months and raised Jewish in Trinidad and Catholic in Nazi Germany, respectively, attest to that fact. Despite their different political views, and despite the fact that many of their meetings did not end amicably, they worked hard at being twins.[1] But Jack and Oskar were fascinated by each other, especially by their matched habits of reading books back to front, sneezing loudly in crowded elevators, and washing their hands before and after using the toilet. They relished long conversations with each other in which both twins tried to keep control of the topic and the conclusion.

Jack and Oskar were not the only twins I've worked with for whom twinship was a significant part of their lives despite their differences. As indicated earlier, in June 2010 I heard from identical reared-apart twin

Hanan Hardy who, at age thirty-five, learned from a Facebook message that she had been adopted and had an identical twin sister living in Morocco. Her July 2010 meeting with her sister Hasania in Morocco did not go as well as she had hoped. When we spoke by telephone after her return to the United States, it seemed unlikely that the twins would get together again. Hanan told me that her career goals and aspirations clashed with those of her twin sister. But toward the end of our conversation, Hanan casually mentioned that she might study Arabic to communicate better with her twin. Jack and Oskar and Hanan and Hasania have convinced me that Delia and Begoña have the potential to find their way to becoming close, possibly as much as many other identical twin siblings.

For most people, finding an identical twin is a special treat, but for the switched-at-birth pairs, the discovery negatively impacts not only their relationship but every relationship within the family. The benefits of being a twin or of reconnecting with a child are understandably dimmed in the context of a switch. Every parent in the two Canary Islands families lost a daughter at some level. Laura missed out on raising Delia, and Débora and Juan lost the opportunity to raise Beatriz and continue to miss their relationship with Delia, who drifted from their home once the discovery was made. Delia's two sisters, and Begoña's older sister and two brothers, cannot recapture the sibling relationships that should have been theirs. Everyone's hurt runs deep.

I imagine that the words *if only* have been recited many times by the members of these two families—if only the babies hadn't been born so close together, if only the nurses had been more attentive, if only we had asked about the babies' different skin color, if only Begoña hadn't wandered into that shop . . . These parents may also be asking themselves why they, and not others, were the victims of such egregious hospital negligence. But they should know they are not alone. The chilling statistics cited in chapter 6 (approximately twenty thousand accidental baby switches each year in the United States, albeit most of them corrected before the babies go home—as far as anyone knows) make it possible that other parents are unknowingly raising children who belong to someone else.

Some people will never suspect that they were raised by the wrong mother and father. Others may always wonder why they looked and acted differently than their parents and siblings, never seeming to fit into the family culture. They may convince themselves that the whimsical ways of gene transmission and expression are responsible—and they could be right. But there is also the chance that they belong to another family. How many among them would want to know the truth? I have always maintained that the truth is best because it lets the past become clearer and the future better controlled. I still believe that, but old beliefs may be challenged when events become personal. Every family member of the switched children in this book was affected by the discovery, and some would have preferred not knowing the truth.

It is not easy to end this book on a positive note because the families' suffering has not ended. But there are some things we can come away with that can help us direct what is unforeseen and changeable and acknowledge what is unforeseen and unchangeable. The first is that people need to speak up when they suspect that a medical procedure, a prescription drug—or a newborn baby—they are told is theirs does not seem quite right. An uncomfortable moment of questioning, even impoliteness, is little to pay when it comes to personal happiness and satisfaction.

The second is that there are few things as important, or as fragile, as knowing who we are and to whom we belong. Both can change irrevocably just by going to a new school (Paul and Phillipe), joining a college club (Brent and George), making a friend (Kasia and Edyta), having the same last name (Tairí and Mari and Jennifer and Samantha)—or walking into a shopping mall.

ACKNOWLEDGMENTS

Expressing words of thanks to my friends, colleagues, and associates who gave so generously of their time is one of the most pleasurable tasks associated with the writing of *Someone Else's Twin*. The book's cover bears just one name, but its contents reflect the efforts of many.

Gran Canaria

Sebastian Socorro Perdomo and José Antonio Rodríguez Peregrina, thank you for sharing your clients with me and for taking the time to reflect on the significance of this extraordinary case. Your interest and support were vital to the success of this project.

Twins and family members in Gran Canaria, I know all of your real names, and wish I could thank you each individually and publicly for telling me your stories with such honesty and trust. Your willingness to disclose previously unknown details of your difficult experience will surely help to prevent such tragic mistakes from happening in the future.

Jessica Crespo, you are a talented interpreter and translator whose skills amazed me as we interviewed the members of the Canary Islands families. I will always be grateful to you for your expert translations of taped interviews, newspaper articles, and legal documents. Your answers to the countless questions that arose during my writing of this book were invaluable.

Iris Blandón-Gitlin, you are a magnificent (and, fortunately for me, bilingual) colleague in the department of psychology at California State

University, Fullerton. You helped me launch this project during the summer of 2008 via telephone calls and e-mail messages to the Canary Islands attorneys, even when it meant getting up early or staying up late because of the time difference. Your interest and enthusiasm for this work never wavered. I cannot thank you enough for your scores of translated notes and letters and for your continued friendship and support.

Fernando Grijalvo Lobera, you became a great friend when I visited the University of Las Palmas's psychology department during my one free afternoon. Thank you for helping to arrange the twins' intelligence testing after I left Las Palmas and for your quick and detailed responses to my questions about life and culture in Gran Canaria. Our day trip to Maspalomas was memorable.

Casimiro Cabrera Abreu, I was delighted to meet you at the Servicio Canario de Salud, Hospital Universitario. You translated my impromptu seminar into Spanish for your colleagues and have continued to provide insight into many aspects of the switched-at-birth twins case. I am now pleased to have you as a North American colleague following your recent move to Toronto.

Ruth Jaén-Molina, I was introduced to you over the Internet while I was researching interpreters, prior to taking my trip. We became friends even before we met, in part because we are both fraternal twins and share a love of the subject. We did not work together on the project, but you and your family graciously accompanied me to Las Palmas's beautiful botanical gardens where you work. Thank you for your friendship and for answering the twin- and non-twin-related questions I posed to you over the past year.

Jorge De Vega, thank you for the courtesy of administering an intelligence test to one of the three sisters after I left Las Palmas. María Olga Escandell Bermúdez, thank you for choosing Sol Fortea Sevilla and Débora Marta Morales, both outstanding professionals, to administer the intelligence test to the other two.

Pilar Costa-Valera and Monique Del Rio, both at California State University, Fullerton, I am grateful to you for occasional Spanish-to-English translations and telephone calls to Las Palmas. It is a luxury to have such skilled colleagues and staff members just down the hall from my office.

José Martín-Albo Lucas, thank you for providing your excellent research paper with the Spanish translation and validation of the Rosenberg Self-Esteem Scale. I appreciated your invitation to visit the psychology department at the University of Las Palmas. Anton Aluja Fabregat at the University of Lleida in Lleida, Spain, thank you for providing the Spanish version of another psychological protocol.

Antonio Gidi, at the University of Houston Law Center, you graciously reviewed sections of this book related to Spanish legal procedure. Your generosity reminds me that there is a wonderful and talented community of scholars out there.

Jaakko Kaprio, at the Department of Public Health at the University of Helsinki, you responded immediately to my request for height and weight data for adult female twins reared together. Your contribution is greatly appreciated.

The Other Switched-at-Birth Twins

Cezary Zekanowski, at the Medical Research Center, Polish Academy of Sciences in Warsaw, a million tributes would not be enough to acknowledge you for contacting Andrzej Ofmański, father of the switched twins in Poland, and for arranging my telephone interview with him. That was a complex process, but you saw it through and helped me in countless ways thereafter. I hope to meet you some day.

Dorota Huizinga, you are an incredibly busy person as associate vice president of graduate programs and research at California State University, Fullerton. Nevertheless, you set aside several hours one Saturday morning to conduct a telephone interview in Polish with Andrzej Ofmańksi.

Michael Mikulewicz, I was lucky to find you! You are the only student from Poland enrolled at California State University, Fullerton, and you are a real treasure. Thank you for your superb translations of the

Polish interview transcript and newspaper articles and for your thoughts and perspectives on this famous twins case.

Neil Mitchenall, I discovered you while searching the Internet for business associates of Charles Joye, Philippe Joye's deceased identical twin brother who was switched at birth. You graciously contacted Charles's family in Geneva in order to provide me with an English translation of Charles's memoir. I hope to thank you in person someday.

Harold D. Vicente, as the attorney who represented the Hernández family (parents and grandfather of Tairí and Mari) in the switched-at-birth twins case in Puerto Rico, you put me in touch with the family members. You also provided valuable commentary on the nature of this case and its outcome. José A. León Landrau, as the attorney who represented the other Hernández family (mother of Jennifer and Samantha), thank you for addressing my many questions about this case.

Iris Blandón-Gitlin, thank you again for conducting telephone interviews with family members in Puerto Rico and for cohosting the switched twin Tairí during her 2010 California visit. Once again, you proved yourself to be a colleague extraordinaire!

Jessica Crespo, I turned to you for translations of the transcripts from Puerto Rico simply because you were the best person I knew for the task. You never disappointed me. Your fluency in French also enabled you to complete an expert translation of an important newspaper article concerning the switched Joye twins from Switzerland.

Twins and their families in Puerto Rico, Switzerland, Poland, and Canada, I am grateful to all of you for your efforts on behalf of this project. I had many "last questions," and you answered them all with patience and grace.

Writing and Production

Angela Rinaldi, you have been my literary agent and friend for fourteen years, and it has been a delightful experience. Your knowledge of book publishing, awareness of new developments in this changing field, and belief in me helped make *Someone Else's Twin* a reality.

Linda Regan at Prometheus Books, thank you for being an editor with a sharp mind and a gentle touch. I profited on numerous occasions from your insight and advice as this book was moving forward. It was wonderful to work with you.

Prometheus Staff Members, thank you all for your contributions to the completion of *Someone Else's Twin*. I wish to especially acknowledge Catherine Abel-Roberts (production), Paula Fleming (copyediting), Jill Maxick (publicity), Brian McMahon (editing), and Steven L. Mitchell (vice president and editor-in-chief). It was a pleasure working with such a professional group of people.

Lauren Gonzalez, if I said you were a world-class reader and editor of the early version of this manuscript, my words would hardly capture my gratitude and admiration. Your detailed comments, helpful suggestions, and wise counsel were extraordinary contributions to the writing of this book. This was the third time you worked with me in this capacity, and I know it will not be the last.

Kelly Donovan at California State University, Fullerton, your editing of photos and figures brought life and vitality to the people and places I wrote about. As an identical twin yourself, I know you resonated personally with the material, and I am grateful for the discussions we had as I watched you perform your magic on the screen. Ammar Altowaiji, you are a valued student assistant who never failed to gather the articles and other materials I needed to have "immediately" as I wrote this book.

Frances Sanchez and Amanda Hayes, as a secretaries in the Department of Psychology at California State University, Fullerton, you printed numerous copies of chapters, articles, communications, and other materials for me during the writing of this book. Your assistance was invaluable.

Committee for California State University, Fullerton's Intramural Faculty Grants Program, thank you for the award that partially funded my travel to Gran Canaria. Your support allowed this research to go forward successfully.

Twins, Parents, Lovers, and Other Strangers

Anne, as my twin sister you followed me into the world seven minutes after I was born, so I have never really been alone. You have been the inspiration for my professional interest and personal fascination with twins' special developmental circumstances and what they reveal about human behavior. We share memories, secrets, and laughs that only we understand. You are a constant presence in everything I have written, including *Someone Else's Twin*.

My parents, Al and Esther Segal, were not present to celebrate the process and publication of *Someone Else's Twin*, but I know they would have been proud. I have dedicated this book to them.

Craig, as my boyfriend, swing dance partner, and best friend, you gave me the love, excitement, and fun I cherished during the writing of this book. You are also a sharp but fair critic, and our discussions of selected passages and themes were meaningful and enjoyable times together. Every writer should have a partner like you—but then, there is only one you.

I also wish to recognize the unseen and sometimes unknown individuals who in small but significant ways helped make my research and writing of *Someone Else's Twin* such a pleasant experience. They include, among others, the California State University, Fullerton library staff who obtained difficult-to-find research articles and the Las Palmas hotel receptionist who gave me free rein with the photocopy machine in the lobby.

Best wishes to you all,

Nancy

Nancy L. Segal

NOTES

CHAPTER 1

1. "Twin, Separated at Birth, Sues for Mix-Up," *Yahoo! News*, http://news.yahoo.com/s/nm/20080528/od_nm/twin_dc/ (accessed June 1, 2008).

2. Mónica López Ferrado, "De Repente, una Hermana [Suddenly, a Sister]," *El Pais*, July 7, 2008, http://www.elpais.com/articulo/sociedad/repente/hermana/elpepisoc/20080706elpepisoc_3/Ies (accessed July 15, 2008).

3. José Ramirez Bethencourt was a mayor of the Second Republic of Spain from 1935 to 1936.

4. Secret Tenerife Blog, "How Did the Canary Get Its Name?" http://secret-tenerife.blogspot.com/2006/04/how-did-that-canary-get-its-name.shtml (accessed November 1, 2010).

5. Ibid.

6. Sandy Moyer, "The Presa Canario," Dogs Site, http://www.bellaonline.com/articles/art2609.asp (accessed December 3, 2010).

7. Joyce A. Martin et al., "Births: Final Data for 2008," *National Vital Statistics Reports* 59 (2010).

8. Nicholas Martin, Dorett Boomsma, and Geoffrey Machin, "A Two-Pronged Attack on Complex Traits," *Nature Genetics* 17 (1999): 387–92.

9. Bruno Reversade, "Genetics of MZ Twins" (paper presented at the 13th International Twin Congress, Seoul, South Korea, July 4–7, 2010).

10. Nancy L. Segal, *Entwined Lives: Twins and What They Tell Us about Human Behavior* (New York: Plume, 2000).

11. Jodie Painter et al., "A Genome Wide Linkage Scan for Dizygotic Twinning in 525 Families of Mothers of Dizygotic Twins," *Human Reproduction* 25 (2010): 1569–80.

12. Segal, *Entwined Lives.*

13. Judith G. Hall, "Twinning," *Lancet* 362 (2003): 735–43.

14. Joyce Martin et al. "Births: Final Data for 2007," *National Vital Statistics Report* 58 (2010): 1–44. Available at http://www.cdc.gov/nchs/data/nvsr/nvsr58/nvsr58_24.pdf (accessed April 16, 2011).

15. Francis Galton, "The History of Twins as a Criterion of the Relative Powers of Nature and Nurture," *Journal of the Anthropological Institute* 5 (1875): 391–406, p. 391.

16. Segal, *Entwined Lives.*

17. Arturas Petronis et al., "Monozygotic Twins Exhibit Numerous Epigenetic Differences: Clues to Their Discordance?" *Schizophrenia Bulletin* 29 (2003): 174.

18. Robert Plomin et al., *Behavior Genetics*, 5th ed. (New York: Worth, 2008).

19. Nancy L. Segal, *Indivisible by Two: Lives of Extraordinary Twins* (Cambridge, MA: Harvard University Press, 2007).

20. Dale S. Wright, *The Six Perfections: Buddhism and the Cultivation of Character* (Oxford, UK: Oxford University Press, 2009), p. 229.

21. Nora Laster, in discussion with the author, June 3, 2010.

22. Segal, *Indivisible by Two.*

23. Questions and Answers, "When Was the Internet Invented?" http://www.letusfindout.com/when-was-the-Internet-invented/ (accessed March 8, 2011).

24. Thomas R. Lee, Jay A. Mancini, and Joseph W. Maxwell, "Sibling Relationships in Adulthood: Contact Patterns and Motivation," *Journal of Marriage and the Family* 52 (1990): 431–40.

25. Daniel G. Freedman, *Human Sociobiology* (New York: Free Press, 1979), p. 129.

26. John P. Triseliotus, *In Search of Origins: The Experience of Adopted People* (London: Kegan Paul, 1973), p. 82.

27. Associated Press, "Ore. Babies Switched at Birth Meet 56 Years Later,"

Yahoo! News, May 12, 2009, http://news.yahoo.com/s/ap/us_switched_at
_birth (accessed November 1, 2010).

28. "Hallan Niños Intercambiados al Nacer," *Prensa.com*, August 14,
2008, http://mensual.prensa.com/mensual/contenido/2005/08/14/hoy/
mundo/308568.html (accessed November 1, 2010).

29. López Ferrado, "De Repente, una Hermana." The article indicated
that there had been twelve switched-at-birth cases in Spain, but only eleven
were listed, including that of Begoña and Delia.

30. Madeleine Joye, *He Was Not My Son* (New York: Rinehart & Sons, 1954).

31. Frederick J. George, *Switched at Birth: My Life in Someone Else's World*
(Charleston, SC: BookSurge, 2008), back cover.

32. Groesback Walsh and Robert M. Pool, "Shakespeare's Knowledge of
Twins and Twinning," *Southern Medicine and Surgery* (April 1940): 173–76.

33. Virtual twins may have genes in common, like any unrelated people,
but they do not share genes by descent.

34. Karin Evans, *The Lost Daughters of China* (New York: Jeremy P.
Tarcher/Putnam, 2000).

35. After they returned home, some parents suspected that their child was
a twin due to matching photographs posted on websites for families with
adopted Chinese children. When some parents raised the possibility that their
child was a twin, Chinese adoption officials denied it.

CHAPTER 2

1. David Klein, "Living History—Autobiography: Genetics and Environment from a Personal History," *American Journal of Medical Genetics* 37
(1990): 327.

2. Amram Scheinfeld, *Twins and Supertwins* (Philadelphia: Lippincott,
1967).

3. Madeleine Joye, *He Was Not My Son* (New York: Rinehart, 1954).
The book was first called *My Three Sons*, but the title was changed to *He Was
Not My Son* because of the justice's decision to return Ernstli and Paul to their
biological families.

4. George Kent, "The Case of the Third Twin," *Reader's Digest* (November 1951): 18–21.

5. Madeleine Joye, "My Son Was Not My Son," *McCall's Magazine* 81 (1954), pp. 30–31, 120, 122, 124, 127–28.

6. Charles Joye, *Medical Chronicle of an Ordinary Patient and the Clan of Charles Joye vs the Clan of Sigmoid Metastasis* (Genthod, Switzerland: Editions du Sautoir d'Or, 2011).

7. Joye, *He Was Not My Son*, p. 111.

8. Ibid., p. 43.

9. Ibid., p. 5.

10. Ibid., p. 26.

11. Ibid., p. 5.

12. Ibid., p. 26.

13. Ibid., p. 9.

14. Ibid., p. 62.

15. The central incisor teeth erupt between six and ten months of age. Darren R. Williams, ed., "Dental Health and Your Child's Teeth (Teeth Eruption Charts)," March 15, 2009; WebMD/MedicineNet.com, http://www.medicinenet.com/ script/main/art.asp?articlekey=43131 (accessed December 10, 2010).

16. Joye, *He Was Not My Son*, p. 42.

17. Arte Sipa Arte and Sinikke Pirinen, "Hypodontia," *Orphanet*, May 2004, http://www.orpha.net/data/patho/GB/uk-hypodontia.pdf (accessed December 1, 2010).

18. Joye, *He Was Not My Son*, p. 70.

19. Albert Franceschetti, Frédéric Bamatter, and David Klein, "Valeur des Tests Cliniques et Sérologique en Vue de l'Identification de Deux Jumeaux Univitellins, Dont l'Un a Eté Echangé par Erreur" ["Value of Clinical and Blood Tests for Identifying Two Identical Twins, of Which One Was Exchanged in Error," *Bulletin Académie Suisse Sciences Médicales* 4 (1948); Archibald McIndoe and Albert Franceschetti, "Reciprocal Skin Homografts in a Medico-Legal Case of Familial Identification of Exchanged Identical Twins," *British Journal of Plastic Surgery* 2 (1949–1950): 283–89.

20. Klein, "Living History—Autobiography."

21. The average frequency of the d gene across forty-four countries world-

wide is 30 percent and ranges between 22 and 44 percent in some European nations. Supriyo Chakraborty, "Gene Frequency and Heritability of Rh Blood groups in 44 Human Populations," *Notulae Scientia Biologicae* 2, no. 3 (2010): 16–19, http://notulaebiologicae.ro/nsb/article/viewFile/4756/4546/ (accessed December 1, 2010).

22. Stanford University School of Medicine: Blood Center, "ABO and Rh Blood Type Frequencies in the United States," July 17, 2008, http://anthro.palomar.edu/blood/table_of_ABO_and_Rh_blood_type_frequencies _in_US.htm (accessed November 1, 2010).

23. Robert J. Fitzgibbons Jr., "Skin Graft," *Medline Plus,* December 2, 2008, http://www.nlm.nih.gov/medlineplus/ency/article/002982.htm (accessed November 1, 2010).

24. James F. Fries, John E. Hoopes, and Lawrence E. Shulman, "Reciprocal Skin Grafts in Systemic Sclerosis (Scleroderma)," *Arthritis and Rheumatism* 14, no. 5 (1971): 571–78. doi:10.1002/art.1780140504 (accessed November 1, 2010).

25. Franceschetti, Bamatter, and Klein, "Valeur des Tests Cliniques et Sérologique en Vue de l'Identification de Deux Jumeaux Univitellins," p. 434.

26. Sipa and Pirinen, "Hypodontia."

27. The article including these images was published in McIndoe and Franceschetti, "Reciprocal Skin Homografts in a Medico-Legal Case of Familial Identification of Exchanged Identical Twins."

28. Ibid.

29. Klein, "Living History—Autobiography," p. 328.

30. McIndoe and Franceschetti, "Reciprocal Skin Homografts in a Medico-Legal Case of Familial Identification of Exchanged Identical Twins"; Franceschetti, Bamatter, and Klein, "Valeur des Tests Cliniques et Sérologiques."

31. Beatriz had been living away from home, but she returned to her mother's house after the discovery to avoid contacts from journalists.

32. Xavier Lafargue, "L'incroyable Destin des Jumeaux Joye" [The Incredible Destiny of the Joye Twins], *Le Matin*, March 27, 2008, p. 4.

33. Philippe Joye (younger), e-mail communication to the author, September 8, 2010.

34. Joye, *Medical Chronicle of an Ordinary Patient and the Clan of Charles Joye*, p. 38.

35. Richard D. Arvey et al. "Job Satisfaction: Environmental and Genetic Components," *Journal of Applied Psychology* 74 (1989): 187–92; Laurie M. Keller et al., "Work Values: Genetic and Environmental Influences," *Journal of Applied Psychology* 77 (1992): 79–88.

36. Philippe Joye has discussed the circumstances of his twinship on the French television program *Down Masks* (1993) and in newspapers such as *Le Matin* (2008) following the 2008 death of his twin brother, Charles.

37. Joye, *He Was Not My Son*, p. 37.

38. Ibid., p. 88.

39. Nancy L. Segal, *Indivisible by Two: Lives of Extraordinary Twins* (Cambridge, MA: Harvard University Press, 2007).

40. Children's Aid Society of Ottawa, "What Is the Children's Aid Society (CAS)?" http://www.casott.on.ca/en/faq.php (accessed November 1, 2010).

41. Segal, *Indivisible by Two*, pp. 33, 37.

42. Carroll Tremblay, unpublished diaries, 1999.

43. Segal, *Indivisible by Two*, p. 48.

44. Carroll Tremblay, in discussion with the author, September 22, 2010.

45. Michael Leidig, "Polish Twins Swapped by Doctors as Babies Receive Damages," *Telegraph*, April 4, 2009, http://www.telegraph.co.uk.news (accessed November 1, 2010); Warsaw (AFP), "Kasia, Nina, and Edyta, or the Story of Three Polish Twins," SAWF News, November 24, 2006, http://www.news.sawf.org/Lifestyle/28336.aspx (accessed November 1, 2010); Matthew Day, "Identical Twins Separated for 16 Years by a Hospital Blunder," *Scotsman*, April 4, 2009, http://thescotsman.scotsman.com/news/Identical-twins-separated-for-.5141540.jp (accessed November 1, 2010).

46. Warsaw (AFP), "Kasia, Nina, and Edyta."

47. Jacek Hugo-Bader, "Siedem Luster [Seven Mirrors]," *Wysokie Obcasy*, December 4, 2009, http://www.wysokieobcasy.pl/wysokie-obcasy/1,103260,7330278,Siedem_luster.html (accessed November 1, 2010).

48. Jacek Hugo-Bader, e-mail message to author, December 17, 2010.

49. The Barbicon, built in 1548, is the gate between Warsaw's Old Town and New Town.

50. Hugo-Bader, "Siedem Luster."

51. Zygmunt's Column, erected in 1644, was named for King Zygmunt III Waza, who moved Poland's capital from Krakow to Warsaw in 1595.

52. Day, "Identical Twins Separated for 16 Years by a Hospital Blunder."

53. Hugo-Bader, "Siedem Luster."

54. Day, "Identical Twins Separated for 16 Years by a Hospital Blunder."

55. Martyna Bunda, "Zamiana [Switched]" *Polityka*, May 16, 2009, http://archiwum.polityka.pl/art/zamiana,424274.html (accessed November 1, 2010).

56. Hugo-Bader, "Siedem Luster."

57. Leidig, "Polish Twins Swapped by Doctors as Babies Receive Damages."

58. Ibid.

59. Nancy L. Segal, "Sports Pairs: Insights on Athletic Talent," *Twin Research and Human Genetics* 10 (2007): 528–33.

60. Andrzej Ofmański, in discussion with the author, October 23, 2010.

61. Warsaw (AFP), "Kasia, Nina, and Edyta."

62. Harold D. Vicente, in discussion with the author, January 8, 2010.

63. Pablo De León López v. Corporacion Insular de Seguros et al., Civil No. 88-764 HL, 742 F. Supp. 44 (United States Dist. Ct. for the Dist. of Puerto Rico, June 12, 1990).

64. López v. Corporacion Insular de Seguros, No. 90-1897 (United States Ct. of Appeals for the First Circuit, 931 F.2d 116, March 7, 1991).

65. Hector M. Laffitte, in discussion with the author, January 8, 2010.

66. Geoffrey A. Machin and Louis G. Keith, *An Atlas of Multiple Pregnancy: Biology and Pathology* (New York: Parthenon, 1999).

67. Dulce Mária Hernández Ramos, in discussion with the author, March 5, 2010.

68. De León López v. Corporacion Insular de Seguros (March 7, 1991).

69. Juan Ramón De León Flores, in discussion with the author, February 9, 2010.

70. Gloria E. Hernández Ramós, in discussion with the author, June 24, 2010.

71. Ibid.

72. Hector M. Laffitte, in discussion with the author, January 8, 2010.

73. Dulce María Hernández Ramos, in discussion with the author, March 5, 2010.

74. Gloria E. Hernández Ramos, in discussion with the author, June 24, 2010.

75. Lavonne Luquis, "Mixup Causes Double Trouble," *San Juan Star*, March 25, 1990.

76. Luquis, "Mixup Causes Double Trouble."

77. Juan Ramón De León Flores, in discussion with the author, April 20, 2010.

78. Tairí Mari De León Hernández, in discussion with the author, February 18, 2010.

79. Tairí Mari De León Hernández, in discussion with the author, February 18, 2010, and June 22–27, 2010.

80. Laura E. Berk, *Child Development*, 8th ed. (Boston: Pearson, 2009), p. 291.

81. Gloria E. Hernández Ramos, in discussion with the author, June 24, 2010.

82. Juan Ramón De León Flores, in discussion with the author, April 20, 2010.

83. Ibid.

84. Miguel F. Ayala, "Otros Does Gemelos Vivieron Separados Desde 1973 por un Error en el Viejo Pino [Other Twins Lived Apart since 1973 Because of an Error in the Old *Pino*]," *La Provincia*, May 29, 2008, http://www.laprovincia.es/las-palmas/2008/05/29/ (accessed November 1, 2010).

85. Marcos, in discussion with interpreter Jessica Crespo, August 29, 2010. The names of these twins have been disguised.

86. "El Caso de las Gemelas Grancanarais Separadas al Nacer Podría no ser un Caso Aislado," Redacción Televisión Canaria, May 29, 2008, http://www.tvcanaria.tv/det_noticia.asp?identidad=30971 (accessed May 30, 2008; link discontinued).

CHAPTER 3

1. "Twin, Separated at Birth, Sues for Mix-Up," *Yahoo! News*, http://news.yahoo.com/s/nm/20080528/od_nm/twin_dc/ (accessed June 1, 2008; link discontinued).

2. Robert Plomin et al. *Behavior Genetics*. 5th ed. (New York: Worth, 2008).

3. Nancy L. Segal, *Entwined Lives: Twins and What They Tell Us about Human Behavior* (New York: Plume, 2000).

4. Peter Watson, *Twins: An Uncanny Relationship* (Chicago: Contemporary Books, 1981).

5. Sandra Scarr, "Developmental Theories for the 1990s: Development and Individual Differences," *Child Development* 63 (1992): 1–19.

6. Beatriz, in discussion with the author, September 14, 2009.

7. Begoña, in discussion with the author, September 15, 2009.

8. Delia, in discussion with the author, September 21, 2009.

9. Débora, in discussion with the author, September 15, 2009.

10. Juan, in discussion with the author, September 15, 2009.

11. José A. R. Peregrina and his wife Noelia Vigil Torres, in discussion with the author, September 14, 2009.

12. Mónica López Ferrado, "De Repente, una Hermana [Suddenly, a Sister]," *El Pais*, July 7, 2008, http://www.elpais.com/articulo/sociedad/repente/hermana/elpepisoc/20080706elpepisoc_3/Tes (accessed July 15, 2008).

13. María Medina Alcoz, "Compensation for Moral Damages in Spanish Law: Special Reference to Moral Damages Arising from Road Traffic Accidents," November 15, 2010, http://www.xprimm.ro/download/cna2010_noi/Maria_Medina.pdf (accessed April 27, 2011).

14. José A. R. Peregrina, e-mail communication to the author, April 27, 2010.

15. "List of Newspapers in Spain," Wikipedia, September 27, 2010, http://en.wikipedia.org/wiki/List_of_newspapers_in_Spain (accessed November 1, 2010).

16. Society of Professional Journalists (SPJ), "SPJ Code of Ethics," 1996–2010, http://www.spj.org/ethicscode.asp (accessed November 1, 2010).

17. Sebastian Socorro Perdomo, in discussion with the author, September 15, 2009.

18. "Twin, Separated at Birth, Sues for Mix-Up," *Yahoo! News.*

CHAPTER 4

1. Beatriz, in discussion with the author, September 14, 2009.

2. Robert Plomin et al., *Behavior Genetics*, 5th ed. (New York: Worth, 2008).

3. Linda Mealey, R. Bridgstock, and G. C. Townsend, "Symmetry and Perceived Facial Attractiveness: A Monozygotic Co-Twin Comparison," *Journal of Personality and Social Psychology* 76 (1999): 151–58; Melinda S. Meade and Michael Emch, *Medical Geography*, 3rd ed. (New York: Guilford Press, 2010).

4. Casimiro Carbrera Abreu, psychiatrist in Spain, e-mail message to author, November 24, 2010.

5. Laura, in discussion with the author, September 15, 2009.

6. Begoña, in discussion with the author, September 15, 2009.

7. "Spain: Major Cities," City Population, January 1, 2009, http://www.citypopulation.de/Spain-Cities.html#Stadt_gross (accessed December 1, 2010).

8. "Spain: Major Cities," City Population, January 25, 2010, http://www.citypopulation.de/Spain-Cities.html#Land (accessed December 1, 2010).

9. "Population of Las Palmas de Gran Canaria, Spain," Mongobay.com, http://population.mongabay.com/population/spain/2515270/las-palmas-de-gran-canaria/, 2007 (accessed November 1, 2010).

10. "Canary Islands," Britain.tv, http://www.britain.tv/travel_canary_islands.shtml, 2006 (accessed November 1, 2010).

11. Nancy L. Segal, *Born Together—Reared Apart: The Landmark Minnesota Twin Study* (Cambridge, MA: Harvard University Press, in press).

12. Débora, in discussion with the author, September 15, 2009.

13. Juan, in discussion with the author, September 15, 2009.

14. Henry L. Roediger and Kathleen B. McDermott, "Distortions of

Memory," in *The Oxford Handbook of Memory*, ed. Endel Tulving and Fergus I. M. Craik (Oxford, UK: Oxford University Press, 2000), pp. 149–64.

15. Elizabeth Loftus and Jacqueline E. Pickrell, "The Formation of False Memories," *Psychiatric Annals* 25 (1995): 720–25.

CHAPTER 5

1. Julia, in discussion with the author, September 16, 2009.

2. Dr. Angel Trujillo Cabas, in discussion with the author, September 16, 2009.

3. The analysis of needs was based on psychologist Abraham Maslow's (1908–1970) hierarchy of motivations. Maslow postulated that physiological needs, such as the need for food and water, must be satisfied first, followed by safety needs such as love and self-esteem. Finally the need of self-actualization, the development of inborn positive potentialities, can be met. Benjamin B. Wolman, *Dictionary of Behavioral Science*, 2nd ed. (New York: Academic Press, 1989).

4. Gara, in discussion with the author, September 17, 2009.

5. Begoña, in discussion with the author, September 19, 2009.

6. The *s* in the designer label *Desigual* is reversed to make the label distinctive.

7. Twin relationship information in some of the previous switched-at-birth twin cases came largely, but not exclusively, from the twins' parents.

8. Franz J. Neyer, "Twin Relationships in Old Age: A Development Perspective," *Journal of Personality and Social Relationships* 19 (2002): 155–77.

9. Nancy L. Segal, *Indivisible by Two: Lives of Extraordinary Twins* (Cambridge: Harvard University Press, 2007).

10. American Red Cross, "Eligibility Criteria by Alphabetical Listing," http://www.redcrossblood.org/donating-blood/eligibility-requirements/eligibility-criteria-alphabetical-listing/ (accessed April 23, 2011).

11. Delia, in discussion with the author, September 21, 2009.

12. The DNA test took place on December 16, 2003, two years after the twins' first meeting on December 1, 2001. Delia Jiminez, "La Doble Que

Resulto Ser Su Gemela [The Double That Turned Out to Be a Twin]," *Cronica*, June 1, 2008, pp. 6–7. Also available at http://www.arcadiespada .es/wp-content/uploads/2008/06/impre.html (accessed May 4, 2011).

13. "Noticia en *La Prensa*," R. Peregrina Abogados, September 17, 2009, http://www.peregrinaabogados.es/noticias/ (accessed November 1, 2010; link discontinued).

CHAPTER 6

1. Amram Scheinfeld, *Twins and Supertwins* (New York: J. B. Lippin-cott & Co, 1967), p. 57.

2. Joan DiPasquale Davis et al., "Pregnancy Anxieties and Natural Recognition in Baby-Switching," *British Journal of Nursing* 10 (2001): 718–26.

3. Robert R. Rusting, "Baby Switching: An Under-Reported Problem That Needs to be Recognized," *Journal of Healthcare Protection Management* 17 (2001): 89–100.

4. DNA Diagnostics Center, "Identification Techniques for Preventing Infant Mix-Ups," http://www.dnacenter.com/science-technology/articles/ infant-mix-up.html (accessed November 1, 2010).

5. Rusting, "Baby Switching."

6. Adrian E. Feldhusen, "The History of Midwifery and Childbirth in America: A Timeline," 2000, http://www.midwiferytoday.com/articles/time line.asp, 2000 (accessed November 1, 2010).

7. Judith Rooks, *Midwifery and Childbirth in America* (Philadelphia: Temple University Press, 1999).

8. Ibid.

9. Joseph R. Wax et al., "Maternal and Newborn Outcomes in Planned Home Birth vs Planned Hospital Births: A Metanalysis," *American Journal of Obstetrics and Gynecology* 203 (2010): 243e1–243e8.

10. Trish Torrey, "The History of the Patient Empowerment Movement," About.com, updated April 9, 2009, http://patients.about.com/od/patient empowermentissues/a/history_patemp.htm (accessed November 1, 2010).

11. Rusting, "Baby Switching"; Tara R. Crane, "Mistaken Baby Switches," *Journal of Legal Medicine* 21 (2000): 109–24.

12. Christi Gill Baunach, "The Role of Equitable Adoption in a Mistaken Baby Switch," *University of Louisville Journal of Family Law, 1992–1993* (1992–1993): 501–13.

13. Associated Press, "Tests Indicate That Girl, 10, is Child of Claimants," *New York Times*, November 20, 1989.

14. Susan Schindehette, "All in the Family," *People Magazine*, August 24, 1998, pp. 48–53.

15. Elizabeth Boardman, "Switched: Keeping Babies Safe in Hospital Nurseries," *Childbirth Instructor Magazine* 8 (1998): 20–22.

16. Chris Strathmann, Ruch McHugh, and Imaeyen Ibanga, "A Mother's Nightmare: Babies Switched at Birth," *Good Morning America*, April 14, 2008, http://abcnews.go.com/GMA/story?id=4646369 (accessed November 1, 2010).

17. Kimmelin Hull, "Switched at Birth," *Writing My Way Through Motherhood and Beyond* [blog], http://kimmelin.wordpress.com/2008/07/27/switched-at-birth/ (accessed November 1, 2010).

18. Nancy L. Segal, *Entwined Lives: Twins and What They Tell Us About Human Behavior* (New York: Plume, 2000).

19. "Inconceivable?" *Dateline NBC*, November 19, 1996.

20. David Livingstone Smith, "Beyond Westermarck: Can Shared Mothering or Maternal Phenotype Matching Account for Incest Avoidance?" *Evolutionary Psychology* 5 (2007): 210, http://www.epjournal.net/filestore/EP05202222.pdf (accessed November 1, 2010).

21. Behavioral changes in females, such as in vocal qualities, have been associated with ovulation, so ovulation may not truly be hidden. Gregory Bryant and Martie G. Haselton, "Vocal Cues of Ovulation in the Human Female," *Biology Letters* 5 (2009): 12–15.

22. David M. Buss, *Evolutionary Psychology: The New Science of the Mind*, 3rd ed. (Boston: Allyn and Bacon, 2004).

23. Nicholas J. S. Christenfeld and Emily A. Hill, "Whose Baby Are You?" *Nature* 378 (1995): 669.

24. Serge Brédart and Robert M. French, "Do Babies Resemble Their Fathers More Than Their Mothers? A Failure to Replicate Christenfeld &

Hill," *Evolution and Human Behavior* 20 (1995): 129–35; Paola Bressan and Massimo Grassi, "Parental Resemblance in 1-Year-Olds and the Gaussian Curve," *Evolution and Human Behavior* 25 (2004): 133–41.

25. D. Kelly McClain et al., "Ascription of Resemblance of Newborns by Parents and Nonrelatives," *Evolution and Human Behavior* 21 (2000): 11–23.

26. Nancy L. Segal et al., "Social Closeness of Monozygotic and Dizygotic Twin Parents toward Their Nieces and Nephews," *European Journal of Personality* 21 (2007): 487–506.

27. Shirley M. Larsen and Polly M. Leyva v. Banner Health System, No. 02-252 (Supreme Ct. of Wyoming, December 23, 2003).

28. David Buss, "Oxford Companion to the Mind: Evolutionary Psychology; 5. Strategies for Generating and Testing Evolutionary Psychological Hypotheses," 1987, http://www.answers.com/topic/evolutionary-psychology/ (accessed November 1, 2010).

29. Ruth Feldman et al. "The Nature of the Mother's Tie to Her Infant: Maternal Bonding under Conditions of Proximity, Separation, and Potential Loss," *Journal of Child Psychology and Psychiatry* 40 (1999): 929–39.

30. John P. Chapman and Konny Lange, "Discharging Twins Separately from Neonatal Units," 2003, http://www.ncbi.nlm.nih.gov/pmc/articles/ PMC1721624/pdf/v088p0F445.pdf (accessed November 1, 2010); Gunnel Elander and Tor Lindberg, "Short Mother-Infant Separation during First Week of Life Influences the Duration of Breastfeeding," *Acta Paediatrica Scandinavica* 73 (1984): 237–40.

31. Stefano Vaglio, "Chemical Communication and Mother-Infant Recognition," *Communicative and Integrative Biology* 2 (2009): 279–81.

32. Michael J. Russell, T. Mendelsson, and H. V. S. Peeke, "Mothers' Identification of Their Infant's Odors," *Ethology and Sociobiology* 4 (1983): 29–31.

33. David Formby, "Maternal Recognition of Infant's Cry," *Developmental Medicine and Child Neurology* 9 (1967): 293–98.

34. Carl M. Corter and A. S. Fleming, "Maternal Responsiveness in Humans: Emotional, Cognitive, and Biological Factors," *Advances in the Study of Behavior* 19 (1990): 83–136.

35. Birgit Mempe et al., "Newborns' Cry Melody Is Shaped by Their Native Language," *Current Biology* 19 (2009): 1994–97.

36. Barbara S. Kisilevsky et al., "Effects of Experience on Fetal Voice Recognition," *Psychological Science* 14 (2003): 220–24.

37. Tiffany M. Field et al., "Effects of Tactile/Kinesthetic Stimulation on Preterm Neonates," *Pediatrics* 77 (1986): 654–58.

38. Marsha Kaitz et al., "Parturient Women Can Recognize Their Infants by Touch," *Developmental Psychology* 28 (1992): 35–39.

39. Marsha Kaitz and A. M. Rokem, "Infants' Face Recognition by Primiparous and Multiparous Women," *Perceptual and Motor Skills* 67 (1988): 495–502.

40. Laura E. Berk, *Child Development*, 8th ed. (Boston: Allyn & Bacon, 2008).

41. Marsha Kaitz et al., "Mothers' and Fathers' Recognition of Their Newborns' Photographs during the Postpartum Period," *Journal of Developmental and Behavioral Pediatrics* 9 (1988): 223–26.

42. Catharina Lewin and Agneta Herlitz, "Sex Differences in Facial Recognition—Women's Faces Make the Difference," *Brain and Cognition* 50 (2002): 121–28. In this study, females outperformed males in recognizing female faces, but males and females were equally successful in recognizing male faces.

43. Jennifer Connellan et al., "Sex Differences in Human Neonatal Social Perception," *Infant Behavior and Development* 23 (2000): 113–18. Available at http://www.math.kth.se/matstat/gru/5b1501/F/sex.pdf (accessed May 5, 2011).

44. DiPasquale Davis et al., "Pregnancy Anxieties and Natural Recognition in Baby-Switching."

45. Reva Rubin, "Binding-in in the Postpartum Period," *Maternal-Child Nursing Journal* 6 (1977): 67–75.

46. Janet Mann, "Nurturance or Negligence: Maternal Psychology, and Behavioral Preference among Preterm Infants," in *The Adapted Mind: Evolutionary Psychology and the Generation of Culture*, ed. Jerome H. Barkow, Leda Cosmides, and John Tooby (New York: Oxford University Press, 1992), pp. 367–90.

47. It is not known whether or not the mothers in these studies were told of their correct or incorrect choices. However, researchers often debrief participants once data collection has ended.

48. "Javier Urra," Wikipedia, July 11, 2010, http://es.wikipedia.org/wiki/Javier_Urra (accessed November 1, 2010).

49. Mónica López Ferrado, "De Repente, una Hermana [Suddenly, a Sister]," *El Pais*, July 7, 2008, http://www.elpais.com/articulo/sociedad/repente/hermana/elpepisoc/20080706elpepisoc_3/Tes (accessed July 15, 2008).

50. Ibid.

51. Antonio Garrido-Lestache, "Identification of New-Born Babies by Fingerprints," *International Criminal Police Review* 481 (2000): 19–24.

52. Dr. Antonio Garrido-Lestache, in discussion with the author, September 28, 2009.

53. Antonio Garrido-Lestache and Antonio Manuel Moral Roncal, *La Identificación de Recien Nacidos en la Casa Real Española, 1700–2000* [*The Identification of Newborns in the Royal Spanish Household*] (Madrid, Spain: Artes Graficas Luis Pérez, 2001).

54. Harold Cummins and Charles Midlo, *Fingerprints, Palms and Soles: An Introduction to Dermatoglyphics* (New York: Dover, 1961).

55. Stefan F. Bracha, "Second-Semester Markers of Fetal Size in Schizophrenia: A Study of Monozygotic Twins," *American Journal of Psychiatry* 149 (1992): 1355–61.

56. Don Van Ryn et al., *Mistaken Identity* (New York: Howard Books, 2008).

57. Spanish Ministry, "Identification of Newborns" [pamphlet], July 2005; also see http://www.correos.es/comun/filatelia/2005/0450_05-seleccionaSello.asp?idSello=2072005&idiom=ENG&idiomaWebActual=ES (accessed November 1, 2010).

58. Garrido-Lestache, "Identification of New-Born Babies by Fingerprints."

59. Harrison C. Allison, *Personal Identification*, 2nd ed. (Boston: Holbrook Press, 1976), p. 124.

60. Garrido-Lestache, "Identification of New-Born Babies by Fingerprints."

61. Ibid.

62. ICN (Identificacion y Custodia Neonal), "Neonatal Custody and Identification: Newborn Unequivocal Identificatión System," http://www.icnid.com/eng/portada.htm (accessed November 1, 2010).

63. "Zenith I: The 1989 United Nations Convention on the Rights of the Child; Sports for Development and Peace," CAPPAA, September 25, 2010, http://www.cappaa.com/zenith-i-the-1989-united-nations-convention-on -the-rights-of-the-child-sports-for-development-and-peace/ (accessed November 1, 2010).

64. "Zenith I: The 1989 United Nations Convention on the Rights of the Child," sect. ZENITH I and II.

65. The Infant Protection and Baby Switching Prevention Act, H.R. 4680, 105th Congress, 2d sess. (1998).

66. Tara R. Crane, "Mistaken Baby Switches: An Analysis of Hospital Liability and Resulting Custody Issues," *Journal of Legal Medicine* 21 (2000): 109–24. Crane (see n. 66) specifically referenced the 1999 version of the bill (H.R. 76).

67. Peter T. Kilborn, "Monitoring Efforts Fail to Stop Baby Switching," http://www.nytimes.com/1998/08/05/us/monitoring-efforts-fail-to-stop-baby-switching.html (accessed November 1, 2010).

68. Rusting, "Baby Switching."

69. Megan Garvey and Peter M. Warren, "O.C. Hospital Acts to End Baby Mix-Ups," *Los Angeles Times*, February 23, 1999.

70. Joseph Dalton, In-Hyung Kim, and Baek-Keun Lim, "RFID Technologies in Neonatal Care," white paper by Intel Corporation, LG CNS, ECO Inc., and WonJu Christian Hospital, September 2005, http://cache-www.intel .com/cd/00/00/25/78/257831_257831.pdf (accessed November 1, 2010).

71. DNA Diagnostics Center (DDC), "Identification Techniques for Preventing Infant Mix-Ups," http://www.dnacenter.com/science-technology/ articles/infant-mix-up.html (accessed November 1, 2010).

72. Boardman, "Switched: Keeping Babies Safe in Hospital Nurseries."

73. Tina E. Nelson, "Safeguarding Newborns: Managing the Risk," *Registered Nurse (RN)* 62 (March 1, 1999), item number 1999030084.

74. Boardman, "Switched: Keeping Babies Safe in Hospital Nurseries."

75. Rusting, "Baby Switching."

76. Barbara H. Cottrell and Laurie M. Grubbs, "Women's Satisfaction with Couplet Care Nursing Compared to Traditional Postpartum Care with Rooming-In," *Research in Nursing and Health* 17 (1994): 401–409.

77. Kathleen Bajo, Judy Hager, and Judy Smith, "Clinical Focus: Keeping Moms and Babies Together," *Association of Women's Health, Obstetric and Neonatal Nurses* (*AWHONN*) *Lifelines* 2 (1998): 44–48.

78. Cottrell and Grubbs," Women's Satisfaction with Couplet Care Nursing," 401.

79. American Academy of Pediatrics Committee on Fetus and Newborn and Committee on Obstetrics, *Maternal and Fetal Medicine: Guidelines for Prenatal Care*, 2nd ed. (Evanston, IL: AAP/ACOG, 1988), p. 85; see also Michael E. Stapleton, "Best Foot Forward: Infant Footprints for Personal Identification," *The FBI Law Enforcement Bulletin* 63 (1994): 14–17.

80. Arlene M. Butz et al., "Newborn Identification: Compliance with AAP Guidelines for Perinatal Care," *Clinical Pediatrics* 32 (1993): 111–13.

81. DNA Diagnostics Center, "Identification Techniques for Preventing Infant Mix-Ups."

82. Rick Staub and Caroline Caskey, Method of Newborn Identification and Tracking, US Patent 6,187,540 B1, filed November 9, 1998, and issued February 13, 2001.

83. Amina Khan, "Researchers Manage to Map Fetus Genome," *Los Angeles Times*, December 9, 2010. Available at http://articles.latimes.com/2010/dec/08/health/la-he-fetal-dna-20101209 (accessed May 4, 2011).

84. Ultrasound can assess twins' chorionicity (same or separate fetal membranes) at eleven to fourteen weeks into the pregnancy. Shared chorions indicate identical twins, while separate chorions are inconclusive with respect to twin type. Kypros Nicolaides et al., "The 11-14-Week Scan," Diploma in Fetal Medicine Series, 2001, http://www.centrus.com.br/DiplomaFMF/SeriesFMF/11-14weeks/chapter-05/chapter-05-final.htm (accessed December 1, 2010).

85. Dalton, Kim, and Lim, "RFID Technologies in Neonatal Care."

CHAPTER 7

1. A set of reared-apart triplets who participated in the Minnesota Study of Twins Reared Apart consulted with attorneys about filing a lawsuit over their separation but did not pursue it.

2. José Antonio Rodríguez Peregrina, in discussion with the author, September 14 and 22, 2009.

3. Sebastian Socorro Perdomo, in discussion with the author, September 15 and 22, 2009.

4. Olga Cabrero, "Features—A Guide to the Spanish Legal System," January 15, 2002, http://www.llrx.com/features/spain.htm (accessed November 1, 2010).

5. Ugo A. Mattei, Teemu Ruskola, and Antonio Gidi, *Schlesinger's Comparative Law*, 7th ed. (New York: Foundation Press, 2009), p. 531.

6. Ibid.

7. "Spanish Twins Separated at Birth Meet Again 28 Years Later," *SUR.com*, May 28, 2008 http://www.surinenglish.com/20080528/news/ spain/spanish-twins-separated-birth-200805281436.html (accessed December 11, 2010).

8. Sebastian Socorro, in conversation with law professor Antonio Gidi, April 27, 2011, and e-mail communication to the author.

9. Agencia, Las Palmas, "El Gobierno Indemnizará a Las Gemelas Separadas al Nacer [The Government Will Compensate the Twins Separated at Birth]," *El Dia*, December 30, 2009, http://www.eldia.es/2009-12-30/islas/3 -Gobierno-indemnizará-gemelas-separadas-nacer.htm (accessed April 28, 2011); Antonio F. de la Gándara, "Sanidad Pierde el Pleito de las Gemelas Ante el TSJC," *Canarias 7*, December 29, 2009, p. 38.

10. Sebastian Socorro in conversation with law professor Antonio Gidi, April 27, 2011, and e-mail communication to the author.

11. María Medina Alcoz, "Compensation for Moral Damages in Spanish Law: Special Reference to Moral Damages Arising from Road Traffic Accidents," November 15, 2010, http://www.xprimm.ro/download/cna2010 _noi/Maria_Medina.pdf (accessed April 27, 2011).

12. Oanda, "Currency Converter," 1998–2010, http://www.oanda.com/ currency/converter/, (accessed November 1, 2010).

13. "Sentencia [Case]," Socorro Ley & Asociados, March 30, 2009, http://www.socorroleyasociados.com/PDF/Sentecia%20integra%20CASO %20GEMELAS.pdf (accessed November 1, 2010).

14. José A. R. Peregrina, "Caso Gemelas Cambiadas al Nacer en España;

Ciudad: Las Palmas de Gran Canaria—Islas Canarias [Case of the Switched-at-Birth Twins in Spain; City: Las Palmas de Gran Canaria—Canary Islands," June 2, 2009, http://www.peregrinaabogados.es/noticias/ (accessed November 1, 2010; link discontinued).

15. "Birth and the Biological Relationship," Court Document 141/2005, made available to the author by José A. R. Peregrina.

16. Ibid.

17. Marisol Ayala, "Las Gemelas Mal Identificadas en el 'Viejo' Pino [Twins Misidentified in the 'Old' *Pino*]," February 1, 2010, http://www.telde actualidad .com/hemeroteca/hemeroteca_secciones .php?dayID=2&id=4196 &monthID=1&seccion=opinion&yearID=2010 (accessed November 1, 2010).

18. Nancy L. Segal, Scott L. Hershberger, and Sara Arad, "Meeting One's Twin: Perceived Social Closeness and Familiarity," *Evolutionary Psychology* 1 (2003): 70–95; http://www.epjournal.net/filestore/ep017095.pdf (accessed November 1, 2010).

19. Nancy L. Segal, Joanne Hoven Stohs, and Kara Evans, "Chinese Twin Children Reared Apart and Reunited: First Prospective Study of Co-Twin Reunions," *Adoption Quarterly* 14, no. 1 (2011), 61–78.

20. Nancy L. Segal, *Entwined Lives: Twins and What They Tell Us about Human Behavior* (New York: Plume, 2000); Nancy L. Segal, *Indivisible by Two: Lives of Extraordinary Twins* (Cambridge, MA: Harvard University Press, 2007); Segal, Hershberger, and Arad, "Meeting One's Twin."

21. Joan Woodward, *The Lone Twin: Understanding Twin Bereavement and Loss* (London: Free Association Books, 1997).

22. Matthew Day, "Identical Twins Separated for 16 Years by a Hospital Blunder," *Scotsman*, April 4, 2009, http://thescotsman.scotsman.com/news/ Identical-twins-separated-for-.5141540.jp (accessed November 1, 2010).

23. Segal, *Indivisible by Two*, p. 48.

24. George Kent, "The Case of the Third Twin," *Reader's Digest*, November 1951, p. 18.

25. Xavier Lafargue, "L'incroyable Destin des Jumeaux Joye [The Incredible Destiny of the Joye Twins," *Le Matin*, March 27, 2008, p. 4.

26. Charles Joye, *Medical Chronicle of an Ordinary Patient and the Clan of*

Charles Joye versus the Clan of Sigismond Metastasis (Genthod, Switzerland: Editions du Sautoir d'Or, 2011), pp. 99–101.

27. Warsaw (AFP), "Kasia, Nina, and Edyta, or the Story of Three Polish Twins," SAWF News, November 24, 2006, http://www.sawfnews.com/lifestyle/28336.aspx (accessed November 1, 2010)

28. Andrzej Ofmański, in discussion with the author, October 23, 2010.

29. Ibid.

30. Pablo De León López v. Corporacion Insular de Seguros, No. 90-1987 (United States Ct. of Appeals for the First Circuit, 931 F.2d 116, April 19, 1991).

31. Ibid.; Pablo De León López v. Corporacion Insular de Seguros, et al., Civil No. 88-764 HL (United States District Ct. for the District of Puerto Rico, 742 F. Supp. 44, June 12, 1990).

32. Hector M. Laffitte, in discussion with the author, January 8, 2010.

33. Dulce María Hernandez á Ramos, in discussion with the author, March 5, 2010.

34. Pablo De León López v. Corporacion Insular de Seguros, No. 90-1987 (April 19, 1991).

35. Sebastian Socorro Perdomo, "Nuestras Noticias," http://socorroley asociados.com/index.html (accessed November 1, 2010); José A. R. Peregrina, "Noticias del Bufete," http://www.peregrinaabogados.es/node/5/ (accessed November 1, 2010).

36. UNICEF, "Convention on the Rights of the Child," August 26, 2008, http://www.unicef.org/crc/ (accessed November 1, 2010).

37. Ibid.

38. United Nations General Assembly, "Convention on the Rights of the Child," November 20, 1989, http://www2.ohchr.org/english/law/crc.htm (accessed November 1, 2010).

39. Sebastian Socorro Perdomo, "Motivos del Recurso," April 24, 2009, http://www.socorroleyasociados.com/PDF/gemelas%20recurso%20web.pdf (accessed August 19, 2009).

40. Christi Gill Baunach, "The Role of Equitable Adoption in a Mistaken Baby Switch," *University of Louisville Journal of Family Law* 31 (1992): 512.

41. "State Recognition of Common Law Marriage," *Black's Law Dictio-*

nary 277 (6th ed.), 1990, http://commonlawfacts.com/tag/blacks-law-dictionary/ (accessed November 1, 2010).

42. Loretta Schwartz-Nobel, *The Baby Swap Conspiracy* (New York: Random House, 1993).

43. Larry Rohter, "Girl Swapped at Birth Now Switches Parents," *New York Times,* March 10, 1994.

44. Baunach, "The Role of Equitable Adoption in a Mistaken Baby Switch."

45. Tara R. Crane, "Mistaken Baby Switches." *Journal of Legal Medicine* 21 (2000) 109–24.

46. Ibid., p. 115.

47. Ibid., p. 123.

48. John A. Robertson, *Children of Choice* (Princeton, NJ: Princeton University Press, 1994).

49. Segal, *Indivisible by Two*.

50. Ibid., p. 18.

51. Laura E. Berk, *Child Development.* 8th ed. (Boston: Allyn & Bacon, 2008).

52. David Howe, "Parent-Reported Problems in 211 Adopted Children: Some Risk and Protective Factors," *Journal of Child Psychology and Psychiatry* 38 (1997): 401–11.

CHAPTER 8

1. Robert Plomin et al., *Behavior Genetics*, 5th ed. (New York: Worth, 2008).

2. Horatio N. Newman, Frank N. Freeman, and Karl J. Holzinger, *Twins: A Study of Heredity and Environment* (Chicago: University of Chicago Press, 1937).

3. James Shields, *Monozygotic Twins: Brought Up Apart and Together* (London: Oxford University Press, 1962).

4. Niels Juel-Nielsen, *Individual and Environment: A Psychiatric-Psychological Investigation of Monozygotic Twins Reared Apart* (Copenhagen, Denmark: Munksgaard, 1965). This work was initially published in the journal

Acta Psychiatrica Scandinavica, Monograph Supplement 183/vol. 40 1964. It was later reprinted with follow-up data on the twins as *Individual and Environment: Monozygotic Twins Reared Apart* (New York: International Universities Press, 1980).

5. Nancy L. Segal, *Born Together—Reared Apart: The Landmark Minnesota Twin Study* (Cambridge, MA: Harvard University Press, in press).

6. Nancy L. Segal, Joanne Hoven Stohs, and Kara Evans, "Chinese Twin Children Reared Apart and Reunited: First Prospective Study of Co-Twin Reunions," *Adoption Quarterly* (in press).

7. Nancy L. Segal, "More Thoughts on the Child Development Center Twin Study," *Twin Research and Human Genetics* 8 (2005): 276–81.

8. Thomas J. Bouchard Jr. et al., "Sources of Human Psychological Differences: The Minnesota Study of Twins Reared Apart," *Science* 250 (1990): 223–28.

9. Plomin et al., *Behavior Genetics*.

10. Nancy L. Segal, Scott L. Hershberger, and Sara Arad, "Meeting One's Twin: Perceived Social Closeness and Familiarity," *Evolutionary Psychology* 1 (2003): 70–95; http://www.epjournal.net/filestore/ep017095.pdf (accessed November 1, 2010).

11. David C. Rowe, E. Jeanne Woulbroun, and Bill L.Gulley, "Peers and Friends as Nonshared Environmental Influences," in *The Separate Social Worlds of Siblings: The Impact of Nonshared Environment on Development*, ed. E. Mavis Hetherington, David Reiss, Robert Plomin (Hillsdale, NJ: Lawrence Erlbaum, 1994), 159–73.

12. Plomin et al., *Behavior Genetics*.

13. Nancy L. Segal, "Twins: The Finest Natural Experiment," *Personality and Individual Differences* 49 (2010): 317–23.

14. The correlations for the identical and fraternal twins reared apart are based on factor scores from multiple tests. See Segal, *Born Together—Reared Apart*. IQ correlations for the other twin and sibling pairs were reported in Thomas J. Bouchard Jr. and Matt McGue, "Familial Studies of Intelligence: A Review," *Science* 212 (1981): 1055–59; and in Nancy L. Segal, "Twins: The Finest Natural Experiment."

15. Identical twins share exactly 100 percent of their genes; fraternal

twins and full siblings share half their genes, on average, by descent; and virtual twins have no genes in common, by descent.

16. Nancy L. Segal et al., "Intellectual Similarity of Virtual Twin Pairs: Developmental Trends," *Personality and Individual Differences* 42 (2007): 1209–19.

17. Sandra Scarr, Richard A. Weinberg, and Irwin D. Waldman, "IQ Correlations in Transracial Adoptive Families," *Intelligence* 17 (1993): 541–55.

18. Nancy L. Segal et al., "Genetic and Environmental Contributions to Body Mass Index: Comparative Analysis of Monozygotic Twins, Dizygotic Twins, and Same-Age Unrelated Siblings," *International Journal of Obesity* 33 (2008): 37–41.

19. Wendy Bumgardner, "BMI—Body Mass Index," December 20, 2008, http://walking.about.com/od/diet/g/bmi.htm (accessed May 2, 2011).

20. Thomas C. Schelling, *The Strategy of Conflict* (Cambridge, MA: Harvard University Press, 1960), p. 54.

21. Nancy L. Segal et al., "Tacit Coordination in Monozygotic Twins, Dizygotic Twins, and Virtual Twins: Effects and Implications of Genetic Relatedness," *Personality and Individual Differences* 45 (2008): 607–12.

22. Allison Foertsch et al., "Closeness in Sibling Relationships: A Twin-Sibling Study" (poster presented at the 89th annual convention of the Western Psychological Association, Portland, OR, April 23–26).

23. Shirley McGuire et al., "Sibling Trust and Trustworthiness," in *Interpersonal Trust during Childhood and Adolescence*, ed. Ken Rotenberg (Cambridge, UK: Cambridge University Press, 2010), 133–54.

24. Delia's sister Gara was interviewed in the presence of her other sister, Julia, but Julia had already completed my interview, so Julia's answers were not affected by what Gara said. Julia did, however, contribute some comments to the conversation.

25. Nancy L. Segal and Iris Blandón-Gitlin, "Twins Switched at Birth: A Case from the Canary Islands," *Twin Research and Human Genetics* 13 (2010): 115–19.

26. Twin study investigators reported a correlation of .99 between self-reported and examiner measured height and a correlation of .89 between body mass indices (BMI) based on self-reported and examiner measured height and

weight. Suoma E. Saarni et al., "Association of Smoking in Adolescence with Abdominal Obesity in Adulthood: A Follow-up Study of 5 Cohorts Finnish Twins," *American Journal of Public Health* 99 (2009): 348–54.

27. Susan L. Farber, *Identical Twins Reared Apart: A Reanalysis* (New York: Basic Books, 1980).

28. These data were made available by Professor Jaakko Kaprio at the University of Helsinki in Finland. The twin sample on which they are based is described in Saarni et al., "Association of Smoking in Adolescence."

29. I once studied a pair of identical female twins who differed by four inches at age eight and by seven inches at age twenty-seven; see Segal, *Entwined Lives.*

30. Farber, *Identical Twins Reared Apart.*

31. These data were made available by Professor Jaakko Kaprio at the University of Helsinki in Finland. The twin sample on which they are based is described in Saarni et al., "Association of Smoking in Adolescence."

32. Mel F. Greaves et al., "Leukemia in Twins: Lessons in Natural History," *Blood* 102 (2003): 2321–33.

33. Segal, *Indivisible by Two.* George's, Marcus's, and Brent's heights and weights were measured during their research participation in the Minnesota Study of Twins Reared Apart. Wade's height and weight were obtained by self-report.

34. Segal, *Indivisible by Two.*

35. Madeleine Joye, *He Was Not My Son* (New York: Rinehart & Company, 1954), p. 26.

36. Helen L. Koch, *Twins and Twin Relations* (Chicago: University of Chicago Press, 1966), p. 208.

37. Archibald McIndoe and Albert Franceschetti. "Reciprocal Skin Homografts in a Medico-Legal Case of Familial Identification of Exchanged Identical Twins," *British Journal of Plastic Surgery* 2 (1949–1950): 283–89.

38. Robert C. Nichols and William C. Bilbro, "The Diagnosis of Twin Zygosity" *Acta Genetica et Statistica Medica* 16 (1966): 265–75.

39. McIndoe and Franceschetti, "Reciprocal Skin Homografts in a Medico-Legal Case of Familial Identification of Exchanged Identical Twins," 286; Albert Franceschetti, Frederic Bamatter, and David Klein, "Valeur des Tests Cliniques et Sérologiques en Vue de l'Identification de Jeux Jumeaux

Univitellins, Dont l'Un a Été Échangé par Erreur [Value of Clinical and Serological Tests in Identifying Identical Twins, One of Whom Was Switched in Error," *Bulletin der Schweizerischen Akademie der Medizinischen Wissenschaffen* 4, 5/6 (1948): 433–44. The nature of the psychomotor and mental tests and their precise outcomes were not provided.

40. David Wechsler, *Manual for the Wechsler Adult Intelligence Scale* (New York: Psychological Corporation, 1955).

41. Robert S. Witte and John S. Witte, *Statistics*, 7th ed. (Danvers, MA: John Wiley & Sons, 2004).

42. Morris Rosenberg, *Society and the Adolescent Image*, rev. ed. (Middleton, CT: Weslyan University Press, 1989).

43. José Martín-Albo et al., "The Rosenberg Self-Esteem Scale: Translation and Validation in University Students," *Spanish Journal of Psychology* 10 (2007): 458–67.

44. Horatio H. Newman, Frank N. Freeman, and Karl J. Holzinger, *Twins: A Study of Heredity and Environment* (Chicago: University of Chicago Press, 1937), p. 128.

45. James Shields, *Monozygotic Twins: Brought Up Apart and Together* (London: Oxford University Press, 1962), p. 165.

46. David T. Lykken et al., "Emergenesis: Traits That May Not Run in Families," *American Psychologist* 47 (1992): 1565–77.

AFTERWORD

1. Nancy L. Segal, *Indivisible by Two: Lives of Extraordinary Twins* (Cambridge, MA: Harvard University Press, 2007).

INDEX